REPROGRAM YOUR SUBCONSCIOUS

HOW TO USE HYPNOSIS TO GET WHAT YOU REALLY WANT

GALE GLASSNER TWERSKY, A.C.H.

MEDIA

REPROGRAM YOUR SUBCONSCIOUS

REPROGRAM YOUR SUBCONSCIOUS

How to Use Hypnosis to Get What You Really Want

Gale Glassner Twersky, A.C.H.

MEDIA

MEDIA

Published 2018 by Gildan Media LLC
aka G&D Media
www.GandDmedia.com

REPROGRAM YOUR SUBCONSCIOUS

Copyright © 2010, 2017, 2018 by Gale Glassner Associates, Inc.

ISBN: 978-1-7225-0030-6

DEDICATION

I dedicate this book in loving memory of my dad and mentor, Lewis M. Glassner, who has been with me in spirit.

CONTENTS

ACKNOWLEDGMENTS

I want to acknowledge my deep appreciation to all those who contributed to the creation of this updated and expanded book edition of my nine-CD series: *Reprogram Your Subconscious: How to Use Hypnosis to Get What You Really Want.* I am tremendously grateful to my wonderful clients who entrusted me with the privilege of participating as a facilitator in their subconscious discoveries and evolution. I thank them too for allowing me to share in their happiness.

Additionally it was vital for me to have the support I received from my loyal family and loved ones, especially my mom, my husband and my children who learned to carry on without me while I was still writing/editing this book. Another debt of gratitude goes to many very special, dear friends and terrific business associates who read my book and gave me their invaluable feedback. They also carried me through the often intense and challenging times when I needed to be so focused on this project. Also my gratitude goes to my incredibly supportive group of friends from Randolph, NJ, *Soul Sisters*: Sandi, Joyce, Vicki, Charlotte, Gloria, Gloria (in Florida), Arlette, Paula and Zella; and additionally my Chicago, IL, Soul Sisters, Bev and Natalie.

Finally I want to gratefully acknowledge my exceptionally talented team of editors. Glassner Associates' amazing professional editors Deborah Carton Riemer, Susan Edwards and my *volunteered* professional assistant editors: Roberta Rich Gornish, Barbara Klink, CMCH, Michal Lesher, Anne Logue, Bobbi Pershing and Rachel Twersky who all guided me with their insights, perspectives and wonderful skills. Also I was so blessed to have on our team, my graphic artist extraordinaire, Nikki Orzel of Phoenix Studios.

All of these terrific people participated in this book as my support team sustaining me. Everyone's contributions enabled me to miraculously complete this project while simultaneously operating my practice and taking care of family matters like moving across the country. All who contributed share in the joy, peace of mind and fulfillment that this book brings to others' lives. To all those incredible people in my life who made this book possible, whether named here or whether they remain unnamed, they have my eternal gratitude.

ADDENDUM

Just before this book was published, an extraordinary woman whose life was a day-to-day monumental struggle to stay alive, succumbed to complications of genetic defects. After more than twenty-five years of almost constant excruciating pain and unrelenting stress, she died. She was so dedicated to staying alive, never giving up her faith so that she could present research that could have an immensely positive impact on so many others who might suffer from illness related to hers. I was a blessed beneficiary of some of her research and experiential knowledge.

She provided me with insights that I have passed on to you through this book. I am awed by her unparalleled generosity, tenacity, and sacrifice. However, since she wished to remain anonymous, I will omit her name and refer to her as my incredibly courageous and brilliant friend, a one in a hundred million, who lived and died alone in New Jersey in her little but sweet apartment converted from a one-car garage.

FOREWORD

Ask anyone "Where is your mind?" and they may look at you as if you might have lost yours. In fact, no one knows what a mind is or where it lives. It takes someone like Gale Glassner Twersky to help you embrace and use this elusive butterfly to your best advantage. In her tidy primer, *Reprogram Your Subconscious: How to Use Hypnosis to Get What You Really Want*, she teaches you simple techniques to tap into your potentials and subconscious — which she aptly calls your silent partner — to get what you want now. She gives you the mastery tools called Reprogramming Hypnosis and Reprogramming Self-hypnosis so you don't have to figure it all out; you just do it. It is all there, clearly laid out for you. Gently sprinkled with real life Reprogramming Hypnosis stories and hypnosis coaching stories, the book is a terrific way to cut to the chase and learn things you always wanted to know about hypnosis but have been afraid to ask.

—*Shelley Stockwell-Nicholas, PhD*
President, International Hypnosis Federation
www.hypnosisfederation.com
Featured speaker on hypnosis, radio and TV personality, author of 14 books including: Hypnosis: Put a Smile on Your Face, Money in Your Pocket.

In *Reprogram Your Subconscious: How to Use Self-Hypnosis to Get What You Really Want*, Gale Glassner Twersky, A.C.H., has provided an engaging and readable overview of self-hypnosis with examples and techniques relevant to lay and professional readers alike. Describing hypnosis as an adjunct rather than a replacement for professional health care, Gale removes the negative connotations and addresses the myths about hypnosis. Multiple rich vignettes describe how the subconscious operates, and how Reprogramming Self-hypnosis helps people to overcome their negative Subconscious Programs. Her pleasant, conversational style offers steps for Reprogramming Self-hypnosis, detailed scripts with guided imagery, and alternative techniques to facilitate mind-body-spirit connections for the individual. The appendices provide a wealth of further information such as scripts to deal with specific issues, articles that illustrate practical applications for hypnosis, along with a glossary and bibliography of relevant works. As a bonus, her audiobook *Relax, Release, and Dream On*, is made available for personal use.

—*Kathleen L. Patusky, PhD, APRN-BC Assistant Professor*
University of Medicine and Dentistry of New Jersey, Newark, New Jersey

I am not a medical or counseling professional, just an ordinary guy who discovered the power of hypnosis. I learned the techniques of Reprogramming Hypnosis that carried me through a difficult period in my life. I am one now who has learned to incorporate self-hypnosis into my life to attain peace of mind and happiness on a daily basis.

Reprogram Your Subconscious: How to Use Hypnosis to Get What You Really Want is an excellent guide to the value of Reprogramming Hypnosis as a tool for unlocking the power of our minds to resolve conflicts, handle challenges and achieve goals. Comprehensive yet accessible to the non-professional, this very readable book establishes why this particular variety of hypnosis works so well and how one can unleash the power of hypnosis when needed to meet the challenges of life. Especially effective are the many real-life examples of individuals who dramatically changed their lives for the better by using Reprogramming Hypnosis, as they provide those new to hypnosis with confidence that they too can be helped and help themselves.

Read the book. Use the techniques the author lays out for you. Be happy.

—*Charles Marro, retired publishing executive*

DISCLAIMER

The information and suggestions given in this book are designed to help you make informed decisions about your overall well-being. It is not intended as a substitute for any treatment that may have been prescribed by your doctor or licensed health professional.

The author of this book does not dispense medical advice or prescribe the use of any techniques as forms of treatment for physical or mental medical problems without the advice of a physician. The intent of the author is to offer information to help you in your quest for Mind/Body/Spirit well-being.

All names, descriptions of people for case studies and other cited examples have been altered to protect the privacy of individuals unless written permission has been granted.

PREFACE

Before Beginning: A Request

It is highly recommended that at your earliest convenience you listen to your FREE Audio Bonus Download of "Relax, Release and Dream On: healing hypnotic guided imagery for relaxing mind and body, releasing negative emotions and sleeping peacefully."

This audio serves to take away doubts and concerns about going into hypnosis. Since 2002 this audio has assisted people to experience hypnosis. Of course, you can learn self- hypnosis and Reprogramming Self-hypnosis without this audio. Yet, you will find listening to Relax, Release and Dream On takes away uncertainty about the hypnosis process while it relaxes you with enjoyable guided imagery. It also will be a source of other long-term benefits for you.

Instructions on How to Obtain Your Free Bonus Audio Download that accompanies this book/eBook are found in Appendix Three:

1. Put the url, found on the first page of Appendix Three, into your browser.
2. Then follow the directions when you land on the next page. Fill in the requested information so we may send you a link to your email address for this audio.
3. Make sure you know the destination where your audio download will be downloaded so that you easily may find it.
4. If you need any assistance, send Gale a message on her website Contact page (galeglassner.com) and someone will get back to you. Be sure you have confirmed the

destination where your bonus audio, Relax, Release and Dream On, will be downloaded.

INTRODUCTION AND ALERTS

Hello, my name is Gale Glassner Twersky. I am so pleased that you have chosen this time with me so that I may share what I have discovered within my practice as a HypnoCounselor/Hypnotherapist since 1999. This is my updated and greatly expanded book edition of my Best Selling audiobook, Reprogram Your Subconscious: How to Use Hypnosis to Get What You Really Want, first published in 2005. So this is the tenth anniversary since the successful launch of my first audiobook that continues to be a Best Seller. Now I have added about 50% new material, added new case studies, revised scripts and introduced new, very important concepts. My goal for this updated and expanded edition is to present a very thorough and more detailed resource, with practical applications covering a greater expanse of topics that further support your success. It does more than just tell you about your subconscious; it offers the logic and formulas how to communicate successfully with your subconscious and walks you through the experience itself.

My theories and practice of Reprogramming Hypnosis (RH) really work and already have helped many thousands as clients and even more as purchasers of my audiobook. That was my dream and now the dream continues reaching out to yet more people who are recognizing the importance of that little known power residing within each of us, the power that is supposed to function as our advocate and friend, our subconscious mind. RH has brought freedom to those who suffered from sleeplessness, freedom from anxieties, freedom from fears, freedom from grief, freedom from feelings of helplessness, freedom from sabotaging, self-punishment programs, freedom from feelings of failure, freedom from feelings of discomfort due to medical procedures, etc., etc., etc. One client summed it up concisely:

"If I had to choose only one thing to help me in my life, it would be the information that Gale provides about hypnosis. It is the foundation of everything I need." L. Koster

And another client added this:

"I had so many "A-HA" moments reading this book. This book is a miracle and a magical journey. It changed my life. I didn't know what happy was until now." Fran Ferrara, advertising manager, NYC

For seventeen years, I have witnessed what works firsthand, teaching hypnosis skills for self-empowerment and guiding people how to reprogram their subconscious in positive, safe and really easy ways that were previously unknown to them. Do you remember any classes in your schooling that explained how much power your subconscious controlled over your thoughts, feelings and behaviors? Or that it was possible for you to make changes in your subconscious programming, deleting the negative and downloading the positive? After having witnessed such incredible transformations right in my office, covering over 80 categories of stress related issues, I knew I somehow had to broadcast this incredibly valuable information that could transform so many lives for the better and do so effectively and in relatively short order. Furthermore, the possibilities are limitless because wherever your mind is somehow involved in an issue, your subconscious is involved too, as your Silent and Invisible Partner.

Consider this: You are who you are. Yet, who are you when you are free of those detrimental Faulty Subconscious Programs? Are you who you are because of your Faulty Subconscious programs? Who would you be without those Faulty Subconscious Programs directing your life? Who could you be without those Faulty Subconscious Programs? Your free will still operates here. You need the strong desire to make the changes for yourself and believe (even if just a tad bit) that it is possible. In this poker hand of life, you do not have to settle for the cards you have been dealt. You can choose new ones. However, it requires that you be proactive and ask. With Reprogramming Hypnosis as your tool, you can choose a winning hand.

RH is a certified specialty hypnosis approach that I created and that establishes a foundation and overall consistent framework for conducting effective hypnosis sessions. The established foundation, framework, operating principles and unique vocabulary greatly assist clients in successfully attaining their hypnosis/hypnotherapy goals. RH offers clients a type of "operating manual" for learning about their subconscious minds so that abstract concepts regarding how their subconscious mind works are made understandable, usable and repeatable for future use.

RH is built upon the already universally accepted beliefs of how computers operate. Thus, the unique system of RH enhances the clients' outcomes by conducting the hypnosis within a consistent foundation and framework that compares the subconscious mind to how computers function. Consequently, the unknown subconscious becomes more knowable, understandable and controllable.

Be aware that the instructions you need for the **free Bonus download audio** are in "**Appendix Three**." You will want to download that audio of *Relax, Release and Dream On*, as soon as possible and follow the instructions and cautions printed there. *Relax, Release and Dream On* will give you the experience of hypnosis and relaxation so the information in this book is even more relevant for you.

Also, there is a tapping exercise explained in a PDF that you automatically will receive with the downloaded audio. Please take advantage of the tapping exercise that you may practice before listening to this audio with your eyes closed. Actually, it is suggested that you listen the first time to this audio with your eyes open, listening to each word, feeling comfortable with all said. Then, the next time after that, keep your eyes comfortably closed while listening to this audio.

Other valuable reference materials are printed in the **Appendices**. So be sure to enjoy my published articles on many aspects of subconscious programming. In Appendix Two is the revised hypnotic guided imagery scripts from my first audiobook. For your convenience your **50-page Journal** is included, which offers you a convenient way to record your thoughts, ideas, experiences, and reactions while they are still fresh in your mind. And now, let's begin our journey together...

CHAPTER 1

FIRST THINGS FIRST

INTRODUCTION, OVERVIEW AND BENEFITS

Welcome. You have just opened the door to unique and remarkable opportunities for gaining more power over your life by using your inborn powerhouse source, your subconscious mind. This book focuses on how to utilize that power to get what you want and let go of what you do not want. An important goal is for you to successfully communicate your desires to your subconscious mind in ways that your subconscious can understand, accept and then make them happen.

Think of your mind in terms of having two parts, your conscious mind and your subconscious mind (also commonly referred to as your *unconscious mind*). Your conscious mind gives you an awareness of your everyday consciousness of thoughts, attitudes, beliefs, feelings, experiences and what you can recall from memories. On the other hand, your subconscious mind functions on its own, totally outside of your awareness. For instance, it operates your bodily functions automatically without checking in with you. Do you intentionally plan when you are going to blink next time? Your subconscious manages that automatically and effortlessly without your input. As you read this book, you will recognize other less obvious demonstrations in your thoughts, attitudes, associations, feelings and behaviors that also are attributable to the workings of your subconscious mind.

YOUR FRIENDLY SUBCONSCIOUS COMPUTER

For now, think of your subconscious mind as an amazingly powerful computer operating within you. It takes care of your needs beautifully as it protects you from pain and harm while it directs you toward what it senses gives you pleasure and happiness. Your subconscious computer works extremely well except in certain situations where it may make errors in its immediate perceptions and disregards long-term consequences. That is when your subconscious computer in attempting to help you, downloads programming that contradicts what you really want. Unfortunately the consequences of such *Faulty Subconscious Programming* can be from slight to devastating. Your mighty subconscious ally then becomes the unintentional culprit responsible for interfering with or blocking your positive progress, your happiness and your well-being.

An example of a subconscious error in perception is illustrated by Robbie's story: *Five-year-old Robbie wanted a drink of water. He found his mom in his baby brother's room where she was diapering his baby brother Quinn. When Robbie asked for his drink of water, his mom told him that she would get it for him as soon as she finished diapering Quinn. Instantly feeling hurt, Robbie concluded that his mother loved Quinn more than she loved him. Robbie's conclusion was that he must not be good enough or lovable enough for his mother to help him first when he needed her. She favored his little brother and that must be why she chose to help Quinn before she helped him.*

Remember, these conclusions came from the immature mind of a five-year-old. Unfortunately starting from that age of five, Robbie carried those misperceptions that had been entered as truth into his Subconscious Programming. Robbie continued to build upon a perspective based on the belief that his mother loved his younger brother more than she loved him. Hence, Robbie's feelings of *Low Self-esteem* and consequential sibling rivalry were initiated with that incorrect perception. Furthermore, once he unknowingly had planted this Faulty

Subconscious Program, it continued to interfere with the brothers' relationship into adulthood.

As for the good news, there is a way you can remedy the subconscious computer program mishaps effectively and consistently. It involves the best kept secret in the entire arena of behavior transformation. It is a type of hypnosis called *Reprogramming Hypnosis or Reprogramming Self-hypnosis* (*Reprogramming Hypnosis/Self-hypnosis*). Hypnosis is a medically approved system or modality that easily gives you an entrée to your subconscious mind. Reprogramming Hypnosis provides a proven way you can locate detrimental Faulty Subconscious Programs, delete them and replace them with downloads of beneficial programs that resolve your original issue caused by faulty programming.

Within these pages you will learn techniques of Reprogramming Hypnosis/Self-hypnosis, clinically proven attitudinal and behavioral modification methods that empower you to be like a *Director of Quality Control* regarding your subconscious mind. You will acquire hypnosis tools for directing/programming your subconscious so you can remove previously flawed, erroneous or invalid programs that are adversely affecting you. Through employing these Reprogramming Hypnosis tools you can create effective suggestions/directions so that your subconscious will accept your new, improved programming. Consequently you will be able to eliminate what you really do not want in your life. These suggestions, by the way, can be written out (or recorded in another manner) and referenced after you are in the hypnotic state. Now at last you will know how to have your conscious intentions achieve clear, direct and purposeful communications with that part of your normally unreachable subconscious mind that truly can accept your directions and make changes.

THE BIRD'S-EYE PREVIEW

Within these chapters you will gain insights into the nuts and bolts of Reprogramming Hypnosis and HypnoCounseling, a facilitator-led hypnosis approach that helps you make comprehensive attitudinal and behavioral changes. You will be directed to a diverse and broad sampling of medical research now available on the proven capacity of hypnosis to produce positive effects. Additionally you will examine the myths long surrounding hypnosis so you can feel 100 percent confident about using Reprogramming Hypnosis and Reprogramming Self-hypnosis. In the past, hypnosis has been associated often with entertainment purposes. But our discussion is intended to enlighten and delight you regarding the empowering possibilities Reprogramming Hypnosis/Self-hypnosis offers you for personal growth and wellness.

You will be introduced to your subconscious, an immensely powerful part of your mind that has been operating off your radar screen as your *Silent, Invisible Partner*. We will examine why your subconscious mind, left to its own devices, may or may not help you attain truly satisfactory outcomes. In fact, you will become aware of how it is possible for your subconscious to unintentionally and mistakenly be working against your well-being even though your subconscious is convinced that it is giving you what you want. Furthermore, you will learn how to practice different techniques of Reprogramming Self-hypnosis that are practical skills intended to enrich and support you throughout your lifetime.

Included is a chapter for understanding how hypnosis automatically impacts simultaneously all parts of your mind, your body and your Spirit — referred to herein as your Mind/Body/Spirit. You will read about others' experiences that demonstrate how hypnosis can produce positive changes mentally, emotionally, physically and spiritually. Besides this you will receive the tools to navigate the challenges of negative people, negative thoughts and negative emotional energies. Case studies are provided to illustrate clearly how Reprogramming Hypnosis techniques teach ways to stay positive in Mind/Body/Spirit, supporting the positive Subconscious Programming you desire. A final chapter includes guidelines for your success using

Reprogramming Hypnosis/Self-hypnosis as well as guidelines for motivation to continue Reprogramming Self-hypnosis as a lifelong self-empowerment support system and an instrument for ongoing enlightenment.

To enhance your enjoyment of this path you will be traveling, this book offers you an interactive learning process that appeals to all kinds of learning styles. Besides listening to your bonus audio, it is highly recommended that you choose a journal to record your responses to questions brought up throughout this book. For your convenience a journal with affirmations (also used as self-hypnosis suggestions) has been provided in the back of this book. It's for journaling your thoughts, ideas, experiences and reactions while they are still fresh in mind. For example, now might be a good time to clarify in writing whatever positive changes/goals you already have targeted for your main focus.

THE ROADRUNNER SHORTCUT VERSION FOR REPROGRAMMING

For those readers who want to learn first how to do Reprogramming Self-hypnosis and later acquire a thorough understanding of the whys and essential supporting details, here is an option that you may choose at any time:

First, listen to your free copy of *Relax, Release and Dream On* as suggested in the Preface if that is your choice to do so. Choose a quiet time and place and first listen to it during your waking hours without closing your eyes. That way you hear clearly and feel comfortable with what is being said.

Then for over a period of at least one week, listen to your audio (if possible) a minimum of once a day during waking hours. Listen to it also every night as you go to sleep. The hypnotic suggestions are going into your subconscious even during sleep as long as your ears can hear them. If possible put the recording on repeat. Be assured that after that one week you will have experienced hypnosis.

Second, read Chapter Four that gives you step-by-step

instructions to learn Reprogramming Self-hypnosis. Review the scripts provided there and the scripts in Appendix Two.

Third, start practicing your entry into the relaxed state of self-hypnosis while listening to track three, the musical backdrop from *Relax, Release and Dream On*. This track of 100% soft music will assist you while initiating self-hypnosis. After listening to this entire audio for a few times, the audio music will have become associated with your relaxed state of hypnosis. The music subsequently will help induce self-hypnosis with less effort. Start with choosing three Reprogramming Self-hypnosis suggestions and express them during your self-hypnosis time. Continue to repeat this process once a day for thirty days to reinforce your new suggestions for your subconscious.

Fourth, read the rest of this book. It contains additional information that prepares you for achieving optimal outcomes for Reprogramming Self-hypnosis and, if applicable, more optimal outcomes for your facilitator-led Reprogramming Hypnosis experiences as well.

GETTING TO KNOW ME

I have felt a persistent, compelling need to share with everyone what I had found to be so valuable and true more than thirty years ago. I was teaching English and Oral Communications at Wheeling High School in suburban Chicago, IL, when I elected to take the Wheeling Adult School enrichment classes on self-hypnosis. Just twenty-two years old, I had never had any experience in the realm of hypnosis. Nevertheless, I had an innate interest about expanding my mind into this new arena. I wanted to better comprehend how the mind worked. My self-hypnosis classes provided life-altering experiences that activated the teacher-in-me to share it with others. Since then I have never surrendered my goal to bring awareness, understanding and inspiration regarding hypnosis to the largest audience possible.

Besides practicing my self-hypnosis for sleep deprivation, for increased energy and for jet lag, I improved my tennis game from advanced beginner to the high advanced level. I used hypnosis to expand my creative ideas for teaching, enhanced my sex life and further developed my intuition that guided me along my life path. What I had envisioned for hypnosis on a larger scale, however, was contributing to society's challenging issues. I could imagine hypnosis being beneficial for preventative health care as well as general physical and mental health care. Hypnosis could be utilized for education, parenting skills, geriatric care, even drug and alcohol rehabilitation. Wherever the mind is involved, hypnosis potentially could be of service. So I told this to everyone I knew such as family members, friends, coworkers, acquaintances and even strangers. However, to my great astonishment, was faced with a startling realization. No one believed me! I was ahead of my time and no one was yet ready to embrace my discoveries. My only option was to practice patience waiting for the right time to come when hypnosis could be more widely accepted and understood for its positive and powerful transformative capabilities.

My vision of communicating this knowledge and discoveries started becoming reality in 2005 when I became published as the author of the nine-CD series, *Reprogram Your Subconscious: How to Use Hypnosis to Get What You Really Want*. It was produced in partnership with Nightingale-Conant, a company that has been a world leader in the personal development field since 1960. For the last five years my nine-CD series (five tutorial audios/ four hypnotic guided imagery), has been on Nightingale's coveted Top Seller list. Now I have given birth to the updated, expanded book version that represents the most comprehensive packaging to date of everything I have learned from my years of work in the field of hypnosis and Mind/Body/Spirit well-being. This book contains about twice the amount of material from the original series. The goal is to supply you with whatever is necessary for your immediate and practical application of Reprogramming Hypnosis to obtain the goals you are seeking.

YOUR BENEFITS PACKAGE

Generally speaking you might use Reprogramming Self-hypnosis for:

- Breaking your stress cycle with physical/mental/emotional relaxation that promotes your good health and general well-being
- Communicating directly with your subconscious, accessing/giving/receiving information
- Communicating with your subconscious to modify your attitudes, mindsets, belief systems, feelings and behaviors
- Communicating with your *Higher Power* (such as *God, Jesus, Allah, Saints, Buddha, Nature, Source, Spiritual Guide, Guardian Angel, etc.*) to receive *Inner Wisdom* and guidance

IF YOU HAD A MAGIC WAND

As you learn more about your subconscious mind and how it works, you can learn to use Reprogramming Hypnosis techniques to change existing Subconscious Programming and replace it with what you really want. What you want may be: excellent health, progress in your career, positive relations with family members, teachers, coworkers and other people, greater financial security, life without worry or anxiety, more spiritual understanding, a positive body image, higher self-esteem, higher self-confidence, greater self-acceptance or other personal goals. Your list might seem endless! Perhaps the following will help you identify something else specific in your life that you would desire to be more positive.

COULD THIS BE YOU?

If you have been unable to: stop feeling sad • stop feeling unmotivated • stop smoking • stop gaining weight • stop sleep problems • stop worrying • stop panic attacks permanently • stop being angry • stop biting your nails • stop being shy • stop feeling road rage • stop losing your keys • or stop any other resistant behavior, now you may have the answer to why you have been unsuccessful. *Your subconscious is steadfast in following its commitments to enforce all your Subconscious Programs.* No doubt your subconscious is maintaining the very thing you want to change. Reprogramming your subconscious may be just what is needed.

POSSIBLE GOALS

The specific reasons and goals for Reprogramming Self-hypnosis vary for each individual. You can use Reprogramming Hypnosis/ Self-hypnosis for almost anything you want that involves your subconscious mind. Following is a list to consider of common situations where you could utilize this type of reprogramming:

• presenting yourself optimally for job interviews • thinking positively • feeling nurtured • remembering to say *I love you* more often • remembering to give your kids hugs more often • playing cards better • releasing your tension from tight muscles • stopping yourself from monopolizing conversations • waking up two minutes before your alarm clock • stopping yourself from criticizing without meaning to criticize • stopping yourself from taking out your anger on someone else • listening more carefully • getting rid of your warts • improving your tennis game • reading faster • improving your speaking ability • trusting your gut feeling • enjoying sex and enjoying it more often • overcoming your jet lag • releasing negative thoughts • relieving your pain from a known source

And of course, Reprogramming Self-hypnosis is wonderful

for its calming ability. It may be used in the following situations for calming nerves and allaying fears:

• before giving your speech • before your exam • before, during and after your surgery • before doing your tax forms • before going out on your first date • before getting pregnancy results • before going in front of a judge • before a policeman comes up to your car and asks you for your driver's license • before getting a biopsy report • before asking for her hand in marriage • before buying your home • before seeing your school principal • before trying on last year's bathing suit • before stepping on your scale • before meeting your child's future spouse • before you meet your child's future in-laws • before reading the directions for your new computer • before seeing your family for Thanksgiving • before going to your high school reunion • before opening your gas or electric bill • before your car mechanic tells you what is wrong with your car • before getting the weather report for your committed vacation spot • before hitting your drive at first tee with everyone watching • before going for a lawsuit deposition • before getting your dental work done

AND THE LIST GOES ON

What has transpired within the HypnoCounseling sessions with my clients goes a long way in explaining how remarkably broad the beneficial applications are for hypnosis and self-hypnosis. While hypnosis has been typically associated with cigarette cessation and weight reduction, there are over seventy-five less publicized areas in which professionals in my field have utilized hypnosis techniques to relieve clients' reactions to stress. The following represents presenting issues or areas needing improvement that have benefited through Reprogramming Hypnosis techniques:

Abuse	Acne
Acid Reflux	ADD, ADHD
Addictions	Adoption
Allergies	Anger
Anxieties	Blood Pressure
Broken Bones	Cancer
Career/Job	Childbirth
Colitis	Concentration
Constipation	Coping as a Caregiver
Coping Long Term	Creativity
Critical Inner Voice	Dental Procedures
Diabetes	Divorce
Fatigue	Fears* (see next page)
Gambling	Grief
Habits	Hair Pulling
Indigo Children	Infertility
Insomnia	Interviewing
Intuition Enhancement	Irritable Bowel
Learning Problems	Memory
Menopause	Migraines
Money Issues	Morning Sickness
Motivation	Nail Biting
Negative Thinking	Nightmares
Obsessive/Compulsive	Pain Management
Partnerships	Past Life
Perfectionism	Post-Traumatic Stress
PMS	Presentation Skills
Procrastination	Racing Thoughts
Relationships	Resistance to Change

Right Brain Dominance	Sadness
Self-Esteem	Self-Confidence
Self-Punishment	Self-Sabotage
Sexual Concerns	Shyness
Sibling Rivalry	Skin Disorders
Sleep Issues	Smoking Cessation
Spiritual Development	Sports Enhancement
Stage Fright	Stress
Stuttering	Surgery Preparation and Recovery
Teeth Grinding/Clenching	Test Taking
Tic	Tinnitus
Trauma	Weight Control
Worrying Excessively	Wounds That Won't Heal

*FEARS about:

• flying in airplanes • death • dogs • doctors • dentists • success • failure • commitment • closed-in spaces • insects • needles • childbirth • aging • the dark • getting trapped in an elevator • heights • gaining weight • being sexually assaulted • being criticized • germs • fears coming back • choking • gagging • men • women • marriage • losing a job • spiders • bankruptcy, etc.

STRETCH YOUR MIND

You will benefit most from reading this book if you keep an open mind so the contents of this book might touch you in ways that might be unknown at this moment. Allow your mind to *stretch outside the box*. I can best explain why this is important by summarizing a poem, *The Blind Men and the Elephant* by the American poet John Godfrey Saxe (1816-1887). The poem is based on a fable told in India about six blind men who went to meet an elephant, an animal that they had never before encountered.

REALITY IS IN THE EYES OF THE BEHOLDER

The poem tells how each blind man gave a description of the part of the elephant he first touched. Each blind man concluded that what he had touched was the *only accurate description* of the entire elephant. The one touching the main part of the body described the elephant as a wall. The second touched the tusks and described it like two spears. The third blind man touched the trunk and declared it was like a snake. Yet, the fourth blind man clung to a leg and described the animal was like a tree. The fifth blind man caught the elephant by the ear and was convinced the elephant was like a fan. The sixth blind man reached out and touched the elephant's tail and proclaimed the elephant was like a rope. All of these blind men had a part of the elephant correct. But each man refused to venture beyond his particular interpretation. Thus, each blind man missed the understanding of the whole elephant that was made up of many parts. Each man was limited to imagining only what solely came through his own perceptions and generalized based only on that. Instead of acknowledging and combining the *insights* of what others had experienced collectively, the blind men stubbornly were unable to imagine the total reality.

I take the moral of this story to heart. Clearly this book was written basically from my perceptions, my conclusions and is only one part, my part, of the total reality.

ARISTOTLE, MOVE OVER

As far as a philosophy goes, HypnoCounseling has been my greatest teacher and laboratory for enlightenment. Dr. Alexander Docker, President of the American Board of Hypno-therapy, observed in *Access*, Fall, 2004, that the way we can measure the worth of any type of self-improvement or wellness modality is to analyze its effectiveness regarding whether it really works or does not work. We may or may not understand exactly why a modality/technique works. Why it works is not the key issue. Rather if it truly works and benefits us, then our intelligence tells us to use it for our benefit. After all, we are practical and wise enough to use electricity even though we do not fully comprehend how electricity works. What I offer for your consideration is from my experience and the wisdom of what has worked — and what has worked many, many times for many hundreds of people I have personally seen as clients, as well as thousands who have been introduced to me through my seminars and audios.

Just as I may not comprehend all the science in electricity, I may not always know all the scientific reasons hypnosis so powerfully and successfully assisted my clients. Frequently I come upon conclusions first, and then realize later the powerful supporting facts that exist for those conclusions. Some things have just appeared through intuitive knowing. In any regard, I am open to wherever my clients' needs lead me. Dr. Docker observed that it may be impossible for a therapy to work every time for all kinds of people. Yet, when a practitioner's techniques are limited by the imposed boundaries that dictate using only generally acceptable ways of looking at reality, then the effectiveness rate of those therapies will drop. As a HypnoCounselor I have not limited my views of reality but rather left everything within the realm of possibility.

YOUR HIGHEST GOOD

Throughout our journey you may be encouraged to know that you have within you the option to recover from glitches and unintentional errors in your Subconscious Programming by reprogramming your computer-like subconscious mind. Your positive substitutions will ultimately establish the most appropriate programming that will promote your *Highest Good*. I use the term Highest Good instead of saying that it will promote a positive result because "positive" is relative. How do you know what is *truly positive* until you have seen the long-term outcome? On the other hand, Highest Good implies what is positive in the broadest perspective and in the long run. You might equate the term Highest Good to that which has been determined to be good from the viewpoint of God or from the viewpoint of whatever Higher Power in which you believe. Think of the times when something that happened seemed so awful, yet it opened the door to some positive outcome that would never have been possible before that awful event first happened. One friend of mine wanted desperately to attend a certain college and was declined admittance. She chose to attend another college where she eventually met the love of her life, her future husband. So it is that you may be unaware or mistaken about what ultimately is best for you or for your Highest Good.

TWO HEADS MAY BE BETTER

Importantly, you will learn how you can initiate these changes yourself and under what circumstances you might need the help of a professional in the hypnosis field. To clarify, the title the hypnosis practitioner uses is dependent upon state laws. As of 2010, persons certified in hypnotherapy are referred to as *HypnoCounselors* when practicing under New Jersey law. In California, however, the same person's title is *hypnotherapist*. For the purposes of this book when the term HypnoCounselor appears, be advised HypnoCounselor may be interchanged with hypnotherapist depending upon the state in which the practitioner practices. Hypnotherapists may be certified by a state approved hypnosis school or they may be licensed professionals such as nurses, social workers, psychologists, and psychiatrists who have taken additional training in hypnosis.

If you are dealing with a serious issue such as drug abuse, clinical depression, thoughts of suicide, violent behaviors, serious physical illness, *bipolar, schizophrenia, psychosis*, etc., you need to incorporate medical doctors and/or licensed mental health professionals to supervise your care and decide if hypnosis is appropriate for you. Non-licensed practitioners of hypnosis do not diagnose illnesses or render a prognosis.

Otherwise, the reasons for seeking a professional *facilitator* depend greatly on your ability to comfortably and effectively complete your own reprogramming changes. At times, unknown subconsciously held resistances may make it very difficult for you to make the changes on your own. Sometimes being your own facilitator transports you too close to the situation to see the forest and instead you focus on the nearest tree. Nonetheless, you will be successful as your own facilitator for accomplishing many of your desired goals. Thus, this book explains hypnosis from both viewpoints: Reprogramming Hypnosis led by a professional facilitator and Reprogramming Self-hypnosis designed and led entirely by you as your own facilitator. Both approaches offer insights that will assist you in mastering your Reprogramming Self-hypnosis.

CHAPTER 2

WELCOME TO YOUR NEW WORLD OF POSSIBILITIES

EXPLORING HYPNOSIS, SELF-HYPNOSIS AND HYPNOCOUNSELING FOR REPROGRAMMING YOUR SUBCONSCIOUS

onsider hypnosis your master key that unlocks your subconscious mind. That being said, it is important to examine and truly understand what exactly hypnosis is so you can effectively use this valuable tool in all its capacities. The word *hypnosis* comes from the Greek root *hypnos*, meaning sleep. Unfortunately, that description has led to many misconceptions that you are put intentionally into sleep when you are hypnotized. This is not the case. When hypnosis is performed by a facilitator or performed by you as in self-hypnosis you are, with few exceptions, actually more aware, focused and concentrated than in your normal everyday conscious state. Perhaps hypnosis may be best summed up this way: Hypnosis is a state of mind that involves focused concentration characteristically with deep relaxation, heightened and expanded awareness.

Hypnosis connects the communication lines between you and your subconscious mind. Once you are in hypnosis, either through facilitator-led hypnosis or self-hypnosis, you have enabled your subconscious to receive and potentially accept your appropriately formulated suggestions. However, be aware that in order for your suggestions to be accepted, they must be harmonious with your ethical, moral and religious/spiritual beliefs. After your suggestions are accepted into your subconscious, these suggestions are empowered to change the way you think, feel and/or behave.

IT IS A STATE OF MIND, REALLY

The hypnosis technique called an *Induction* is your entryway into one of the more relaxed States of Consciousness similar to when you are in deep meditation or deep prayer. The graphic illustrations depicting the brain wave frequency patterns in this chapter will give a visual understanding of the different *Beta, Alpha, Theta and Delta States of Consciousness*. When you enter hypnosis either induced by a facilitator or by self-hypnosis, you naturally and comfortably shift from your active, everyday Beta Consciousness State of awareness (measured in a brain wave frequency of approximately 13-25 hertz) into the more relaxed, slower frequency of the Alpha Consciousness State (a brain wave frequency of approximately 8-12.5 hertz). Alpha is a very common *Altered State of Consciousness* achieved when you first transition into being in hypnosis. It feels familiar because throughout your typical day, you are fluctuating often between Beta and Alpha states. For example, you are in the Alpha State of Consciousness when you are engrossed watching television or doing some monotonous task.

Another altered state, more deeply relaxed and very appropriate for hypnosis suggestions is the Theta Consciousness State (a brain wave frequency of approximately 4-7.5 hertz).

BRAIN WAVE GRAPHS

The following graphs are an approximation of an EEG (electroencephalograph) one second sample. The signal is filtered to present only the specific waves.

The electroencephalogram measures the activity of billions of brain cells called neurons that use electricity to carry information so as to talk to each other, also known as cell signaling. The EEG machine measures the levels of the electricity over the scalp and it appears like waves. The wave patterns change as the level of consciousness changes as seen in the graphs below:

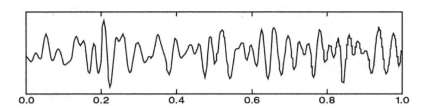

Beta Brain Wave

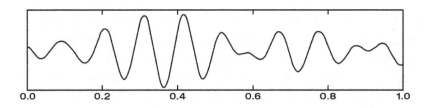

Alpha Brain Wave

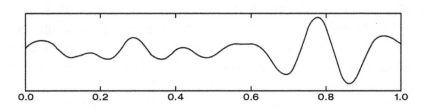

Theta Brain Wave

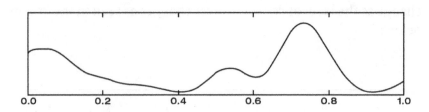

Delta Brain Wave

(Used with permission under the terms of the GNU Free Documentation License)

The deepest relaxed and Altered State of Consciousness for hypnosis is Delta consciousness which is deep sleep (a brain wave frequency of approximately .5-3.5 hertz). When you are in the Delta state, the suggestible part of your subconscious receives the suggestions but you are asleep and unable to interact with active dialogue as you would if you were in the Alpha or the Theta state, not sleeping. When you are given a general anesthesia for a medical operation, the anesthesia brings you into the deep sleep of Delta consciousness where you are unable to converse, yet your subconscious is still active, taking in the data of what is happening.

In contrast, while you are in the Alpha or Theta state you still are able to remember and focus directly upon what is being said without being distracted by disturbances in the immediate environment. In fact when in Alpha or Theta consciousness you still can have a regular conversation with someone else. Suffice it to say it is very difficult to nail down the exact moment when you transition into the hypnotic state of Alpha or Theta.

YOU GOTTA BE IN THE RIGHT FREQUENCY

Of more importance is that when you are in the hypnotic state, the subconscious part of your mind dominates and its frequencies are slower than that of your Beta consciousness. It is significant that when you are in hypnosis, it is through your subconscious mind rather than your conscious mind that your thoughts originate. Also, once in hypnosis it is through your subconscious mind that you perceive the world. Additionally, once you are in Alpha or Theta State of Consciousness, your subconscious is available to you and is in its suggestible state. Regarding self-hypnosis and HypnoCounseling, this means your subconscious then is open to accepting the suggestions you reference or voice out loud or silently with a pre-planned word or phrase. Theoretically your hypnosis suggestions are intended to favorably direct your thoughts, feelings and behaviors for outcomes that you really want. However, when you are in the Beta Consciousness State of mind that uses a faster frequency, you are unable to transmit on the necessary brain wave frequency for directing your subconscious to make changes. It is analogous to radio reception. First you must be on the correct radio station channel frequency to get clear reception. Then you can call and reach that channel to offer your comments and someone is there to answer the phone and respond.

MAYBE IT IS A GOOD THING

As an aside, your subconscious is always observing and recording information about you even when you are in your Beta State of Consciousness. Therefore, your subconscious continues to silently build its database about everything you say, think, do, dream, smell, taste, hear, touch, feel emotionally and emote. It is just that your subconscious is unreceptive to your suggestions/ directives when you are sending them while you are in your Beta State of Consciousness frequencies. And perhaps that is a good thing. How many times have you spoken without thinking and wished to take your words back? Imagine if your subconscious believed everything exactly as you said it and downloaded even your sarcastic or reckless words into your reality? Most likely then you would have many more Faulty Subconscious Programs to correct. That means you also would have considerably more problematic issues to release than you have now!

SUGGESTIBILITY RULES!

One theory still popular among hypnosis professionals is that a part of your conscious mind that has been labeled the *Critical Factor*, intentionally blocks your requests from ever reaching the suggestible part of your subconscious mind. The theory explains that in order to avoid this blocking from happening, you must bypass the Critical Factor of your conscious mind. During my years as a HypnoCounselor I have come to understand this concept differently. It is just you being in the Beta State of Consciousness that disallows your direct access to your subconscious where it is in its suggestible state. As previously stated, when you are in your normal Beta Consciousness State, it is like being unable to tune in to the correct radio station for effective subconscious communications. The point to remember is that changes in your Subconscious Programming are possible only when you reach your subconscious in its suggestible, receptive mode. Your subconscious is in its suggestible, receptive mode, the same mode that is necessary for hypnosis, when you are in the Alpha, Theta and Delta States of Consciousness. For purposes of you using Reprogramming Hypnosis and/or Reprogramming Self-hypnosis, being able to transition into the Alpha and/or Theta state is crucial for successful reprogramming of your subconscious mind. Nevertheless, even when you are in the Alpha/Theta Consciousness States, your suggestions to your subconscious may be rejected if your suggestions lack clarity. More often though the rejections are due to your subconscious mind that is defending your previously downloaded Subconscious Programming. Your subconscious refuses to accept your suggestions if they appear to oppose or conflict in some way with your previously downloaded and still existing Subconscious Programming. So your refusal to accept your desired hypnotic suggestions is motivated by your ever vigilant subconscious mind rather than independently motivated by a part of your conscious mind.

The confusion is understandable since it may look on the surface as though the resistance to new suggestions is due to a consciously initiated rejection. Fortunately, Reprogramming Hypnosis techniques explained in this book can help you resolve the subconsciously perceived *conflicts of interest* between your new suggestions and your already established Subconscious Programming.

CHILDREN HAVE UNIQUE SUBCONSCIOUS SPONGES

Children under the age of twelve seem naturally to be more suggestible than older children and adults. It is far easier to reach their *Suggestible Subconscious* and download suggestions either intentionally or unintentionally. One explanation is because they accept as reality the powerful words and actions of authorities such as parents, teachers and religious figures. There is also a theory that explains this phenomenon. This theory acknowledges that young children are more often in the Alpha or Theta Consciousness States just naturally. Children have wonderful imaginations and enjoy fantasy and daydreams characteristic of the altered states of Alpha and Theta. Furthermore, Alpha and Theta are more natural states of consciousness because they are the states of relaxation rather than of stress. Perhaps younger children are spared significant stress until they are close to being teenagers. Regardless of what the explanation may be, as a child you are very susceptible to accepting Subconscious Programming imposed *intentionally and unintentionally* by your authority figureheads. By the way, those figureheads include your movie/TV/musician role models. No wonder your authority figures have wielded lasting, powerful influence over you.

YOU HAVE THAT SPECIAL FEELING

You might recognize the feeling of hypnosis as that feeling you get when you have been bored driving your car and you realize you cannot remember driving the last three miles. Or that feeling you get when you have been watching a TV show and you zone out without really being aware of missing the show. Daydreaming is an example of being in the Alpha or Theta state. It feels like a pleasant, relaxed feeling. Your mind just is focused somewhere else, deep in thought and your immediate, physical surroundings have less importance to you.

MEDITATION'S HIGH-ACHIEVING SIBLING, HYPNOSIS

Both meditation and hypnosis are wonderful techniques for relaxing the Mind/Body/Spirit. Nevertheless, meditation currently is more widely known and practiced than is hypnosis. It has been as if the word *hypnosis* had too many misconceptions associated with it. I will amplify this topic later as we focus on myths about hypnosis. On the other hand, hypnosis has important, valuable capabilities that distinguish it from meditation. Hypnosis, like meditation, gives you the option to maintain inner silence, the absence of thoughts and the introspective state characteristic of meditation. Hypnosis, similar to meditation, allows you to perceive information from your subconscious levels that your cluttered conscious mind normally obscures. Yet, hypnosis gives you an additional option to be more proactive. You can communicate your directives framed as suggestions to your subconscious. Although many people use hypnosis just to achieve the meditative state of Alpha and Theta, hypnosis is most commonly known for going even further.

HYPNOSIS IS LIKE A LASER BEAM

Hypnosis helps you create subconsciously orchestrated positive changes and achieve goals using your Mind/Body/Spirit to support your desires. Your hypnotic suggestions precisely delineate for your subconscious what needs to be changed, what needs to be deleted and what needs to be added to your life (thoughts, feelings and behaviors) for a specific outcome. Once your subconscious accepts a suggestion, it automatically manifests it, typically within a short period of time, as a shift in one or more of the following: your attitudes, mindsets, belief systems, emotions, behaviors and/or physical well-being. While other forms of relaxation and inner communication might be compared to turning a light on inside your subconscious, hypnosis compares to you turning that light on and then directing a laser beam inside to achieve your specific, desirable results and goals. The speed with which people are able to accomplish their desires using hypnosis is often remarkable. Not every time, but in so many cases, people successfully reach their goal or a significant part of their goal within thirty to sixty days. And this includes issues that may have been plaguing the person for years or even throughout a lifetime.

HARD TO DETECT

There might not be a clear indication when you transition from Beta State of Consciousness to Alpha or Theta State of Consciousness. If you are just learning self-hypnosis, it may be challenging to pin down when you start being in hypnosis because it may be difficult to recognize or feel that you are actually in hypnosis. After some practice you will arrive at a sense of being relaxed and slowed down. Your body may feel heavier than usual. Other signs that you have indeed transitioned into hypnosis are when your breathing slows, your body temperature rises or drops and/or your heartbeat slows. Nonetheless a familiar refrain from clients is that they did not think they were actually in hypnosis. Some will insist they never were hypnotized or in hypnosis. They did not feel any different than they felt before. They heard all sounds from the surrounding environment and remembered everything that was said during the process. It just felt like normal relaxation.

SO CONVINCE ME

As a result of this typical perception, there is usually something in a hypnosis session to provide proof that the client is really in hypnosis. These proofs are called *convincers*. It may be as simple as asking you to try to open your eyes, yet suggesting to you that at that time that you prefer to keep them closed or you just are unable to open them. You may feel as though your eyelids are stuck, closed tightly until the HypnoCounselor gives you the new suggestion that you can easily and comfortably open your eyes again.

Sometimes the clients override the suggestion that their eyes feel unable to open. Instead they open their eyes. That is always your option. It basically means those clients needed to feel reassured that they, at any time on their own volition, can open their eyes. Even though the clients may still be in hypnosis with their eyes closed, they are comforted knowing they do have the power to open their eyes at will. If clients open their eyes, the facilitator may then suggest they close their eyes once more and go even deeper into relaxation because they are still and always will be ultimately the ones in control.

Another indicator to check the level of hypnosis is asking the clients' subconscious to signal when they are in a deeper level of hypnosis just by subconsciously and automatically lifting up their finger on one hand. This is an example of an *Ideomotor Response*. Used this way, an Ideomotor Response convinces you that you indeed are in a deep level of relaxation because you can feel your finger lift up without intentionally moving your finger.

YOU ARE IN CHARGE

When you utilize the tremendous power of hypnosis to communicate with your subconscious to effect changes within your Mind/Body/Spirit, you are always the one in charge. You are selecting all that feels right to you and rejecting anything that does not. Even if you are listening to a HypnoCounselor who is facilitating your communications, you still have the power to accept or reject anything that is said. In fact, your subconscious does it automatically for you since it understands your ethics, morals and religious/spiritual beliefs and recognizes you would not want any of those compromised. Would you agree that this is rather impressive? In actuality all hypnosis is really self-hypnosis because you have to give yourself permission to follow the suggestions.

HYPNOSIS: AS OLD AS THE PYRAMIDS

Interestingly, the practice of hypnosis actually has ancient roots. The ancient Egyptians, Greeks and Persians all had customs that appear to emulate the state of hypnosis. Some speculate that the ancient Egyptians used hypnosis as a form of healing in their *Sleep Temples*. The Sleep Temples were places where sick patients would quietly relax or begin sleeping while a healer whispered through a partition, telling the patient that all was healed and the patient was well. In fact, today it is known that during your sleep cycle, you enter the Alpha, Theta and Delta altered states of consciousness. It is during such times when your Suggestible Subconscious dominates the forefront of your mind that it enables you to receive and respond to such communications. So, the ancient Egyptians may have discovered the workings of hypnosis and the suggestibility of the subconscious long before our time.

HYPNOSIS UPDATED

FRANZ ANTON MESMER (1734-1815)

German born *Franz Anton Mesmer* is considered the father of hypnosis. Mesmer had studied theology, philosophy and law before studying medicine and becoming a doctor. Mesmer would use the power of what we currently call an *Indirect Suggestion*. For example, his patients would respond by going into trance with Mesmer's wild waving arm antics, a confusion technique. He also introduced his new theory of *Magnetic Fluid* that was described as a *Universal Energy* that would bring about the desired healing once it was balanced within one's body. Mesmer was well known by 1794 for his miraculous healings. However, through unfortunate circumstances not necessarily of his own doing, his reputation was defamed by a commission of doctors ordered to investigate Mesmer's theories and practices. Because the doctors could not perceive any tangible evidence of the Mesmer's Magnetic Fluid, they declared Mesmer had to be a fraud. Mesmer left for London and continued healing patients without charge. Although he died in obscurity, today we still use his name to identify someone who is in a trancelike condition as being *mesmerized*. Others have theorized that Mesmer's healings were due to *Auto-suggestions* that actually functioned in the same way as self-hypnosis suggestions. Auto-suggestions support the theory: *what your subconscious mind accepts as your truth, becomes your actual reality.*

JAMES BRAID (1796-1860)

In 1841 *James Braid*, a Scottish physician, reportedly coined the term *hypnosis* in his practice. The word *hypnosis*, as mentioned before, actually comes from the Greek root *hypnos*, meaning sleep. Braid tried but failed to change the nuances of the word *hypnotism*. He did this because the word promoted the confusion that you are asleep during hypnosis when actually most people are more aware and focused when in hypnosis than when in their regular waking hours. Braid was fascinated with the ability of people to go into a trance and wrote on the subject.

For years, hypnosis was widely used for surgical anesthesia. But with the discovery of chloroform in 1848, hypnosis lost its popularity. Both chloroform and ether quickly became the newest medical practice for anesthesia just at a time when hypnosis might have gained a more dominant role in health care.

WHY THE TURTLE AND NOT THE HARE?

Have you ever wondered why something as valuable as hypnosis has taken so long to be accepted by the general public? One answer would point to the example of the *Heimlich maneuver,* now called the *Abdominal Thrust Technique.* The Heimlich technique is now one of the most widely accepted ways to dislodge whatever may be blocking a choking person's breathing passageway. Although Henry Heimlich introduced the procedure in 1974, it only became generally accepted practice in 1985, eleven years after its introduction. Hard to imagine something as easy, noninvasive and so effective in saving lives would take so long to be accepted.

Hypnosis has certainly had its challenges as a credible modality burdened with misconceptions and associations with individuals who sadly have used it inappropriately. The movies erroneously depicted hypnosis as mind-control by the bad guys. *Entertainment hypnosis* provided laughs for audiences as hypnotized individuals performed zany antics that normally the participants would never do. No wonder it has taken hypnosis this long to gain general public acceptance! Unfortunately, until fairly recent times, there has been an absence of large bodies of research promoting a more extensive use of hypnosis for health care, for self-improvement and for other fields as well. But today there are impressive amounts of convincing research that demand our attention as we seek all safe, valid and cost-effective approaches for maintaining harmony and balance physically, mentally, emotionally and spiritually. As you will see, clinical research now concludes hypnosis provides a positive, noninvasive adjunct to conventional medicine.

HYPNOSIS UNDER THE MICROSCOPE

Fortunately a strong body of research now exists to support the efficacy of clinical hypnosis for Mind/Body/Spirit well-being. In gathering materials to demonstrate this point, I focused mainly on a sampling of recent research within the last five to ten years. It was important to choose references across the broad spectrum of beneficial applications for hypnosis. The research verifies the enormous possibilities for hypnosis/self-hypnosis for improving quality of life.

Below is listed seventeen titles of clinical studies supporting the positive uses for hypnosis. More complete information for accessing these articles is in the bibliography:

- Hypnotherapy an Effective Treatment for Irritable Bowel Syndrome
- Self-hypnosis Relapse Prevention Training with Chronic Drug/Alcohol Users: Effects on Self-esteem
- Hypnosis Shown to Reduce Symptoms of Dementia
- Mind-Body Interventions in Oncology
- Hypnosis as an Adjunct Therapy on the Management of Diabetes
- Hypnosis for Smoking Cessation
- Stanford Study Shows Hypnosis Helps Kids Undergoing Difficult Procedure
- Hypnotic Alteration of Body Image in the Eating Disordered

- Effect of Hypnosis on Systemic and Rectal Mucosal Measures of Inflammation in Ulcerative Colitis
- Ericksonian Hypnosis in Tinnitus Therapy
- Clinical Hypnosis for Reduction of Atrial Fibrillation After Coronary Artery Bypass Graft Surgery
- Hypnotic Approaches for Alopecia Areata
- Review of the Efficacy of Clinical Hypnosis with Headaches and Migraines
- Hypnosis as a Vehicle for Choice and Self-agency in the Treatment of Children with Trichotillomania
- The Hypnotic Belay in Alpine Mountaineering: the Use of Self-hypnosis for the Resolution of Sports Injuries and for Performance Enhancement
- Hypnosis, Hypnotizability and Treatment
- Ericksonian Hypnosis in Women with Fibromyalgia Syndrome

ADDITIONAL EXAMPLES OF RESEARCH

- Hypnotherapy has been reported to improve skin disorders. According to an article in the Archives of Dermatology by Dr. Philip D. Shenefelt (vol. 136, Mar 2000), eighty percent of skin disorders that they tested showed improvements through hypnotherapy.

- Stanley Fisher, a leading psychoanalyst trained in medical, forensic and psychological applications of hypnosis reported in *Bottom Line Health*, November 2003, that patients benefit by using self-hypnosis to communicate with their body and prepare their body for surgery and post-surgery. He suggested that using self-hypnosis promoted a faster recovery. In fact, eighty-nine percent of patients who used self-hypnosis for surgery preparation, during and after surgery, recovered more quickly than the patients who did not use self-hypnosis techniques for surgery.

• In *Newsweek*, September, 2004, Dr. David Spiegel, a professor and associate chair at Stanford University School of Medicine and an expert in the practice of hypnosis, was quoted on his views regarding the uses of hypnosis. He pointed out that in addition to pain management, relieving the effects of stress and gaining control over habits, hypnosis has been successful when an alternative to sedation is needed. One example he observed that used hypnosis effectively for an intrusive medical procedure was angiography.

BELIEVE IT OR NOT: MYTHS EXPOSED

Before continuing, it is appropriate to dispel some of the myths regarding hypnosis that might prevent one from making use of this powerful self-improvement tool. Even though these myths relate mostly to facilitator-led hypnosis, the explanations apply for self-hypnosis concerns too. Below is a list of common myths and a discussion of the facts that expose the inaccuracy of the myths:

THE TRUTH AND ONLY THE TRUTH

Myth #1: Hypnosis can control you and make you do and say things that you really do not want to do. It is easy to understand the source of this misconception. You may have witnessed stage hypnotists who seem to make people do and say silly things that make audiences erupt with laughter. But what is it about those volunteers that would allow them to talk and act that way in front of an audience? Remember they willingly volunteered to have fun and be part of the entertainment. These volunteers are more likely to be risk takers and people who enjoy the spotlight.

If they were not comfortable making fun of themselves, their subconscious would never permit them to relax into the highly suggestible state of hypnosis. Typically, the hypnotist would prepare them with a *Post-hypnotic Suggestion* so the volunteers would feel no embarrassment about what they said or did. That is Entertainment Hypnosis. Hypnosis for entertainment purposes is completely different from clinical hypnosis used for behavioral and attitudinal modification by hypnosis professionals in a private office setting.

Myth #2: While in hypnosis, you may divulge something you want kept totally private, such as an embarrassing family secret or your finances. When you seek the services of a professional HypnoCounselor or hypnotherapist for counseling, the truth is that you are the one in control. Your judgments are still intact as is your ability to discriminate and withhold anything you choose. You disclose only what you feel comfortable disclosing. No one can force any information out of you that you prefer to keep private. Typically during my pre-hypnosis interview with clients, I explain to them that I can be of the most assistance when I understand the particulars of their situation. However, it is not necessary for them to share personal details when in hypnosis if they choose not to do so. Sometimes, the client prefers not to mention the particulars about specific people, certain situations or events, especially where there are strong emotions involved. And yet we are still able to deal effectively with such cases by giving the clients suggestions that can direct their subconscious to resolve the issue without resurrecting the specifics of the client's past. The clients still can reach the goals of their sessions even though they are communicating in broader generalizations.

Myth #3: A substantial percentage of people are unable to be hypnotized. The truth is that anyone who can follow directions can allow his/her conscious mind to transition into the altered Alpha state and, thus, successfully achieve hypnosis in an office setting. The key question is: Do you really want to allow yourself to go into hypnosis? And is there something like a fear subconsciously blocking you from allowing your transition into Alpha? Personally, the question of whether someone will be able to go into hypnosis is a non-issue in my practice. Yes, I am talking about a sampling that includes hundreds of people. Yes, this is a self-selecting group. They have made a commitment emotionally and financially to use my hypnosis services. Yet many people are quite nervous when they come. Many are skeptical about whether they can be hypnotized. What most researchers may overlook when testing people's potential for going into hypnosis is the techniques that can calm your nervousness before hypnosis. The following are the factors that make it possible for most everyone to achieve the hypnotic state:

TAP INTO YOUR SUBCONSCIOUS

- *Factor One: Acupressure tapping techniques*, based on principles closely aligned with *Acupuncture*, can help put you into a positive frame of mind for hypnosis. Acupressure *Muscle Testing* techniques also can uncover and reverse resistances like fears and negative attitudes before you even begin with the hypnosis Induction. For instance, in my preliminary interview with a client, I demonstrate Muscle Testing through Acupressure points, also called *Applied Kinesiology*, and explained in detail in Chapter Six. These Acupressure techniques help immensely with a person who might typically and unknowingly resist hypnosis. In essence, Muscle Testing techniques allow you to focus in a positive way to release negative thoughts that might block your hypnosis success. There are many different approaches that a facilitator may utilize that work better for the clients who need to feel safe and more in control of the hypnosis process. When you are able to trust your facilitator's expertise, training and good intentions, it is easy to follow the simple relaxation techniques with a high degree of success.

THE SLAM DUNK

- *Factor Two:* In 2002, I established a *protocol* for clients to listen to the audio *Relax, Release and Dream On,* to virtually guarantee that they would experience hypnosis comfortably and successfully in the privacy of their own home. Listening to the audio wipes away fears concerning successful entrance into hypnosis. It works best when clients listen to *Relax, Release and Dream On* at times during both waking hours and every night at bedtime, at least for several days consecutively before their first appointment. As you sleep, your subconscious is listening and integrating the acceptable suggestions that are in the audio. Listening to this audio makes the entire process of hypnosis familiar, pleasurable and easy. You may feel calmer and more relaxed the next day after listening to this audio, a type of healing hypnotic guided imagery including positive affirmations. Thus, before you even initiate hypnosis, your attitudes and feelings regarding the hypnosis process may register as positive. I have included *Relax, Release and Dream On* to introduce you to an immediate experiential understanding and application supporting this book's virtual hypnosis course.

IMPERATIVE PRIVACY

- *Factor Three:* The HypnoCounselor has a clearly defined responsibility to protect your privacy. It is in the HypnoCounselor's code of ethics to maintain confidentiality. This is essential for trust and confidence in the relationship between the HypnoCounselor and client. All records are kept private. This rule of privacy for all clients ensures you more peace of mind conducive for relaxing into hypnosis.

DO YOUR HOMEWORK

- *Factor Four:* When the need arises for seeking professional hypnosis counseling, your responsibility is to research and carefully evaluate the qualifications, reputation, integrity and compatibility of the hypnosis professional for your situation. Just as in any service field, HypnoCounselors and hypnotherapists have different techniques, training, experience levels, personalities, perspectives and intuitive abilities. Select the professional who matches your needs and comfort level. Choose with wisdom and trust your intuition too. Doing so will increase your ability to enjoy hypnosis (remember it is a pleasurable, relaxed feeling) and receive the most benefits.

YOUR MIND AND HEART UNITED IN THE RIGHT PLACE

- *Factor Five:* Besides trusting your facilitator, another determining factor for allowing yourself to enter hypnosis is the power of your commitment to your identified goals for hypnosis. Your willingness to allow yourself into hypnosis is related to how much you are personally and internally motivated. Oftentimes clients seek out a hypnosis professional because a family member has insisted they go for hypnosis help. This is often the case for those attempting smoking cessation. But using hypnosis to stop cigarette smoking or alter any other type of habit, requires that the client truly wants it and is self-motivated.

Thus, people refusing to continue the cigarette habit will stick to their commitment. Those choosing hypnosis for the sake of pleasing others will cave in too easily when they are challenged. They typically are interested only in demonstrating that they *tried* rather than being focused on succeeding. Consequently, they may resist even entering the hypnotic state. For instance, if you are seeking to stop the cigarette habit, you must have a "burning" desire to stop for your own sake and well-being. Otherwise you should save your money until you are undoubtedly ready to quit.

BE CAREFUL WHAT YOU WISH FOR

- *Factor Six:* Another form of resistance to going into hypnosis may ensue after someone's hypnosis goals have been achieved. There is an uncommon yet instructive case about one teenager who wanted to improve his grades. Kyle knew he had to study much more than he was currently doing. He chose suggestions so he would do his science homework before he socialized on the Internet. Kyle also wanted to overcome his shyness and be more outgoing. Interestingly, immediately after his hypnosis session he began behaving with an outgoing style. That night for the first time ever Kyle had a lengthy conversation with his dad's friend. The next morning he awakened and started studying his science homework. So I was quite surprised when I received a phone call from his dad declaring that his son was unhappy. His son was not comfortable with his new behavior and wanted to return to his old ways. That is always a person's option.

But, remember that saying: *Be careful what you wish for because you might just get it?* Needless to say, be forewarned and prepared to perhaps instantaneously get what you have requested through the suggestions you have planted in your subconscious mind.

CHANGE FOR THE BETTER

- *Factor Seven:* Quite clearly what frightens many people is simply change, any change, even though it may be completely positive for them and is exactly what they had desired and intended to achieve. Regardless of all the positives, change still represents the *unknown*. This fear may be addressed with specific suggestions that preempt this issue. One such hypnosis suggestion I recommend mentions how easily you are making the transition into your new positive thoughts, mindsets, feelings and behaviors. You may find it feels so much more comfortable and natural experiencing this improved way than the way it used to be for you in the past.

In any case, specific and purposeful suggestions may provide a seamless transition that prevents anything other than ease and comfort about changes. When you make a change in a particular behavior or belief system through hypnosis, your subconscious automatically without any fanfare orchestrates the changes that create the positive, natural shifts in your life. With the proper hypnosis suggestions you still are able to recognize the role of your self-empowering hypnosis as a valuable part of the equation. You know you are doing this for you and you are taking charge. The unknowns are made known through your specific Reprogramming Hypnosis suggestions that you have discussed and approved beforehand.

WHAT WORKS FOR LILY MAY NOT WORK FOR BILLY

- *Factor Eight:* Another element to consider for success in achieving hypnosis is that different people with different personalities may require different approaches and different techniques. In order for hypnosis to be successful, you need the appropriate Induction and appropriately worded suggestions individualized for you. The person who has concern about being controlled by others is oftentimes the same person who struggles with trusting and accepting another's authority. It is a high priority for such people to be autonomous and thus maintain control. You may recognize this type of personality as the fiercely independent person who may have been the strong-willed kid, the rebel who stood up for himself/herself, or the free spirit, or the risk taker who regularly challenged authority figures. These types of people need an Induction into hypnosis that allows them to see that the hypnosis process is one that they are controlling rather than one that they are submissively following. There are specific kinds of Inductions and other hypnosis techniques that adopt an indirect, yet effective approach for those who need to be reassured that they are always in charge and in control.

Other people, who tend to be more willing to go by the rules, follow directions of the leader, who prefer to be peacemakers, often find it very easy and comfortable to follow a facilitator's lead into relaxation. It is agreeable for them to be told what to do. Here again the level of trust between the facilitator and you is tantamount to your permitting the hypnosis process. You need to trust the safety of the process believing you are indeed safe; trust the sincerity of the facilitator and trust the facilitator's comprehensive expertise in hypnosis. This all promotes success for your entering hypnosis and subconsciously accepting your selected hypnosis suggestions.

Myth #4: You could get stuck in hypnosis and not be able to come out of it. Although many people have expressed this fear, it is unfounded. Even if something were to happen to your facilitator and he/she were unable to give you instructions to get out of hypnosis, you automatically would come back soon to your conscious state sensing nothing was going on. Or you would be able to return to your conscious state after taking a short nap. When you listen to a hypnotic guided imagery audio as you go to sleep at night, the recording may last less than an hour; yet, you sleep normally and awaken on your own. Thus, it happens all the time that you naturally come out of hypnosis.

Myth #5: Hypnosis is a short-lived fix providing you only temporary help. In reality the opposite is closer to the truth. Hypnosis creates lasting changes especially when you reinforce these changes for at least thirty days or more to cement your new habit. Once the suggestions given during hypnosis have been accepted into your subconscious mind, the subconscious transforms those suggestions into newly approved mindsets, belief systems, feelings and/or behaviors. The result is that your thoughts, feelings and behaviors respond to the new habits as part of your permanent Subconscious Programming.

Just as you only can operate your computer based on the programming that is currently downloaded into your computer, so it is that you automatically follow only what exists in your internal Subconscious Programming.

On the other hand, please note that like all of us, you are vulnerable to life's crises and other dramatic forces that can create new, uninvited changes in your Subconscious

Programming. That is why it is so important to keep practicing your hypnosis on a frequent, consistent basis to monitor and correct those unforeseen and unwanted changes. In fact, hypnosis is recommended as your daily tonic. If you are already practicing meditation, then hypnosis and meditation may easily overlap or may be performed entirely simultaneously. You may meditate after getting into the hypnotic state. Then while remaining in meditation, proceed to give yourself your preferred hypnotic suggestions.

MORE GROUND RULES FOR HYPNOSIS

TAKE HYPNOSIS SERIOUSLY

A hypnosis facilitator unfamiliar with the nuances of proper hypnosis technique may produce unwanted consequences. One such case happened when a person unskilled in hypnosis techniques tried to help a smoker to quit smoking. The person dabbling in hypnosis gave the smoker a suggestion that cigarettes made him extremely nauseous. After the hypnosis was finished, anytime the smoker smelled a cigarette or even thought of a cigarette, he indeed got so nauseous that he became physically compromised. He did stop smoking. But he literally could not bear being near any smokers without getting so nauseous that he had to leave the area. Fortunately, it was possible for a professional HypnoCounselor to remove and correct the inappropriate suggestions.

THERE REALLY IS AN ART TO HYPNOSIS

Good hypnosis training and clinical experience in hypnosis are essential for the professional facilitator. Writing effective hypnotic suggestions for the general public requires a thorough comprehension of hypnosis, the subconscious mind and all kinds of variables that exist within our population. What exactly is said to you while you are in hypnosis is very important as each word specifically is geared to direct your subconscious to follow the suggestion just as it is worded. The goal is to choose suggestions with phrasing appropriate for you so they are easily understood by your Suggestible Subconscious mind. You will be doing the same for yourself in practicing Reprogramming Self-hypnosis. However, you will have the advantage of already knowing yourself and your issue considerably well. Some suggestions are considered direct while others are indirect. Some suggestions are in simple metaphors and analogies. Additionally, certain suggestions are recommended for your very easy, comfortable and prompt return to your conscious state. All of these technicalities will be discussed in Chapter Four. Furthermore, Chapter Four elaborates in great detail how to compose and phrase your original hypnotic suggestions for your Reprogramming Self-hypnosis experiences. You will learn the art of selecting and creating suggestions that work best for you.

NO AGE DISCRIMINATION HERE

I have already mentioned the wide range of issues that hypnosis has assisted. Hypnosis helps you prevent or stop harmful consequences of your subconscious reactions to stressful situations. More specifically, your stress is induced by your perception of what really or (even not really) happened. Your subconscious automatically programs your thoughts and beliefs regarding reactions to your perceptions of what happened. Hence, you unwittingly may end up with subconsciously held negative thoughts, faulty mindsets, erroneous associations and/ or negative behaviors related to your perceptions. Hypnosis is your tool to remove and replace those adverse subconsciously initiated programs. But so far there has been no mention regarding age appropriateness for hypnosis. Is there any age that is too old for hypnosis? Well, I have worked successfully with a ninety-two-year-old woman. A better parameter would be how well a person can hear, understand and follow the facilitator's directions. It also should be emphasized that hypnosis is an incredibly effective tool for working with children too. Children ages approximately six to seven years and older are potential candidates for HypnoCounseling in the office setting. Children need to sit fairly still long enough to follow directions and concentrate for about fifteen minutes. For younger children or those unable to concentrate long enough, it is possible to utilize personalized recordings that the parent or guardian plays at bedtime as the child begins sleeping. It is recommended that for thirty consecutive days the child continues to listen to the audio at bedtime. This is effective because your subconscious, regardless of your age, listens while you are sleeping. Since a fetus can hear while still in the womb, hypnosis may be used for a child in utero also. It is common to use hypnosis in order to prepare and guide the unborn child and mother for a comfortable birth experience and successful breastfeeding.

AFTERMATH OF A FRIGHTENING MOVIE

I remember a ten-year-old boy who had come for help regarding sleeping through the night. He had watched a frightening movie three years previously and ever since had been unable to sleep straight through until the morning. His fears would awaken him every night. However, the night after his first hypnosis session was the first time in three years that he did sleep all night long. It also was the first time in the past three years that his mom slept through the night! Her son used to awaken her when he awoke in the middle of the night. What miraculous thing happened in my office? It is the miracle of how you were blessed with the ability to make corrections for your life through communicating with your Suggestible Subconscious mind and directing it to manifest what you needed. Now how great is that?

YOUR SUBCONSCIOUS EARS

Your subconscious has ears? Even without ears like you have on both sides of your head, your subconscious can hear nevertheless. This fact was verified personally for me when I worked with a five-year-old little girl who was still bed-wetting. Suzanne was too hyperactive to stay still for the hypnotic visualization, so I created a audio for her to listen to at night. I nestled special directions within the hypnosis suggestions of the audio to prompt Suzanne when she awoke in the morning to ask for a glass of water and to request permission to see her favorite TV show for that day.

When I called Suzanne's mother a week later to hear how Suzanne was responding, the mom said there had been no changes. Oddly enough though, her little sister Deidre was following the hypnotic suggestions about asking for the glass of water every morning and asking permission to see her favorite TV show. What had happened was the two sisters shared the same room. Unbeknown at that time, Suzanne had a hearing impairment. She was unable to hear and process the hypnosis recording. However her three-year-old sister Deidre, who had never met me, heard the audio while she was sleeping at night and subconsciously accepted some of the relevant, positive audio suggestions. Remember that as you begin sleeping, you are in the Alpha state. Therefore, you are in the appropriate brain wave frequency to effectively download new suggestions into your *Suggestible Subconscious* mind.

YOUR SHANGRI-LA

A common thread runs through each guided imagery hypnosis session I lead. Before beginning any hypnosis, I request that my clients select a safe and healing place, real or imaginary. During hypnosis the clients enjoy their safe and healing place with every part of their sensory being: sight, sound, taste, smell, touch and intuition. They truly experience while in hypnosis what is it is like to be there. By using their imagination, they actually travel easily, gently, confidently and time efficiently to their specified safe place. They remain there soaking up the peaceful and calm feelings, so comfortable, so relaxed and so safe.

HOW ABOUT NOW?

If possible, take some time now to create a safe and healing place for you. Have it ready to access for the visualization exercise in Chapter Four that practices self-hypnosis. Your Mind/Body/ Spirit will become acclimated to having your safe place represent peace, calm, harmony, balance, self-healing and self- enlightenment. You may want to choose an outdoor, natural scene such as on a beach, in a wooded hiking area, in the mountains, or maybe in a special room. You might choose a place with a beautiful view of where you travel in your dreams. You might create something totally from your imagination, something new and wonderful for your safe and healing place.

Just remember your safe and healing place must represent only positive feelings and associations for you. Ask yourself, *What kind of feelings am I experiencing? What am I seeing?* Notice all the senses of touch. What do you feel — a comfortable, light breeze, a gentle warmth? What do you taste, smell and hear? Notice the relaxed sensations in your body. Notice all of the good feelings that are associated with this special safe place. Revisit your safe place through self-hypnosis on a daily basis or whenever possible, knowing it is always available to you. Know that each time you revisit this safe, healing place, it is more and more enjoyable and feels so great. It is your feel relaxed, feel-good, feel safe place. It is where you feel grounded, receive healing energy, select positive self-healing lights and confirm your connectedness to God or to your Higher Power and to all that is. You also anticipate great joy when you return to this safe, healing place.

JUST IMAGINE

Occasionally people have reported difficulty in selecting a truly safe place because they have never experienced a real sense of safety in any place they could remember. If that is your situation, my suggestion would be to imagine being protected by an invisible force field that prevents anyone or anything from entering or disturbing you while you relax. Envision and feel yourself relaxing while you are protected by your Higher Power, perhaps on a beach, up in the mountains, in a beautiful garden or in a lavishly comfortable vacation spot where you have dreamed of visiting. Even a room that surrounds you with your favorite things can be your safe and healing place. Perhaps you can picture or feel like you are experiencing this sense of safety as if you would imagine it for someone else who has 24/7 security.

Take a moment now if you have not already done so, as now could be an opportune time to select your safe and healing place. It needs to be a place where you always experience peace of mind, calm and only positive feelings. Use all your five senses in addition to your intuitive knowing as you acknowledge this place as so comfortable, safe and inviting. However, you can always substitute another place for your safe place whenever you so desire.

CHAPTER 3

MEET YOUR SILENT, INVISIBLE
PARTNER

YOUR MOST POWERFUL ALLY FOR REPROGRAMMING

Our subconscious mind is one of the least understood parts of our human condition. Yet, it is one of our most valuable, powerful parts. Your subconscious mind directs your Mind/Body/Spirit for your entire life.

In the dictionary it is mainly defined in terms of what it is not. It simply is not your conscious mind. As an adjective, it means existing in the mind but not immediately available to consciousness: affecting thought, feeling and behavior without entering awareness. *Merriam-Webster Medical Dictionary*, c.2002, further explained the adjective form of the word *subconscious* as meaning a state of being that exists without even the possibility or the evidence of a resident consciousness — the same as described for states of the soul.

Hmm, do you find it very interesting to equate the subconscious state with the state of the soul? In fact, many say that communicating with their subconscious mind through hypnotic techniques is like speaking to their soul. As you learn how to communicate effectively using Reprogramming Hypnosis, keep in mind these mysterious and perhaps mystical relationships that exist within your subconscious mind and your Inner Wisdom.

BETTER THAN MAC OR PC?

Actually the part of your mind called *your subconscious* is one of your most impressive computer-like possessions you are so blessed to have. More powerful than any computer that has ever been invented and more powerful than any that humankind ever will create, your subconscious mind among other things is in charge of all your autonomic bodily functions. It regulates your breathing, heart, circulation, digestion, nerves, reproduction, actually all of your physiology including all of your senses of sight, touch, smell, hearing, taste and intuition. It records in your computer-like memory all your thoughts, emotions and dreams. Amazingly most every single thing you have ever experienced, starting when your brain began functioning, can be accessed through the cooperation of your subconscious mind. Now that is quite some capability! How could one estimate the amount of *RAM* or *Gigabytes* in your subconscious mind? It is virtually impossible to calculate the power of your subconscious mind just as it is impossible to accurately calculate the power of your total mind. Its vastness is beyond our conscious comprehension.

THE MYSTERY OF MEMORY STORAGE

Scientists have concluded that your conscious as well as your subconscious memory is accessed through your brain, primarily through the frontal and temporal lobes. Nonetheless, scientists have yet to identify with certainty the exact physical location of your memory storage. The process of encoding and retrieving memories is complicated, involving many structures to function properly. Fortunately, you can interact with your subconscious mind without needing a definitive answer as to where its information is located or even if it may be outsourced. Remember at the beginning of this book it was mentioned that we still do not completely understand electricity but we use it because it works? So it is with your subconscious mind. The following list however, will assist you in understanding the basic tenets upon which your subconscious behaves. I will continue elaborating upon these principles in subsequent chapters.

GETTING TO KNOW YOU, SUBCONSCIOUS

One:

Your subconscious advocates for you. It wants to help protect you and keep you from physical, mental and emotional pain. It also wants to please you as well as secure pleasure and happiness for you.

Two:

When you are in the Altered Consciousness State of Alpha, Theta or Delta, you are operating under the right conditions that make it possible for you to communicate to the subconscious part of your mind. You are in the right brain frequency to communicate your thoughts, feelings, suggestions and directions to the "suggestible" part of your subconscious responsible for creating your subconscious beliefs, mindsets, associations, feelings/emotions and behaviors.

Three:

When your subconscious perceives what it believes you want; or, when it perceives what you believe is your reality, it cooperates by bringing those things literally into your current reality even though they may not have been there before. Additionally your subconscious acts making these choices without considering any present or future adverse consequences of its programming for you.

Four:

Unfortunately once your subconscious has downloaded what

it perceives is your belief, mindset, association, feeling or behavior, its responsibilities pertaining to that download are finished. Its job description does not include revisiting under its own volition its decisions, re-evaluating or revising any Subconscious Programs.

Five:

Your subconscious often perceives and then makes conclusions that correspond with symbolic, metaphoric language. For instance, when you are experiencing strong emotions that can put you into the Altered Consciousness State like Alpha or Theta, your Suggestible Subconscious is activated and listens to you. If you say, for instance, that someone makes you sick to your stomach, your subconscious takes you literally, believes you and instantly creates that condition as your new reality. Then before you know it, you are truly feeling sick to your stomach, thanks to your Subconscious Programming.

Six:

When you are a child, under the age of twelve, your Suggestible Subconscious is open to accepting as reality what the words and actions of authority figures such as parents, teachers and religious leaders, show is their truth, their actual reality.

After age twelve, others are generally unable to so easily reach and direct your Suggestible Subconscious responsible for creating your Subconscious Programming.

The exception to this occurs when as an adult you are experiencing circumstances of strong emotional reactions to what is being perceived. The experiencing of strong emotional reactions instantly can transition you into an Altered State of Consciousness. By entering an altered state like Alpha or Theta, you are in the same frequency that opens up direct communications to your Suggestible Subconscious. Bingo, you may have instantly downloaded new Subconscious Programming without any clue that it has happened.

Seven:

Your subconscious seems to respond to negatively framed commands by perceiving them as opposite to what is commanded. The command, *Do not worry*, therefore is interpreted as *Do worry*. Perhaps it is your Subconscious Programming that rejects you being told what to do and motivates you to do the opposite.

Another possibility would be that it is the strong power of the image or the strong feeling of the word(s) mentioned in the command that actually matter the most to you. The strong, clear images/feelings become your main focus and initiate your attraction to them rather than to the negative wording (do not) in the command. Here is another example: Do not think of a red barn. So what are you thinking of now, a red barn? Now notice how do you react when I say, *Do not think of anything?* What are you thinking about or picturing in your mind? By giving you a command that focuses your attention on a weak or uncertain visual or neutral feeling attached to it, do you notice that you hesitate or have no clear, immediate reaction of thinking of something else? It may seem too confusing to automatically set your thoughts on one specific thing. Maybe you are thinking just of the word, *anything* because it gives you something to focus upon even though the word itself is so vague.

TAKE CHARGE AND MANAGE

The most powerful part of your mind is your subconscious mind. However, you will have more conscious influence and control over your subconscious mind once you learn how to be like a Director of Quality Control for your subconsciously held thoughts, feelings and behaviors. Reprogramming Hypnosis and Reprogramming Self-hypnosis unlock the mysteries for you and provide you with the keys to establish significant editing control over your subconscious mind's choices. That way your subconscious responds with what you really want and discards what you really do not want.

FIRST PRIORITY

My recommendation is to use Reprogramming Self-hypnosis first to maintain a relaxed, peaceful state of mind consciously and subconsciously. Such a state of mind consistently helps you retain mental, emotional, physical and spiritual harmony and balance.

Maintaining this peaceful, relaxed state of mind actually inhibits your subconscious from impulsively responding to cues of strong emotions. Consequently, you may avoid, or at least greatly limit, the creation of new and unintentional Faulty Subconscious Programs that occur most often in highly stressful times. Maintaining a peaceful, relaxed state of mind is essential because it allows for automatic access to your intelligence, logic and intuition in times of great distress. That way you react with wiser responses to stressors and make wiser choices that expedite desirable resolutions.

IT MAY BE GREEK TO YOU

People have found self-hypnosis helps in establishing and clarifying their positive objectives and goals because hypnosis permits communication with their Suggestible Subconscious mind where so many answers and solutions are available. So how do you deliberately access your Suggestible Subconscious? Hypnosis helps you reach your Suggestible Subconscious by relaxing you into the very common altered State of Alpha and/or Theta Consciousness. Hypnosis techniques provide the vehicle for reaching the Alpha and Theta states. The Delta Consciousness State is considered the deepest, most relaxed level of consciousness. It is the one where you actually are in very deep sleep. Delta consciousness can be induced through hypnosis for such typical purposes as medical procedures and surgery. In fact, hypnosis is especially valuable for people who are allergic to drugs and need an alternative to drug-induced anesthesia. However, when you are in the altered consciousness of Delta, unlike Alpha and Theta, you are unable to converse with anyone because you are deep asleep.

For the purposes of Reprogramming Self-hypnosis, you primarily will be using the Alpha and/or Theta altered states. When you sleep hearing the audio *Relax, Release and Dream On,* you additionally are implementing Reprogramming Hypnosis while in Delta consciousness. In any case, hypnosis, whether with the help of a professional or self-hypnosis directed by you, is the entryway to your subconscious mind's wealth of information and understanding. Also once you are in hypnosis you will have transitioned into an altered state of mind that is equipped for receiving and implementing your suggestions subconsciously. Thoughts that come to your mind while you are in Alpha or Theta Consciousness are springing from your subconscious mind rather than your conscious mind. Ironically it does not feel very different from how you feel being in your Beta consciousness, just more relaxed or more focused and present. Yet the information available to you while in Alpha or Theta is vast compared to the limited information available through your conscious Beta state of mind.

A THUMBNAIL SKETCH

The following is a general guideline for using Reprogramming Self-hypnosis to communicate with your subconscious:

One:
    Connect directly with your subconscious state of mind through the Induction that leads you into hypnosis. Simply trust

you are in communication with your subconscious in your relaxed state. Use deepening techniques (explained in Chapter Four, p. 96) to reach if possible a deeper level of relaxation.

Two:

Focus on what is your desired, positive goal.

Three:

Direct your subconscious first to identify and then delete from your Subconscious Programming whatever programs are still blocking you from that goal. Next download your positive replacement programming for achieving that goal.

Four:

Believe that your subconscious has accepted your directions/ suggestions. Believe your goal is becoming or already has become your reality.

Five:

Guide yourself back to your conscious state or request that you transition into sleep, awakening at your appropriate time feeling great.

ALTERNATIVE ROUTES

It should be noted that there are circumstances that allow for communication of your desires to your subconscious without the use of hypnosis. For example, your subconscious will come to the forefront during times of very strong emotions, under anesthesia and during accidents that produce physical/emotional shocks or traumas. If a smoker just after hearing the shocking news that she has lung cancer, swore she would stop smoking, her subconscious very likely would receive that strong, emotional message. The tremendous emotions of fear that accompanied her thoughts of needing to quit cigarettes would have the ability to activate her Suggestible Subconscious. When her subconscious would perceive the message that she was in dire need to quit the smoking habit, it would want to please her and thus would follow her directions to stop her from smoking. She automatically would receive the motivation/subconscious urging to succeed.

Of course, people may select other methods for successful smoking cessation. Many smokers have stopped smoking using the nicotine medication of the *Patch*. Others have used their strong willpower alone or used other stop smoking aids. Hypnosis is one of several effective tools to reach this goal. Nevertheless, many former smokers come for hypnosis even ten years after they originally have quit the smoking habit because a new crisis/new trauma drove them back to the smoking habit. No doubt for these people something emotionally positive associated with their past smoking habit was still there motivating them to restart the smoking habit.

An *Emotional Payoff* that was still connecting the people to cigarette smoking could return them to the smoking habit when they desperately needed some feel-good emotions, such as feeling comforted, secure or powerful. Clearly for those people who returned to smoking, their Emotional Payoff was still attached to their cigarettes. The Patch, your own willpower and other smoking cessation aides often fail to disconnect an Emotional Payoff that unknowingly can force you to keep and/or return to your old habit. However, Reprogramming Hypnosis can redirect your positive Emotional Payoffs onto other things instead that are really positive for you. You might program taking in two deep breaths as your feel-good activity that replaces the original Emotional Payoff from cigarettes. Through the Reprogramming Hypnosis technique you also would associate something very negative with cigarettes, something that repulsed you. Once your Emotional Payoff is severed completely from smoking cigarettes, and smoking cigarettes has only negative feelings attached to it, you will find it much easier to stop that harmful cigarette habit forever.

EARL'S ATTACHMENT TO CIGARETTES

An example of that very circumstance happened with Earl who had quit smoking over eight years before he had started smoking again. He had been going through a divorce and as we learned in the hypnosis session, his cigarettes still represented companionship, something he could count on always to be there. Now that his wife was leaving him, he reverted to the old support system, his old friends, his cigarettes. However, when the hypnotic suggestions helped Earl to sever that friendship association, he was able to stop his need for cigarettes entirely. Additional hypnotic suggestions gave him different and far more positive ways of feeling better. While there are many ways to accomplish attitudinal and behavioral modifications, hypnosis does have a big advantage. Hypnosis may in relatively short order dissolve the feel-good associations or mindsets that motivate people to continue a way of thinking, feeling and/or behaving that is contrary to their Highest Good.

ONLY YOU CAN SELF-CORRECT

As an internal programmer, your subconscious unfortunately lacks the ability to independently change its original choices that it has downloaded for you. Once your subconscious downloads a program for you, that program is final. Sadly your subconscious continues to support that choice regardless of the harm, pain and havoc it may create for you. Your subconscious is fulfilling its obligation to defend its choices regardless of all the complaining you do. The programs are defended by your subconscious as if they were giving you what you desired (pleasure or protection from pain) or what you perceived was your reality (e.g. *I am a failure*). It continues that way UNTIL you purposely revise or somehow delete the program by communicating your instructions directly to your Suggestible Subconscious. Unfortunately, when you are in your ordinary Beta State of Consciousness, your inner talk is unable to reach the suggestible part of your subconscious mind to change your Subconscious Programming.

PARTS THERAPY: DIVIDED THEY STAND

A relatively new and powerful hypnotic technique is called *Parts Therapy*. This technique is attributed to the famous American hypnotherapist, Charles Tebbetts. Parts Therapy is based on a premise that imagines that your subconscious is divided into many, many parts. Each part has a responsibility to maintain and protect a job it has accepted.

Examples of such jobs may be: *one,* continuing a mindset that expressed what your subconscious perceived and believed you thought was your reality; *two,* continuing an association that the subconscious deemed was relevant or helpful to you; *three,* giving you more pleasure and happiness relating to a specific way of thinking, feeling and/or behaving; and *four,* protecting you from something that could cause you physical, mental, emotional or spiritual harm.

One typical reason a subconsciously held habit persists is that your subconscious first perceived and then continued to associate the very positive feelings from your first experience with that habit. So your subconscious is motivated to continue that association in order for you to receive more pleasurable feelings each time you perform the habit. Bottom line in such a case, your habit is maintained indefinitely because of your feel-good reward subconsciously associated with it. Plus, your habit remains because your subconscious never revisits it, even if the program is no longer valid or has proven harmful to you. Unfortunately there is no way for your subconscious to voluntarily inform you as to the true reasons underlying your habit. No wonder your subconscious is overlooked as a source for dissolving your habit. You probably have had nary a clue to trace your habit back to your subconscious mind.

Thus, cigarette smokers might far more easily have stopped smoking on their own, except for the fact that their subconscious continually was recreating some powerful, good feelings that it had associated with cigarettes when they first started smoking. A young teenage boy may have started smoking with a group of his friends because cigarettes became associated with the good feelings of being liked and accepted by others. The smoking habit was initiated by strong self-esteem enhancement, a powerful Emotional Payoff. He may have enjoyed the feeling of freedom like he did something his parents would never have allowed him to do. Smoking may have initiated feelings of self-empowerment, another positive motivator to continue smoking. The list goes on and on.

CASE STUDIES: SEEING IS BELIEVING

The following case studies illustrate something important to understand about the nature of your subconscious mind and how it works. The privacy of each client is maintained through carefully selected alterations of names and details that still retain the integrity of the example.

DOLORES' STORY: GETTING RID OF MONEY

Dolores had lost control of her finances. As a single mom she could not afford to allow money to just slip through her fingers. Yet, she was always buying things and spending beyond her means. Not surprisingly, she created debt accompanied by tremendous stress. Consciously she knew she should not be buying all those things, but just could not help it. During hypnosis she was able to trace that need to get rid of money, to a particularly mean third grade teacher. This teacher terrorized Dolores and all of her third grade classmates many years ago. What Dolores learned while in hypnosis was that her subconscious had associated money with all the terrible feelings she had about that teacher. This concept may seem hard to believe. Yet this is what Dolores revealed. Every day the teacher would be sitting at her desk in front of the class counting cash. The teacher was in charge of the schools' fundraising efforts. Dolores' subconscious sensed how much Dolores detested this woman. Since subconsciously money had become a symbol for that woman, Dolores was actually trying to get rid of that teacher and the bad feelings associated with her teacher every time she spent her money!

So we spoke directly to Dolores' subconscious part responsible for making that choice of associations and directed it to release and delete that money/teacher association. Dolores directed her Suggestible Subconscious to program that she spent money only when she absolutely needed to spend it. Another suggestion was: *All unnecessary spending has stopped now*. Dolores used this hypnosis process to discern and eliminate the subconscious roots of her bad habit. Subsequently, she favorably changed her behavior regarding money. She has since been in control of her spending, and enjoyed saving extra money that enabled the college funds for her kids to grow significantly. Furthermore, during her session and while she was in hypnosis, Dolores was able to neutralize her strong negative feelings for her third grade teacher. Dolores responded well to the hypnosis suggestions that neutralized all the teacher's negative words and actions of the past. Afterwards it was possible for Dolores to practice forgiveness towards her teacher.

THROW THOSE EMOTIONS INTO NEUTRAL

Forgiveness is a key ingredient in neutralizing, releasing and moving on past your pain. Forgiveness means you are giving yourself permission to overcome the past that was affecting you in a negative way. Forgiveness helps to release the pain of the past while still retaining the lessons and wisdom from of the past. It was very important in the case of Dolores to give her those supporting suggestions to help her forgive. Furthermore, just as a small child needs concrete, specific and precise instructions, your subconscious needs to be directed with clarity in all things. Now why would your subconscious do something that would cause you such pain and suffering as it did for Dolores and others referenced in this book? Remember your subconscious often acts impulsively without using the logic of the neo-cortex part of your brain. When it is responding impulsively to your very strong emotional cues, your subconscious is unable to see long-term consequences. It acts impulsively, giving you your bottom line only.

Besides not seeing the long-term consequences, once your subconscious makes an association or a selection of an action, it consistently and powerfully maintains that choice regardless of the good or bad consequences. In fact, when it comes to a battle between your conscious mind and your subconscious mind, your subconscious mind wins! That is probably why you cannot resist that butter cream cake even though you consciously instructed yourself earlier you were going to resist. If you have ever been involved in sales training, think back to how so many decisions are made. Most decisions are formulated based on emotions and emotional reasoning. Later more logical reasons are found to support those emotional choices you have already made. So your emotions past and present represent a tremendous authority over your choices, consciously as well as subconsciously. Did you have any idea how important your emotions were in determining the direction of your life?

SAMANTHA'S METAPHOR

Another example of how the subconscious mind programs

emotional associations is illustrated by the story of Samantha. Samantha came for help due to her extreme anxiety. She was already on several medications but nothing seemed to help. She kept swallowing hard and fast without being able to control her anxiety or the swallowing. She just was unable to relax. Samantha finally was able to go into hypnosis after I explained that she was safe and that she was, in fact, in control. Hypnosis would most likely give her insights as to why she could not consciously stop swallowing every ten to thirty seconds.

Sure enough while in hypnosis, Samantha recounted a time when she was threatened by bullies at her school. She recalled being terrified. All she could remember was that they grabbed her by her blouse collar and she was swallowing almost constantly. I asked her why she was swallowing and after a few more probing questions, her face lit up with the realization that she was doing her best to swallow her fear. When I asked her how that scene related to her present circumstances of swallowing so much, she intuitively understood the connection that her subconscious must have made and was still promoting. Samantha's subconscious had associated her swallowing as a way to relieve her fear and anxiety. As a consequence, every time she was faced with fear or anxiety, she would commence swallowing in order to release those strong negative emotions by swallowing her fear. Constant swallowing in the presence of fear and anxiety represented an enactment of a Subconscious Program established over thirty years earlier that was ironically subconsciously created to help her.

Samantha's case is an example of the subconscious' tendency to assume, and consequently create, an association using metaphorical language (such as the swallowing of fear) and applying it literally. Before coming for HypnoCounseling, Samantha had no idea that her long ago, fear-producing experience with the bullies was responsible for her uncontrollable swallowing. Again, as in Dolores' situation, Samantha's subconscious had responded immediately to her emotional distress and instituted a Subconscious Program as a solution to protect her. Note also that the Subconscious Programming was done outside of Samantha's conscious awareness. Obviously, it was not her fault in the least. Thankfully Samantha's case has a happy ending. Samantha's subconscious accepted and applied the Reprogramming Hypnosis suggestions that revised the Faulty Subconscious Program. Subsequently she stopped the old programmed anxiety response that included the uncontrollable swallowing. This greatly relieved Samantha's anxiety and she was able to return to work within a couple weeks.

BUT IT IS NOT YOUR FAULT!

It is important to remember that you bear no blame for your involuntary subconscious choices. Many of these subconscious choices that were intended to help you were carried out without your knowledge or awareness and without your permission. Therefore, reject the blame and guilt that might be associated with the outcomes of those subconscious choices, whatever they may be. This is a significant point that speaks to Daniel Goleman's dilemma as revealed in his book, *Emotional Intelligence.* Daniel Goleman, PhD, covered the behavioral and brain sciences for *The New York Times.* Goleman was torn between two approaches for doctors. One approach is Western medicine that basically focuses on priorities other than the Mind/Body/Spirit connection in treating patients. Conventional Western medicine divides care primarily into specialties in order to treat different parts of the body's physiological manifestations of illness and disability. The other is the Mind/Body/Spirit Eastern medicine that suggests a holistic approach, acknowledging that the Mind/Body/Spirit is intertwined as part of the body's condition. In essence Eastern medicine promotes all three parts of Mind/Body/Spirit as total and equally important health aspects of the patient. Therefore, all parts of Mind/Body/Spirit need to be addressed in treating the whole person. The mind or perhaps a specific part of the mind shares a powerful role at times in initiating and/or supporting what triggers one's physical illness and disability.

RESOLVING THE DILEMMA

Goleman was not totally satisfied with the approach of conventional Western medicine because he recognized the validity of a Mind/Body/Spirit more holistic connection. Still he was uncomfortable embracing the implications of the Mind/Body/Spirit approach because of a major flaw that he perceived. Goleman concluded Eastern holistic approach meant people would have to accept huge guilt that they caused their own illness and/or disability. For instance, they may feel guilty that their thoughts were not positive enough or that they allowed negative thoughts that caused their illness. Of course, placing blame on the individual for consciously causing his/her illness could be no further from the truth.

I believe the findings from hypnosis sessions have provided answers for Dr. Goleman's dilemma. As Goleman explained in his book, the *amygdala* part of your brain impulsively chooses a reaction to your stress and does so without your conscious agreement. The decisions of how you are to react often are flawed and inaccurate. Yes, sometimes the subconscious does a great job. But we are not as concerned with the successes as we are with the failures since the consequences of those failures such as obesity, addictions, disease and so forth are so damaging. The memory bank from which the amygdala draws is often outdated emotional garbage that you would have thought you had long ago discarded. Maybe that accounts for grown adults showing such childlike emotional behaviors.

ANDERS' SUBCONSCIOUS WEIGHT GAIN

As demonstrated by the Parts Therapy approach, the subconscious often can and will cooperate in exposing what initiated an unfavorable Subconscious Program. Take the case of Anders. Anders wanted to reduce his weight that had developed into obesity. Anders explained that he was the only boy among three sisters in his family. He perceived that his parents showed an obvious preference for the girls. As a result, Anders described feeling invisible. While in hypnosis, Anders learned from his subconscious that in order to keep him more visible, his subconscious chose to make him big, really big, so his family would have to notice him. Thus, his subconscious gave him the bottom line of what it thought he wanted — to be noticed and feel significant rather than to be invisible. But even when he had reached adulthood and long after the death of his parents, his eating continued to be out of control. His Subconscious Program that produced weight gain was still running. Anders was left with the unhappiness of ill-health brought on by the obesity that he could not consciously change. Yes, he could reduce his weight, but only on a temporary basis because that original Subconscious Program that forced him to remain large was still there. Fortunately, Anders made good progress with hypnosis applications. Through Reprogramming Hypnosis he finally ended the old damaging Subconscious Programming and replaced it by reprogramming positive Subconscious Programs that helped him to reduce his weight and to establish more self-control in his life.

YOUR TEAM PLAYER

This brings up a major point. Hypnosis and HypnoCounseling are very often useful as adjuncts to other professional services. HypnoCounselors and hypnotherapists work with physicians, surgeons, psychiatrists, psychologists, social workers, massage therapists, acupuncturists, physical therapists, art therapists, hospice volunteers and the list continues. Often I use suggestions offered by the client's therapist to create the most effective script for my client. Sometimes the therapist may ask me to uncover a particular reason for a behavior so the client and therapist may come to a better understanding about a specific issue. When it comes to surgical procedures, we already are fully aware of why there is pain. So HypnoCounselors offer valuable assistance for uncomfortable medical procedures, operations and childbirth. I remember one doctor who remarked to me that he never saw a patient so relaxed during a biopsy as his patient was while in hypnosis. He probably would be even more amazed if he knew that it took two earlier hypnosis sessions for his patient (my client) to finally have the nerve to go through her biopsy in the first place!

TIME IS ON YOUR SIDE

The time necessary for Reprogramming Hypnosis suggestions to be understood and accepted by your Suggestible Subconscious varies from one individual to the next. You are to focus on making your desired changes over at least thirty consecutive days. Thirty days of repetition is generally accepted in the behavioral modification world as how long it takes to start and solidify a new habit. Consequently, you will need at least thirty days or longer for your targeted changes to become permanent landscape within your subconscious mind. You could opt to continue the positive reinforcement of your suggestions for six months. This repetition will serve to diminish the negative effects of possible future crises in your life that could cause setbacks to your new programming. Your new changes will be encouraged to be a permanent part of your lifestyle.

Sometimes the effect of the Reprogramming Hypnosis/Self-hypnosis is immediate and dramatic, almost a night and day change. In working with individuals who want to give up smoking, I often see a fairly rapid turnaround after the person comes back to his conscious state. He may never want another cigarette again. In other instances, the person may smoke a few cigarettes after the hypnosis session and then get disgusted and stop smoking. Another person may continue to smoke for a week and then stop smoking. Some people need a short booster follow-up session. Others need another full session or more to address whatever lingering resistances there may be that did not arise in the original or follow-up sessions. It is also possible to conduct phone hypnosis sessions that benefit clients as a time-saving and effective follow-up option. If your subconscious continues to resist your Reprogramming Self-hypnosis suggestions, you need to make adjustments and use other hypnotic techniques until you discover the way to resolve the resistance. The subject of Subconscious Resistances will be explored in greater depth in Chapters Four and Seven.

THE PUNISHMENT THAT NEVER ENDS

One of the most difficult types of Subconscious Resistances originates from a person's subconsciously programmed belief that he/she wanted or needed to be punished. That may sound strange, I know. Why would your subconscious perceive that you would want to be punished? The answer is that your subconscious senses your belief that punishment relieves and/or ends your guilt and pain. It may appear to your subconscious that you are feeling terribly guilty about something you thought, said, felt or did. After receiving a punishment your belief system says that everything will be forgiven and you will feel the pleasure of relief and forgiveness. It may be that your punishment is associated with making things feel better for you as in *cleaning your slate.* However, in all these cases, your subconsciously induced punishments do not make you feel better.

In actuality the punishment continues indefinitely and you continue suffering. After all, once your subconscious has downloaded any program including one of self-punishment, it never revisits the programming to make adjustments or to end it or to say, *Okay, you have had enough punishment. It stops now.* I have named this a *Subconscious Self-punishment Program.* It means that your subconscious has chosen a program that keeps you in some kind of pain or suffering as your punishment. It blocks you from receiving pleasure, happiness or even good luck either in a narrowed definition or in an all-encompassing way. Consequently, self-sabotage may serve as your self-punishment and atonement for something you believed that you thought, felt or did that was inappropriate, wrong or evil. Are you a person who feels like you have a dark cloud hanging over your head regarding any kind of work, relationships, finances, children or a combination of the above? You may have a self-punishment Subconscious Program that may be responsible.

FIRST COME, FIRST SERVED AND FIRST CREATES PRECEDENCE

The Subconscious Self-Punishment Programs take precedence over any new, positive suggestions that come afterwards because your Subconscious Self-punishment Programs were formulated first, and of course, downloaded without your awareness or permission. These Self-punishment Programs rarely leave without a struggle. The subconscious takes its responsibility to you seriously. If it easily were to drop your Self-punishment Program, your subconscious would be violating its job to maintain vigorously its Subconscious Self-punishment Program. Typical new hypnosis suggestions that you might use to instruct your subconscious to seek positive good feelings for you would mean an end to your punishment. But since the original Self-punishment Programs are opposed to finding relief and happiness for you because you must be punished first, your subconscious naturally fights positive change.

The premise is that punishment is necessary in order to acquire forgiveness and relief from your guilt. This justifies your *Subconscious Self-Punishment* Program. *Your subconscious believes that by punishing you, it will be relieving you of painful guilt so sometime later you will feel pleasurable relief.* Your subconscious thinks it is helping you. It simply follows what has been programmed until you initiate a subconscious revision or deletion of that program.

This is where Reprogramming Hypnosis has an advantageous approach. It first deletes the Self-punishment Program that would block the new positive suggestions. Next, you are able to download the new Reprogramming Hypnosis suggestions. These suggestions integrate your favorable programming that serves now as a replacement for what was deleted. For instance, your new Subconscious Programming could sustain your peace of mind, self-empowerment and self-healing. Thankfully, this would enable you to neutralize the pain and suffering incurred from the now deleted Self-punishment Program. Working to release Subconscious Self-punishment Programs has unique challenges. Nonetheless, with time, repetition, reiteration and dedication you can convince your subconscious to delete your Self-punishment Programs and replace them with positive programming for your Highest Good.

THE ONE-LINER MINDSET

Sometimes there is a mindset, almost a one-liner that you heard typically when you were a child and accepted it subconsciously as a truism. An example of such a truism is: *You should never be wealthy because money is associated with the devil.* This powerful mindset actually could block your ability to accumulate wealth since accumulating money would mean to you that you are associating with the devil. Again this self-sabotaging mindset may be deleted through Reprogramming Hypnosis suggestions and other hypnosis techniques.

JUST A MATTER OF TIME

It should be emphasized that some people are slower to integrate and utilize their Reprogramming Hypnosis suggestions than others are. Consequently, it may appear as though your subconscious is resisting while really, it just needs more time to understand and assimilate. It is impossible to know with certainty who will respond quickly, who will respond more slowly, and who will meet resistances that have to be overcome before the Reprogramming Hypnosis reaches its optimal effect. When resistances surface, there are excellent Reprogramming Hypnosis/Self-hypnosis techniques to identify them and assist you in overcoming the resistances. Sometimes you may need to reach out for additional professional help with resistant programs. Have you already identified resistances to your proposed changes? Keep a record of any that may surface.

AN EXTRAORDINARY AND QUICK RECOVERY

As previously mentioned, sometimes the effect of the Reprogramming Hypnosis is immediate. One such case study resulted in a very quick, dramatic and unique reversal. Twenty-eight-year-old Bonnie totally rid herself of numerous obsessive/compulsive behaviors after a two-and-a-half-hour hypnosis session. She first demonstrated this reversal within five minutes after concluding Reprogramming Hypnosis. She tested herself by being able to go up a flight of stairs straightaway to the top without coming back down to repeat the last three steps again as she used to do compulsively. A few days later she informed me that all fifteen of her obsessive/compulsive behaviors had disappeared since our first hypnosis session. Her positive response was more than extraordinary to say the least. She had been struggling with fifteen OCD behaviors for over seven years. The irony was that we were focused on a different unrelated issue. Yet when Bonnie released tremendous guilt, she received this unexpected, incredible bonus.

NOTABLE CHANGES

In the case of another client who was feeling so down about herself due to her negative self-perception, her subconscious made the complete shift to a positive self-image instantly and the client started to feel better before the session was even over. In other cases, people have started to respond to their suggestions within one week. Yet, some clients respond more gradually over a month or more. It is very worthwhile for you to keep a journal or take abbreviated notes regarding any changes, especially noting when your desired changes occur. This practice allows you also to pay attention to the subtle changes and keep a record so as to perceive with more accuracy the differences in your feelings, beliefs and behaviors. The more you notice that hypnosis is working for you, the more it does work for you. Perception is everything. What you believe that is your reality, coupled with strong emotions, becomes your reality!

REPETITION IS GOOD. REPETITION IS GOOD. REPETITION IS GOOD.

One theory explains that when you are thinking the same thought repeatedly, you are literally and physiologically creating a strong bridge of brain cells that collectively establishes a large belief system out of those single thoughts. This theory was illustrated at a seminar I attended in Chicago in 2007. The conference, *Celebrate Your Life,* sponsored by Mishka Productions, featured a seminar led by Gregg Braden, *The New York Times* best-selling author and a pioneer in bridging science and spirituality. Gregg showed a video focused on a screen showing a person's active brain scan while the person was thinking the same thought repeatedly. The video showed an actual formation of a wide bridge of brain cells being drawn to each other, brought together as the person was thinking the same thought over and over again. Greg explained that the more often the thought was produced by the person, the more the brain cells gravitated towards each other forming a bigger and bigger bridge-like formation. The absolutely fascinating video presentation was like watching the formation of a single mindset as it was building into an all-powerful belief system that was greatly reinforced.

A VALUABLE REMINDER

As part of my HypnoCounseling practice, I typically create a personalized audio recording that includes guided imagery followed by the client's approved suggestions that reinforce instructions to his/her subconscious mind. Repetitive listening to your audio also helps to break down resistances that your subconscious may be presenting because of former contradictory programming. You can gain the most benefit by listening to your recording a minimum of once every night as you go to sleep and weekly at least three times or more during waking hours. If you were to listen to the recording daily, at least once during day-time or waking hours as well as at bedtime, that would be ideal. Listening to the relaxation suggestions during your waking hours and then returning to your conscious state again at the end of the recording is even more powerful than listening only at bedtime/naptime during sleep. When you listen to the audio at bedtime, it is unnecessary to concentrate on the meaning of the words. Only your ears have to hear what is being said in the audio. Your subconscious mind actively listens while you are asleep. So you can rest assured your subconscious will pay good attention without your supervision.

USE IT OR LOSE IT

Sometimes if you practice hypnosis without sufficient repetitious reinforcement to permanently solidify the suggestions, the positive effects of the hypnosis may seem to fade after you stop practicing hypnosis. Although there are hypnosis professionals who omit making recordings of the client's hypnotic suggestions, I view the personalized audios created for clients as important reinforcement that represents extra insurance for successful hypnosis. Typically I record a personalized, guided imagery visualization that includes the clients' personalized Reprogramming Hypnosis suggestions created during our initial interview session. Otherwise I employ a hypnotic suggestion that my clients use the more generic recording of *Relax, Release and Dream On* as reinforcement for all their new Reprogramming Hypnosis suggestions.

POWER IN NUMBERS: GROUP HYPNOSIS MEETINGS

Additionally, I have formed a monthly Group Hypnosis Meeting Online. GHM (pronounced gym) Online was created in order to reach as many people as possible, allowing almost unlimited access for Reprogramming Hypnosis. Each month our GHM Online includes a facilitator-led hypnotic guided imagery recording on a universal topic that includes benefits for all. The recordings are typically 30-50 minutes, relevant as well as timeless. Reprogramming Hypnosis yields the most amazingly powerful, positive effects when it is incorporated into your daily, weekly or at least monthly routine. GHM Online is for the beginner as well as for those already advanced in their hypnosis experience.

Currently, registration is required on galeglassner.com for a very reasonable monthly or an annual discounted fee to receive the GHM Online monthly audio download. Registering brings other discount benefits too. In any regard, please make hypnosis part of your lifestyle for your best rewards!

ONE A DAY SELF-HYPNOSIS SUPPLEMENT

Along with listening to *Relax, Release and Dream On,* practice your self-hypnosis techniques for at least ten to fifteen minutes every day and, of course, longer if you choose to do so. This offers another avenue for reinforcement of all your selected reprogramming suggestions. Besides, this is one of the best gifts you can give yourself for personal growth and wellness. You will be practiced in the communication with your Mind/Body/ Spirit. You will be doing yourself a great favor by breaking up any stress cycle that may be operating within you either consciously or subconsciously. Performing your self-hypnosis and Reprogramming Self-hypnosis can easily become second nature. Think of hypnosis as a necessary habit like running a program that scans your computer for viruses. Imagine weaving self-hypnosis into the fabric of each day and notice how you are better able to cope with the daily stresses of living. Use Reprogramming Self-hypnosis to focus on and actualize what you want in your life and what you want to dismiss from your life as well.

KEEP IN THE LIGHT

Whenever you are using any kind of self-hypnosis, I recommend two important qualifiers to include as part of your suggestions to your subconscious. One is to always visualize something protective like a white light surrounding you with protection or verbalize a prayer or affirmation for protection from everything that is other than of God (of the Light, of your Higher Power, or of Goodness). This means framing all requests under the protection of your Higher Power. The second inclusion is another hypnosis suggestion: *All my requests are fulfilled for my Highest Good and are put into effect in ways that are for my Highest Good.*

That way you avoid getting something that you really want that would be given to you in ways contrary to your Highest Good. This is a precaution that takes into consideration the warning: *Be careful what you wish for...*

THE IMPACT OF YOUR WORDS

In learning about your subconscious and how valuable it is to reach it through hypnosis, you will be advised to please pay careful attention to every word you use to create a suggestion for your subconscious. Your subconscious takes your words, and the images your words create, very literally and concretely. If I were to give you the suggestions that said, *you now feel better* and I did not elaborate upon that concept, your subconscious would be confused and unsure of what you were meaning. What does feeling better actually mean? Let us say you have been having a stress-related TMJ (temporal mandible joint) problem in your jaw and you need to relax, stop grinding your teeth and get a solid night's sleep. You would do better by saying to yourself the following suggestions after you are in hypnosis:

> *My eyes are soothed. The muscles across my forehead have smoothed and relaxed. The muscles in my jaw have relaxed also. I am focused on the quiet waves of my easy breathing. I am sleeping at night with my lips parted and with my jaw remaining totally at ease. As I sleep, my upper teeth perhaps remain suspended over my lower teeth. It is like there is an invisible force field that keeps them separated. My teeth feel comfortable. My jaw feels so comfortable, soothed, perfectly aligned and relaxed. Now when it is my time to sleep, I sleep as if all is right in my world. Everything is resting. All is calm. All feels peaceful. And so it is.*

These suggestions embody visual, auditory and kinesthetic suggestions that also include imagery (quiet waves of easy breathing and force field metaphors) that are phrased entirely in positive language. Remember to eliminate misunderstandings by focusing on what you want to create using clear and very specific details.

NINETY PERCENT VERSUS TEN PERCENT

Perhaps you want to change some habits, maybe polish your professional skills, improve your learning abilities or parenting skills. Maybe you want to improve your body's ability for self-healing. All of these things and so much more are possible once you establish direct, effective communication with your responsive Suggestible Subconscious. You may achieve this using Reprogramming Hypnosis or the type of self-programming such as Reprogramming Self-hypnosis. I personally have witnessed hundreds of such improvements from Reprogramming Hypnosis and each one seems amazing and wonderful to me. They often involved issues that a person had for years or maybe for an entire lifetime. Frequently clients will say that they just cannot control a certain behavior or a certain way of feeling. They may worry too much and feel great anxiety. They may want a better relationship and cannot seem to break some old habits. In regards to Reprogramming Hypnosis, the HypnoCounselors/ hypnotherapists have a specific role as a facilitator and a conduit. They guide. They inform. They encourage. However, it is the clients who do the work. The clients bring into their lives what they desire and discard what is other than for their Highest Good. They do ninety percent of the work and their facilitators contribute ten percent.

YOUR POWER TOOL

Your subconscious works in accord with your body's innate self-healing system. Your subconscious may assist you in realigning and transitioning your body's energies into harmony and balance and into a peaceful state of mind that includes positive thinking. Thus, when you keep your energies from being zapped by your reactions to stress, you have more energy for maintaining a strong immune system and for more healing potential. On one hand, negative emotions and Faulty Subconscious Programming are in conflict with your positive, natural, peaceful flow of energies. On the other hand, your subconscious is your power tool to release these negative energies/negative emotions caused by stress and replace them with positive energies/positive emotions that nurture you. When your body's energies are flowing optimally without obstructions from Negative Energy, your energies more effectively support your health, harmony and balance.

THAT'S THE SPIRIT

When you deal with issues of the Mind/Body it is almost inevitable that you gain wisdom from the workings of your Spirit also. Those who seek spiritual answers from their subconscious Inner Wisdom often experience powerful revelations about themselves and their issues. Recall that hypnosis occupies the same altered State of Alpha and Theta Consciousness as your deep prayer state. Thus, being in hypnosis is like using the same communication lines you would in prayer with God or whatever Higher Power you may seek for your answers. Reprogramming Hypnosis requires that your hypnosis suggestions take into consideration and accurately reflect your spiritual beliefs.

ALL FOR ONE AND ONE FOR ALL

It is extremely valuable to include your Spirit in dealing with changing Subconscious Programming. When any one of the three included in your Mind/Body/Spirit is out of whack, your entire balance may be disrupted. This could result in mental, emotional and/or physical manifestations of imbalance. On the other hand, when your thoughts, beliefs, feelings and behaviors are in sync with what your Spirit knows is your truth, your Spirit is bound to be in harmony and balance also. That represents true inner peace of Mind/Body/Spirit. You will probably recognize that condition when you experience feelings of being comfortable with yourself and feeling safe in your world. You are at peace, *In the Zone* or *In the Flow.* Furthermore, when you are actualizing your life's purpose, you often will recognize and experience such feelings. Moreover, *synchronicities* known as *experiences, circumstances or events that happen so coincidentally together that the odds of their occurring in that way, in that order are overwhelmingly extraordinary and amazing. When synchronicities do occur, their existence creates more meaning and significance to those involved as well as to those who are the observers.*

BEING IN THE FLOW OF SYNCHRONICITY: A TRUE LIFE STORY

My longtime friend Gloria often had reminisced about a very special childhood boyfriend she had known during the first six years of her life. Gloria and Jeff were best friends, inseparable until his family moved out of state without telling anyone his forwarding address. Even into her late thirties, Gloria had so longed to see her friend Jeff again.

Now with that background understanding I shift your attention to another part of the story. During my flight home from Chicago I met Mimi, a lovely woman whose son played with my daughter during the plane trip. To my surprise, Mimi called me a year later. She asked if I remembered her and of course I did. Then she explained that her husband's company had transferred him from D.C. to my area in northern New Jersey. She had remembered that I had spoken highly of my town of Randolph. As a result, Mimi and her husband had searched for and bought a home in Randolph. I replied, *How wonderful, Mimi. And what street are you on?* To which she replied a familiar name. *Mimi, go outside to your front porch and look up to your right at the white house two homes above you. Wave because that's my house and I am waving at you!* Is that incredible?

Well that is only half of the story. It turns out that my friend Gloria met Mimi's family at a social gathering just a month after their arrival in town. Imagine Gloria's shock when she was introduced to Mimi's husband, Jeff, the same Jeff who was Gloria's long lost childhood boyfriend! More than just a coincidence, I would label that as a DOUBLE *synchronicity!* Can you imagine what the odds would be of all of this happening?

IT COULD HAPPEN TO YOU

You may experience extraordinary events as you are more open to present awareness and placing significance on each moment. You may seem typically to show up at the right time and at the right place. The right people who can assist you just appear. All doors continue opening for you. You might get the feeling that whatever it is you are doing, you are living your purpose.

When you connect with your *Inner Knowing* and become more aware of your Subconscious Programming that has been directing your life, you become more aware of your life's purpose too. It is like fitting the puzzle pieces together to see the entire picture. What gives you joy and also what gives you challenges point you in the same direction of what your life was meant to accomplish. You may find that all lead you to being of service to others in some way. Your joys represent opportunities to be shared with others. You serve as a role model for others who want to experience what you have experienced. Think about the award winning Olympic athletes who train others and give inspirational talks to students. Think of the very successful corporate CEO who freely mentors others in business decision-making.

On the other hand, when you surmount difficult challenges, you also have opportunities to share with others what you have learned. Again, you are a role model for others who need to overcome their similar challenges. Think about the parents who have lost a child to a disease and respond to their grief by creating a support group for grieving parents or volunteer for a foundation to help other children suffering with that disease. We seem to have an inborn inclination to create and share the good from what we have experienced intensely, regardless whether the experience has been very positive or very difficult for us. When you believe that what happens to you is not just a coincidence but rather is significant to your life, you can identify patterns indicating what your life is about and what opportunities/lessons you were born to receive and achieve. This is far easier to accomplish with the help of your Suggestible Subconscious because in hypnosis you are privy to a broader perspective than you have while in your Beta Consciousness State.

As part of that intention, I encourage people to contemplate their spiritual beliefs while they are in the altered state of hypnosis. For purposes of speaking to your subconscious, you need to identify who you believe is in charge. From whom do you seek divine intervention? To whom do you direct your prayers? Identify *Who* it is that you believe is your Source, your Higher Power, even if it is Fate or Nature. The Mind/Body/Spirit connection is innately inextricable. For the best results your spiritual beliefs and your Spirit all need to be in harmony with your mind and your body.

SAFETY ZONE

I have observed an almost universal spiritual perspective that supports harmony for Mind/ Body/Spirit on all levels. It is very clearly illustrated in clients who have come to me with anxiety-driven panic attacks. One client may have panic attacks when flying in an airplane. Another may feel panic while driving a car. And another client may suffer panic attacks while being home alone. Panic attacks may create physiological changes such as elevated blood pressure, trembling, sweating, nausea, stomach pains and fainting. The mindset that has been accepted is: I am in danger in these specific conditions. Therefore, this message is signaled throughout the body. The body responds by manifesting the negative physiological changes presented in panic attacks. The amygdala part of the brain is involved again stirring up old fear responses to similar circumstances from the past. The person who is experiencing great anxiety and fears is manifesting a Spirit that also is out of balance and alignment. One way to regain your inner control is to establish inner peace of your Spirit. Your Spirit that maintains harmony and balance characteristically is always at peace knowing that you are safe in your Higher Power's hands. This is where your spiritual faith helps you relax and feel your inner strength. Whatever happens, you can cope with it and be fine. It is always a win-win situation. All is happening under the auspices of your Higher Power.

Sometimes people are unsure that they can believe in those concepts but tell their subconscious that is what they want to believe because they recognize that in practical terms, it works well for stopping fears and panic attacks. Whatever works, works.

WHO'S IN CHARGE?

Another spiritual perspective that you may feel comfortable adopting, if you are seeking to identify yours, is that your time here on earth is full of meaningful lessons and opportunities for spiritual growth and awareness. Each life blessing and each life challenge is really your Spirit's learning experiences, opportunities to learn the lessons yet to be understood and integrated. Many times the more intense the experience (pleasant or unpleasant), the more powerful the lesson and the greater is the growth spurt. As you achieve joy and happiness, overcome adversity and appreciate your beautiful blessings, you get closer to emanating love as a natural way of being. You may express that love as devotion to God or to Whomever or to Whatever you describe as your Higher Power. You may express love directed inside to your own self and love expressed outwards to all people.

These perspectives may or may not be compatible with your beliefs. That is perfectly fine as there is no need then to adopt them. What is important is for you to understand and be able to articulate what your spiritual beliefs are, whatever they may be. Then you can effectively communicate your beliefs to your subconscious mind. Your spiritual perspectives serve as your spiritual anchor guiding your life. My suggestion is for you to take the time while in self-hypnosis to contemplate and define your spiritual perspectives on your life. You will need to know how to direct your subconscious in spiritual matters so you can remain in harmony with your spiritual truths. Further discussion relating to matters of your Spirit is in Chapter Five.

NEVER UNDERESTIMATE THE ROLE OF YOUR EMOTIONS!

To further understand how your subconscious works, look at how your emotions play a monumental role in influencing your subconscious mind. Your emotions, especially when they are intense, activate a part of your subconscious that responds to protect you against danger and bad feelings or to move you toward greater pleasure. Your subconscious may also be convinced of the truth of your statements when you are expressing them with strong emotion. This makes perfect sense because your strong emotions can shift you into an altered state of Alpha or Theta. That means you automatically are put into direct communication with your Suggestible Subconscious that without your permission or awareness, downloads your Subconscious Programs. Thus, your emotions directly and/or indirectly affect your Mind/Body/Spirit through the resulting Subconscious Programs.

Scientific research already has shown that emotions can affect the amount of acid your body produces in your stomach. Emotions trigger what may give you high blood pressure and headaches. And emotions like anger, anxiety and sadness are after all stress factors.

More and more research points to illnesses and disabilities having their roots in your emotional reactions to your stresses. But maybe we need to proceed one step further. What Subconscious Programs are responsible for producing and controlling the effects that are associated with our activated emotions? You probably have heard of someone dying from a broken heart. What about someone dying because of extreme sadness, loneliness and maybe also because their strong emotions focused consistently on wanting to die?

To be clear, a stress-induced headache is not imaginary. It is a result of real physiological changes that have occurred within the person's body. As Daniel Goleman, PhD. reveals in his book, *Emotional Intelligence,* if a person is feeling great fear and anxiety before an operation, there are some doctors who will reschedule the operation to when the patient will be calmer because the patient who is experiencing great stress, statistically has less chance of a successful recovery. What is in your mind has the potential to affect your body. It is that simple. Then you may ask, *Why not put into your mind positive thoughts and images by just thinking them and picturing them, thereby affecting your Mind/ Body/Spirit in a positive manner?* That does certainly help. What you focus upon with strong feeling, especially when it is done consistently, does serve to create your reality. Yes, that is certainly part of the answer but not all of it. Oh, were that the case, it would be so easy!

THE CATCH

Alas, when you are in your conscious state of mind, the one you are in most all the time during your waking hours, you are unable to institute or program your desired changes into the subconscious part of your mind. Remember, you are not plugged into the appropriate brain wave consciousness frequency that can access the suggestible part of your subconscious. In contrast, your Suggestible Subconscious opens to discussion with you while you are in an Altered State of Consciousness like the Alpha and Theta states. Also, your subconscious is able to accept communication of reprogramming suggestions/directions while you sleep.

You might have difficulty imagining communicating with your subconscious during sleep. Actually, during sleep you may enlist the help of someone else, a facilitator. Yes, an effective way to reach and communicate with your Suggestible Subconscious is precisely while you are sleeping. Many hypnosis audios take advantage of sleep time for planting subconscious suggestions appropriately worded for your subconscious to understand and to accept. Recall the Egyptian Sleep Temples (Chapter Two) and the healers who used sleep time for whispering suggestions into the ear of the sleeping ill person. During sleep there are times you naturally are in altered states of consciousness that are conducive for effectively downloading Reprogramming Hypnosis suggestions into your subconscious. Whether you are asleep or in a waking state, your Reprogramming Hypnosis suggestions designed for your subconscious have to meet certain requirements in order to be successful. Be aware that the word choice, word arrangement, repetition and other techniques determine to a large extent how well your suggestions are adopted by your subconscious. Chapter Four discusses how to practice Reprogramming Self-hypnosis and explains these requirements.

HOWDY PARTNER!

Now that you have been introduced to your Silent, Invisible Partner, here is a review of essential elements to remember:

First, for effective communications with your subconscious, your subconscious must be in its suggestible state, as when you are in an altered State of Alpha or Theta Consciousness. Hypnosis is able to induce these suggestible states. Remember there are unintentional times when your subconscious automatically becomes suggestible. These occur during trauma such as a car accident, during an operation and during normal sleep. Additionally your Suggestible Subconscious often comes to the forefront as the dominant part of your mind during highly emotional times, including the birth of a baby as well as during a funeral. These are times when you may often incur Faulty Subconscious programs. Please note that it is very difficult if not impossible for you to define the exact moment when you transition into the altered state when your Suggestible

Subconscious takes over. Chapter Four will discuss detecting signs of reaching an altered state.

Second, the language you use when communicating with your subconscious must be stated in specific, clear, succinct wording that most ten-year-old children would understand.

Third, your Suggestible Subconscious responds well to figurative language and imagery such as similes, metaphors and analogies. These all allow your meaning to be understood more clearly. A picture can be worth a thousand words. Besides visual pictures, remember that you can create metaphors employing all your senses of sound, taste, smell and touch as well. A general rule to follow is to appeal to your dominant sense for sensory perception, assuming you can identify which sense is your dominant one. Otherwise use suggestions that appeal to all six senses. Also, comparisons work well because you better understand whatever is new when you compare it to what you already know and understand.

The next chapter will explore further the techniques of Reprogramming Hypnosis and focus upon the practice of Reprogramming Self-hypnosis. Now would be an appropriate time to review the *Relax, Release and Dream On audio*. Each time you listen to it, you will be able to go into hypnosis even more deeply. Listening to it will give you an extra advantage of experiencing hypnosis before reading the next chapter. It is perfectly fine if you start to sleep at the beginning or anytime before the audio concludes because you still will absorb the benefits of the hypnosis suggestions. Perhaps you will want to record in your journal the responses you have to this bonus audio.

CHAPTER 4

PRACTICE MAKES BETTER, SO BETTER TO PRACTICE

LEARN AND PRACTICE REPROGRAMMING SELF-HYPNOSIS

Although this entire chapter is dedicated to sharing techniques of Reprogramming Self-hypnosis appropriate for reprogramming your subconscious, one potential misperception needs to be avoided. Learning how you induce the self-hypnosis state is relatively easy and uncomplicated. For our purposes it does not necessitate a full chapter. Of course there are many different options available for how you might induce self-hypnosis and many are presented in this chapter. But the core of this chapter is learning how to choose exactly what is most productive for your subconscious communications. It is essential that you communicate knowledgeably, purposefully and skillfully to secure your optimal results. You will need to know some of the specifics to say and how to frame the way you say it.

CHAPTER FOUR: THE STRUCTURE

This chapter focuses on a step-by-step process for creating a Reprogramming Self-hypnosis script that is appropriate for reprogramming your subconscious mind. It is built to teach on three levels. It starts with a generalized outline description and ends with a full-blown script that is poised and ready for directing your subconscious to accomplish your general and specific goals. Scripts themselves are optional assistants for you. Once you have the sequence of Reprogramming Self-hypnosis in mind, you can go forth intuitively reprogramming for your desirable outcomes without a specific script.

The first level gives you the big picture. The second level focuses on more specific components, building a more detailed description of the same process. Level Two might be all that you would need in order to begin your Reprogramming Self-hypnosis sessions. The third level offers an example of an extensively developed Reprogramming Self-hypnosis script with hypnotic guided imagery enriched with many optional details.

You may have occasions when you will selectively utilize hypnosis suggestions that have been published by others as well as suggestions composed originally by and for you. This chapter guides you carefully so you are prepared for both options alone or in combination. Additional Reprogramming Hypnosis scripts (revised in 2010) from the original nine-CD series, *Reprogram Your Subconscious*, 2005, are in Appendix Two.

At the conclusion of this chapter you will find two original scripts featuring *Extended Metaphor* examples that function as suggestions to your subconscious regarding positive changes. If you would like, record them for your Reprogramming Self-hypnosis script (solely for your personal use) or refer to them by title during your self-hypnosis session.

NOW PREPARING TO BEGIN, QUIET PLEASE!

When you first begin learning self-hypnosis, it is necessary to find a peaceful place and quiet time to begin practicing. You will need a space where you can focus solely on self-hypnosis. After sufficient self-hypnosis practice, you will be able to ignore (or cancel in your mind) all distractions that at an earlier time may have made self-hypnosis very challenging. Then you may do your self-hypnosis almost anywhere or anytime such as when you are a passenger on a train, plane, boat or car, at a sports game, in a house of worship, a dentist's chair, a doctor's waiting room, in bed or in innumerable situations. These are just a few of the possible places for self-hypnosis. Soon with practice, you will learn to take a shortcut using your three personalized signals that relax you into hypnosis within thirty seconds or less. This shortcut will be explained later.

CAUTION: It is Unsafe While Driving a Car or Operating Machinery to Practice Self-Hypnosis or Listen to Any Hypnosis Audio.

This is imperative for your safety. You will be unable to stay focused properly on your driving or on your mechanical task at hand. One of my clients confessed that he listened to his audio while driving even though he was aware of the strong warning. He ended up driving around the block numerous times without being aware of doing so. How fortunate he was to have learned that lesson while still remaining safe!

REPROGRAMMING SELF-HYPNOSIS: *THE BIG PICTURE TO FINE DETAILS*

LEVEL ONE: SIMPLIFIED OVERVIEW

PART ONE: THE BEGINNING

The Induction is the *first main part*. It includes the words or actions you use to get your mind into the relaxed altered state of hypnosis. Deepening suggestions are used as part of the Induction but may be repeated throughout the entire hypnosis session to ensure you remain in the hypnotic trance state. Typically you will:

- Use deepening techniques, such as imagining that with each breath you exhale, you allow yourself to go more deeply into relaxation, moving from the Alpha to the Theta State of Consciousness. Many believe the Theta state produces even better results for reprogramming. Another deepening suggestion could be that you feel more relaxed with each stairway step you go down or with each number you hear from *ten* to *one*.

- Make statements establishing that you and everyone else you know are protected. Also mention that it is safe for you to use hypnosis to reprogram your subconscious for your purposes. It is also safe for others that you use hypnosis to reprogram your subconscious for your purposes.

- Specify out loud or silently to your subconscious how long you desire to stay in hypnosis. Also specify how to proceed after the conclusion of your self-hypnosis time. State whether you desire to sleep immediately afterward, waking up at your pre-selected time or whether you desire to come back to your conscious state immediately after the hypnosis session is concluded.

- Specify if you desire to meditate after your Reprogramming Hypnosis Suggestions and before you conclude your session.

PART TWO: THE MAIN BODY

The   communication   of   Reprogramming   Self-hypnosis

Suggestions to Your Subconscious is the *second main part.* Communications may be stated silently or out loud. They may dramatically vary in content depending upon the subject matter you have chosen to address. Although in general terms your communications achieve the following:

- Your communications target, identify (if possible) and delete anything that has opposed or would oppose your suggestions/goals.

- Your communications download the new suggestions/ goals and download encouragement for your subconscious to continue supporting those suggestions/ goals.

PART THREE: THE CONCLUSION

CONCLUSION OF YOUR SELF-HYPNOSIS IS THE THIRD MAIN PART:

- It begins when, if it is your appropriate time to come back to your conscious state, you begin counting from *one* to *ten* (or to whatever number you used originally to induce hypnosis), bringing yourself back to your totally alert state of Beta Consciousness.

- Alternatively, if it is your appropriate time for sleep, you conclude your Reprogramming Self-hypnosis by giving yourself the directions to easily, comfortably drift into a deeply relaxing, peaceful sleep, awakening at your appropriate time and feeling great in every way.

VARIETY OF INDUCTIONS: ADD SPICE TO YOUR LIFE

- Eye Fixation is an Induction that requires you to stare at an object, a spot on the wall, a swinging watch or whatever you choose to look at that is a sufficient distance away from you so that both of your eyes may see it in front of you. By staring at that fixed or moving point, you induce eye fatigue within a short period of time. The eye fatigue in turn induces the Alpha or Theta Conciseness State of hypnosis. You will feel your eyelids getting more tired, getting heavier and heavier. As you start to feel that way, just close your eyes and go deeper into relaxation. Then you give yourself additional deepening suggestions like saying: *with every breath I exhale, I allow myself to go deeper into relaxation/hypnosis. Going deeper and deeper, way down.* Continue with more deepening suggestions.

While many examples of self-hypnosis scripts in this book use a stairway or beach scene, there exists a variety of different progressive relaxation Inductions appropriate for self-hypnosis:

- Use a scene from a beach, watching the very gentle waves. With each wave coming to shore, allow yourself to go deeper into relaxation. Count the waves from *ten* to *one*. When you reach the count of *one*, you are there, in your safe place.

- Focus on your breathing as you slowly count your deep breaths from *ten* to *one*. By the time you reach one, you have arrived totally relaxed at your safe and healing place.

- Imagine a gentle warm light starting from the top of your head and traveling to different parts of your body that you have selected. See and feel at least ten areas of your body going from tight, tight, to relaxed, relaxed. Conclude your relaxing light imagery with relaxing

your toes. Then instantly you have arrived at your safe
and healing place.

- Hear a gentle, soothing chime creating a delicate sound.
  Count the sound of each chime from *ten* to *one*. When
  you finish counting to *one*, you have arrived totally
  relaxed in your safe and healing place.

- Imagine you are in a hot air balloon, going higher and
  higher, feeling more and more relaxed the higher you
  go. You might count yourself higher from *one* to *ten* and
  with each number you go higher up and you feel more
  deeply relaxed. When you reach *ten*, you are so totally
  relaxed and you have arrived in your safe place.

- Imagine you are getting a massage. Start the massage
  feeling it relax your feet, and feel yourself going deeper
  into relaxation. Then feel the massage on your knees,
  going even deeper into relaxation. Feel the massage on
  your thighs as you are going even deeper. Then feel the
  massage relaxing your hips, as you are going even
  deeper. Then feel the massage on your stomach, as you
  are going even deeper. Then feel the massage on your
  arms, going even deeper. Then feel the massage on your
  shoulders, going deeper down into relaxation. Then feel
  the massage, massaging your neck, going deeper
  relaxed. Then feel your jaw being massaged, going
  deeper. Then your temples are massaged, going deeper.
  Then feel your forehead being massaged, going deeper
  and deeper, so deep into relaxation. Now you are totally
  relaxed and have entered your safe and healing place.

- Visualize yourself climbing up stairs counting *ten* to *one*,
  feeling more relaxed with each step. When you reach
  step number *one*, you are there, in your safe and healing
  place where no one can disturb you without your
  permission.

- Take an up or down escalator or take an elevator either
  traveling up or down, noticing with each floor that you

count from *ten* to *one*, your body, mind and spirit are relaxing deeper and deeper, releasing all tension, anxiety and stress. When you arrive at *one*, you are in your safe and healing place.

- See yourself comfortably walking through a mist counting your steps from *ten* to *one*. When you finish counting to *one*, you are there, feeling so relaxed in your safe and healing place. All tension, anxiety and stress have left your Mind/Body/Spirit.

- See yourself walking through a mansion with ten connecting rooms each having a connecting door. As you open one door you cross the room to the next door; open that door and continue with door number *nine* through door number *one*. With each door you open, it opens you up to more relaxation and peace of mind. After you open door number *one*, you are in your safe and healing place.

- Visualize a blackboard and slowly erase the ten numbers going backward from *ten* to *one*. With each number erased, allow yourself to go deeper into relaxation, more peaceful and calmer. All tension, anxiety and stress have been replaced with soothing serenity.

LEVEL TWO: A TWELVE-STEP GUIDE FOR REPROGRAMMING SELF-HYPNOSIS

PART ONE: THE BEGINNING

Step 1:

Find a comfortable place where you can remain undisturbed for the time you have allotted for the hypnosis. With your neck supported, either be seated comfortably or be lying down comfortably.

Step 2:

Close your eyes and take in two deep breaths, in through your nose and slowly exhale through your mouth to the count of eight.

Step 3:

Imagine as you exhale you are releasing all tension, stress and anxiety that may have collected anywhere within your entire Mind/Body/Spirit. Just let everything go.

Step 4:

Touch two adjacent fingers together lengthwise on your right or left hand. Many people touch the side of their index finger lengthwise against the side of their middle finger. Note that this fingers-touching-signal is only one possibility. You may choose another preferred way at any time but then keep it consistent.

Step 5:

Think of a favorite number or choose any number between *one* and *ten*. Visualize and/or hear that number. Say that number over and over again silently or out loud. Discard and ignore any distracting thoughts by imagining you are placing an *X* or the word *cancel* over the thoughts. You could imagine envisioning this or hearing the word, *cancel* and/or feeling the stamping of the *X* on the distraction. Immediately return your focus to your special number and feeling relaxed. Steps 2-5 direct you to do three things simultaneously when you wish to enter hypnosis. This is a safety precaution that prevents you from going into hypnosis unintentionally.

Step 6:

Notice that now directly in front of you is your special staircase leading you to your safe place. You may choose whether the stairs are going up or whether they go down or whether you would prefer a level path with ten markers. These ten steps are shallow and there is a handrail on either side of the staircase. Imagine you are strong in body and able to walk easily. When you get to the end of the stairway after counting (either silently or out loud) the steps from *ten* to step *one*, you find yourself in your safe place where no one may disturb you without your permission. This is the most wonderful, *safe and healing place* for you.

You may choose a different Induction if desired. See the other options listed earlier in this chapter under *Variety of Inductions: Add Spice to Your Life.* If you prefer a level path, feel yourself as healthy in body, walking past ten large stone markers that could be along a pleasant road or upon a beach. The stone markers are only a few feet apart. As you pass each marker, allow yourself to be more and more deeply relaxed. When you arrive at number *one*, you are in your safe and healing place.

Step 7: (Optional Positive and Healing Suggestions)
    Describe to yourself that:
    a) You are feeling grounded and centered.
    b) Your Mind/Body/Spirit is feeling peaceful, in harmony and balance.
    c) You are feeling healing energy circulating within your entire Mind/Body/Spirit and throughout your personal energy field that extends beyond your physical body.
    d) You are experiencing healing colored lights from the sun bringing appropriate vibrations of *Positive Energy* that are intended for each of your issues of imbalance. These healing lights are filling any voids left behind from the negative emotions/*Negative Energy* that you have released. You may notice the healing colored lights change colors on different days due to your current immediate needs.

Step 8:
    Express gratitude to your subconscious for having accepted

and downloaded all your previously requested suggestions and goals for your Highest Good and well-being.

PART TWO: THE MAIN BODY

Step 9:

This is a time and place where you communicate to your subconscious your suggestions that delete anything that would oppose or conflict with the goals of your new hypnosis suggestions. You additionally submit or resubmit your new positive suggestions that create or reinforce your new Subconscious Programs. You may refer to a place where they are written or orally recorded. You may also state them out loud and/or silently as you have rehearsed them. After communicating your Reprogramming Hypnosis suggestions, first confirm that your subconscious has accepted these suggestions and then thank your subconscious for having successfully downloaded them. Believe that your suggestions are operating within you now.

Step 10:

Say silently to yourself or out loud how much time you wish to remain in hypnosis focused on the positive outcome of your requests, meditating and/or just purely relaxing while in hypnosis. Alert your subconscious to the exact time you wish to return to your conscious state such as after fifteen minutes or describe the specific time when you easily, gently drift into a nap or into your night's sleep and awaken as you would naturally or awaken at a specified time. Step 10 may be combined with Step 7 if you so choose.

PART THREE: THE CONCLUSION

Step 11:

If you have chosen to sleep after self-hypnosis, begin sleeping now. Since it is your time to sleep, tell yourself that you enjoy your rejuvenating sleep, awakening at your preselected time refreshed, re-energized, renewed and feeling great.

Step 12:

If you have chosen to return to your conscious state after concluding self-hypnosis, first remind yourself that tonight or whenever it is your time for you to sleep, you are able to sleep immediately, deeply and peacefully as soon as your head touches your pillow and your eyes close for sleep. Next, begin returning fully to your conscious state by slowly counting from *one* to *ten*. Count slowly, reminding yourself how you feel so re-energized, yet relaxed, peaceful, cleansed and healed.

RETURNING TO CONSCIOUS STATE AFTER SELF-HYPNOSIS

The following is one possible method for returning to your conscious state (Beta) when you are ready to exit self-hypnosis. You may say it silently or out loud:

One, it is time for me to come out of hypnosis. However, when it is my time for sleep, I sleep deeply and peacefully as soon as my head touches my pillow and my eyes close for sleep.

Two, my entire body feels great. My body has been cleansed and healed, revitalized and re-energized.

Three, my mind feels great! It has been cleansed and healed, revitalized and re-energized.

Four, my fingers are perhaps stretching now, my toes might be wiggling, my eyelashes are beginning to flutter open now. They are fluttering open as I easily am coming back so comfortably to my conscious state, alert, totally aware, able to focus and concentrate better than ever, able to think clearly and be alert and able to drive safely.

Count slowly the remaining numbers: *Five, Six, Seven, Eight, Nine* and *Ten*, I am back to my conscious state, my eyes are opening now. My eyes are wide open now and I am feeling relaxed, alert, able to focus and concentrate better than ever, refreshed, re-energized and renewed. I am totally back to my conscious state. I am feeling clearheaded, alert, totally aware and able to drive easily and safely. I am feeling just great!

It is essential that you are totally back to your Beta State of Consciousness. Give yourself a strong signal after returning to your conscious state like standing up and snapping your fingers three times as you say, *I am wide awake and alert!*

CUSTOMIZE: YOU HAVE OPTIONS

You may customize or alter the imagery that you use for hypnosis to whatever is most comfortable for you or whichever type of sensory perception helps to increase your relaxation response. Some people have difficulty visualizing but rather can feel or hear as their way of entering relaxation. Also, while I suggest counting from *ten* to *one*, you may want to count from *twenty* to *one* or repeat the *ten* to *one* imagery a second time until you feel more deeply relaxed. Fortunately, once you have successfully been directed or self-directed into hypnosis, it becomes easier and easier with repeated practice. It just naturally starts happening more automatically for you thanks to your cooperative subconscious.

VOCAL VARIETY ENHANCES VIVID IMAGERY

Relax, Release and Dream On exemplifies the use of vocal inflection and animation for a detailed guided imagery script. Once you are in the altered state of hypnosis, listening to a vivid auditory experience can be compelling. Vocal variety may be preferable to your using a monotone voice except when used for your Induction phase where monotony helps initiate the hypnosis state. Your subconscious responds well to vivid imagery created by your voice.

SOMETIMES YOU WANT MORE THAN FIFTEEN MINUTES

The following offers guidance for actualizing Reprogramming Self-hypnosis for purposes of reprogramming your subconscious with a very involved, descriptive script. If possible make an audio recording of this involved script that may exceed fifteen minutes and listen to it as your personal recording after you have approved its suggestions. Simply delete from the script whatever may seem inappropriate for you. You may want to use other people's scripts or create your own original versions. There is no such thing as only one right way to conduct self-hypnosis. You may choose to do self-hypnosis without any predetermined script, yet you may find more success having certain goals to accomplish in mind before you begin. One method may prove better for you than others so keep experimenting. Some circumstances do not allow for hypnosis with audio assistance. Consequently, practice your Reprogramming Self-hypnosis both ways, with and without using the thirty-minute, music only, track three from *Relax, Release and Dream On* or using very relaxing music from another audio source.

PUT ALL ELSE ON THE BACK BURNER

Before you begin your Reprogramming Self-hypnosis session, reaffirm to yourself that you are worth this time and deserve this time for yourself. Acknowledge that everything else that could have distracted you has been placed in a big soup pot sealed with a lid and is staying on the back burner until you are finished. Also, find a comfortable place where you may remain undisturbed for the time you have allotted for your self-hypnosis experience. Your neck should be comfortably supported before you start hypnosis.

REPROGRAMMING SELF-HYPNOSIS WITH HEALING GUIDED IMAGERY: A SCRIPT YOU CAN PERSONALIZE

PART ONE: THE BEGINNING

I close my eyes and take in two deep breaths in through my nose, filling my lungs and slowly exhaling through my mouth to the count of eight. I imagine as I exhale I am releasing all the tension, stress and anxiety that may have collected anywhere within my entire Mind/Body/Spirit. It feels like I am just letting everything go. It is so easy to let go. It is as simple as the letting go of the strings from helium balloons. I just let everything go ...

Now I touch two fingers, from the same hand, together, side-by-side as I think of my special number that I have reserved for self-hypnosis. I am visualizing this special number and silently saying the number over and over again [out loud or silently.] I continue staying focused on my special number as I notice my breathing is slowing. With each breath I exhale, I allow myself to go deeper into relaxation feeling, calm, peaceful and safe ...

I am allowing myself to drift and float deeper and deeper, down deeper into total relaxation as I am focused on my special number ... My mind's eye is fixed on that soothing number ... My arms and hands may feel so heavy I may barely be able to lift them at all ... All thoughts have slowed down and I automatically concentrate only on the relaxation without having to think about it at all. In fact, with each breath I exhale, I may feel myself more deeply relaxing, letting go of all tension, tightness and anxiety ... I am confident that I am protected ... I am protected ...

There now is a white light that surrounds me and protects

me. It protects everyone I have ever known or will know. Everyone and everything is protected. I am safe … Positive energy enters and flows continuously through a portal in the circle of white light. It allows Positive Energy to surround me, steadily bringing into fruition all that I request for my Highest Good … Feeling so comfortable, so protected and so deeply relaxed … Way down into relaxation … With every breath I exhale, I allow myself to feel more and more relaxed …

I simply cancel any thoughts contrary to deep relaxation. I cancel them with an X in my mind's eye telling them to leave and replacing them with extremely happy thoughts of relaxation and comfort … Yes, feeling deeply, deeply peaceful and calm … To help me go even deeper into relaxation, I now sense that in front of me is my special staircase of ten steps that leads me to my safe and healing place. These ten steps are shallow and there is a handrail on either side of the staircase. I imagine I am strong in body and able to walk easily. The staircase is leading me to my safe and healing place. As I take each step on the stairway, I imagine myself, with each step I take, going deeper and deeper into that very relaxed feeling … When I reach the bottom of the stairway, step number *one*, I find myself in my safe and healing place where no one may disturb me without my permission. This is the most wonderful, safe and healing place for me in the entire world …

[If you are unable to see a stairway, use others senses such as feeling sensations of slightly warm light or perhaps hearing sounds as you walk down stairs. Make adjustments where necessary.]

I am ready to begin now with counting: *Ten*, going way down … Way down into deep relaxation, all muscles, all ligaments, all tendons are softening and letting go of all tension, all stress … *Nine*, deeper still … All my thoughts are focused on one thought of deep relaxation. If thoughts other than of relaxation appear, I simply cancel them with a big X in my mind's eye. I may notice at some time, maybe now, maybe later, I feel my breathing is slowing, slowing, slowing down … *Eight,* deeper still, so quiet, so peaceful, like a beautiful sunset … *Seven,* the deeper I go into relaxation, the more wonderful it feels … *Six,* so deeply relaxed, everything slowing, so peaceful and tranquil … *Five,* way deeper relaxed, feeling so calm, so soothed. *Four,* I may feel more deeply relaxed more than ever before … way into my deepest level of relaxation … *Three,* deeply, deeply relaxed. My arms, my hands, my legs, feel so heavy, so heavy it may be difficult to lift them … *Two,* I am almost there now, almost there to my safe and healing place, to my very deepest level of relaxation … And *one* deeply, deeply, deeply, relaxed, so deeply, deeply, deeply relaxed …

And now I can imagine I am here in my safe place. Perhaps I can touch it, smell it, taste it, hear it, and see it! I am in my safe place, undisturbed and feeling so comfortable … My senses radiate relaxation, peace, comfort. I experience the feeling of being safe and cared for. I know and feel that I am loved unconditionally … And every time I return to my safe and healing place, I am able to bring myself here more easily, more comfortably and more time efficiently than before. Each time I return to my safe and healing place I sense even stronger feelings of well-being, of unconditional love and of self-healing.

I may find that these pleasurable and positive sensations beckon me to return to my safe place once every day for rejuvenation, for re-establishing peace of mind, harmony and balance within my entire being … Every time I return here to my safe and healing place, I find it easier and easier to relax into deeper and deeper relaxation. And it always feels so peaceful, so great to be here.

Since I have arrived in my safe and healing place, I may notice a feeling now as if my feet were growing roots into the earth and these roots are grounding me and centering me … A white light from above shines down on the crown of my head bringing unlimited white light energy that energizes and heals every cell of my body. The white light returns all my cells to their healthiest status … Feeling the harmony and balance within my entire body is so healing ... It is so clear that I am always connected, plugged into the universal outlet for love, light and energy ...

I summon my healing, positive colored lights from the sun and feel them cover my body with their gentle, healing glow ... Each light represents a specialty vibration of ten-hertz energy that is intended for releasing negative emotions while healing each area where my Mind/Body/Spirit may be other than balanced. These different colored lights gently touch the surface of my skin and enter through my feet, circulating throughout my body, healing and cleansing, healing and cleansing, healing and cleansing ... They are filling up any voids left behind from Negative Energy that I have released ... These lights bring me such strength, such courage. They fill me up with beautiful feelings of unconditional love and connection to my Creator. They are always there for me. They are accumulative. Furthermore, each time I return to this safe place I may ask for whatever colors I need for my healing. The colors may change based upon my needs each day. The colors automatically keep my energy frequencies optimal for self-healing.

PART TWO: THE MAIN BODY

Now that I am in my safe and healing place I reaffirm for you, my subconscious, all the suggestions and goals I have approved and chosen for my Highest Good and well-being. I am directing you, my subconscious to enact them in ways that are for my Highest Good and to keep reinforcing them. With tremendous gratitude I thank my subconscious for having fulfilled all requests that I previously and presently requested for my subconscious to download permanently for me. I am so grateful for your help and I am so happy it has all been done!

MY SUGGESTIONS ARE AS FOLLOWS:

[Here is where you say, out loud or silently to yourself, the specific hypnosis suggestions that target Faulty Subconscious Programs that would interfere with your desired suggestions/ goals. Then you express the suggestions that create the conditions for your goals to be realized. Additionally you imagine your goals as though immediately they are part of your present reality.]

I express my deep gratitude to my subconscious for all its help and relay how ecstatically happy it makes me feel having had all my suggestions realized for my Highest Good in ways that are for my Highest Good.

At this time I am focused on and receive my intuitive knowing and Inner Wisdom related to my goals that support my Highest Good.

[After you have received whatever intuitive knowing is available at that time, conclude your Reprogramming Self-hypnosis session with directions for ending it:]

I remain in this very relaxed state, enjoying all that has been absorbed from this experience until the time I have allotted for hypnosis has ended.

PART THREE: THE CONCLUSION

Continue with the next phase that either allows you to sleep or brings you back to your Beta Consciousness State. If you are performing your Reprogramming Self-hypnosis without a recording, state the appropriate option for concluding your session for that time only, choosing either OPTION ONE or OPTION TWO. OPTION ONE is for drifting into a deeply relaxed sleep where you awaken at your appropriate time. OPTION TWO is for coming back to your conscious state.

NOTE: If you want to record an auditory version of this entire script, include both options in your recording as is written in the remainder of this script.

OPTION ONE: *It is time for me to sleep now. I continue to sleep throughout my selected hours that are dedicated for sleep. I awaken at the appropriate time feeling refreshed, calm and feeling great like my body's batteries have been recharged. I have been cleansed and healed. If it is my appropriate time for sleep and I have yet to begin sleeping, I begin sleeping now. I remain relaxed as I promptly drift so gently into a deep, peaceful and rejuvenating sleep. I continue sleeping wonderfully until it is my intended time to awaken back to my conscious state. I sleep all the intended time in a very restful, healing sleep. I process whatever issues that still need to be processed, in a very compassionate, gentle, easy and time efficient way.*

NOTE: Include the following paragraph in your audio script recording only:

If it is my time for sleep, I follow the directions for my appropriate time to sleep. In fact, when hearing the instructions that direct me to return to my conscious state, it only helps me sleep more deeply and peacefully. I sleep until it is truly my appropriate time to return to my conscious state. Meanwhile, I disregard any instructions that would bring me out of this deep relaxed state. Such instructions only help me to sleep more deeply and peacefully until it truly is my appropriate time to return to my conscious state, feeling great.

OPTION TWO: *If it is my appropriate time to return to my fully awake, aware conscious state, I begin by counting from one to ten. I first remind my subconscious that tonight or whenever it is my desired time to sleep, I sleep immediately, deeply, peacefully as soon as my head touches my pillow and my eyes close for sleep. I sleep all the intended time in a very restful, deep sleep. I process whatever issues still need to be processed in a very compassionate, gentle, easy and time efficient way... If it is my appropriate time to return to my conscious state, I begin now counting from one to ten to bring me gently, comfortably and time efficiently out of deep relaxation. When I reach the number ten, I am totally back to my conscious state, fully awake, clear headed, alert, energized, able to focus and concentrate better than before, feeling great like my body's batteries have been recharged.*

Now, if it is my selected time to return to my conscious state, I begin with the instructions immediately: One, it is time for me to come out of hypnosis. Two, my entire body feels great. My body has been cleansed and healed, revitalized and energized. Three, my mind feels great! It has been cleansed and healed, revitalized and re-energized. Four, my fingers are stretching; my toes may be wiggling; and perhaps my eyelashes are starting to flutter open now as I easily am returning to my conscious state. I am alert, totally aware, and also able to concentrate and think clearly, able to drive safely and easily. Five, Six, Seven, Eight, Nine and Ten, I am back to my conscious state. My eyes are opening now. My eyes are wide open now, wide awake. I am feeling relaxed, alert, clear minded, able to focus and concentrate very well, refreshed and energized. I am able to drive safely and easily. I feel just great in every way! Snap your fingers together three times as you say: *Wide awake, NOW!*

PLAN AHEAD FOR RECALL DURING SELF-HYPNOSIS

It may be difficult to remember precisely everything you want to say when you are in self-hypnosis. You may be wondering how to remember exactly what you want to say to your subconscious every time you are in Reprogramming Self-hypnosis or any type of self-hypnosis. Sometimes it is challenging to think in a linear, concrete and precise left brain fashion when you are in the relaxed State of Alpha or Theta Consciousness which involves more right brain activity. So the easy solution is to first think ahead, analyze, edit and prepare what you want to communicate before you begin your self-hypnosis session. It is very helpful to decide beforehand any positive suggestions for your Reprogramming Self-hypnosis sessions and write them down carefully or make a vocal recording of them. Compose your suggestions just as you would want your subconscious to download those suggestions permanently. Then, while in hypnosis, refer to your suggestions as those written on that paper, in a computer file, recorded on an audio or wherever you have stored your suggestions. This clarifies precisely what you want in the specific wording and meaning that you intend to communicate to your subconscious. You may refer to those suggestions without the need for more details. The following short script will give you some ideas of what you might say:

I am reinforcing for my subconscious all the Reprogramming Self-hypnosis suggestions I have written down (or just spoken out loud a few minutes ago, or listened to as my daily affirmations, or labeled in my journal, Positive Suggestions). They are just what I need. I love having them as my reality. I am grateful to you, my subconscious, for having deleted the opposing Faulty Subconscious Programs and then having downloaded all of these selected improved suggestions/affirmations as lasting Subconscious Programming for me. All of these suggestions make me feel so very happy and give me tremendous pleasure.

ADDITIONAL LIFE BOATS AVAILABLE

There are three revised and reprinted Reprogramming Hypnosis guided imagery scripts from the original *Reprogram Your Subconscious*, 2005 series. These scripts appear in Appendix Two. You may use these scripts as a reference guide to assist you in creating your own scripts for private use. These scripts focus on some of the most powerful and positive emotions: *Inner Peace*

Maintains Harmony and Balance (overcoming anger), *Inner Security Maintains Faith That All Is Well* (overcoming anxieties and worries) and *Inner Nurturing Maintains Self-esteem and Self-empowerment* (overcoming sadness, loss and helplessness). All hypnotic guided imagery scripts are universal in themes and demonstrate techniques that you may adopt and integrate in part or in their entirety for your Reprogramming Self-hypnosis. Always you will be guided to discard anything that is other than acceptable for your *ethics, morals and religious beliefs.* You are the master of your journey; with your permission, I am your guide.

RECOMMENDATIONS FOR USING YOUR BONUS AUDIO

First listen to *Relax, Release and Dream On* during your waking hours with your eyes open. That way you will hear everything that is said and know that all will be okay when you listen to it while sleeping. If you have never experienced hypnosis or a hypnosis audio, there are directions for a very short Acupressure tapping exercise to prepare you for this hypnosis experience. These instructions are included as a PDF file with your audio download and also are included if you order the *Relax, Release and Dream On* audio.

You may choose daytime, evening, bedtime or any combination thereof for your listening enjoyment. Listen to this audio as frequently as is possible for you every day for at least one entire week. For the purposes of preparing yourself to learn self-hypnosis, your intention is to experience the pleasant sensations of being in hypnosis, to understand the process of hypnosis and to experience how easy it is to follow the hypnosis suggestions. Actually, when you are sleeping, it is unnecessary for you to consciously pay attention to the recording. Just be sure you hear it without other distractions interfering like television or others' conversations. Many people listen with headphones/ ear buds so as not to disturb anyone else in the room. Of course, if your roommate is willing to listen to the audio with you at bedtime, both of you will benefit from the positive suggestions and extra relaxation. In fact, this audio will continue to provide benefits for you indefinitely.

MORE TIPS FOR REPROGRAMMING SELF-HYPNOSIS

One:

Offer your suggestions stating the most important suggestion with the highest priority first.

Two:

Suggest that whatever was programmed in your subconscious mind that was faulty or has proven other than for your Highest Good regarding your issue has been deleted. It has been deleted just as easily as you can delete files on a computer.

Whatever messages or communications that were accepted by your subconscious and that led to the undesirable outcome(s) have also been deleted. Instead, you have replaced the old files with positively beneficial ones for your Highest Good.

Three:

Suggest you have instructed your subconscious to create your Forgiveness file also. This is where you resolve all issues of guilt and self-punishment if they were ever present. Suggest that you have forgiven all those who hurt you whether it was intentional or unintentional. And you have forgiven yourself as well.

Four:

State whereas in the past you used to think/feel/do_____, that has now stopped or changed completely. Instead, you now think/feel/do_____; and whenever you do_____, it makes you feel great!

Five:

Suggest and describe how your future is now unfolding and experience everything vividly with all of your six senses. Suggest how you envision and feel everything after your suggestions have taken effect (e.g., how you look, feel, think, believe and behave after your subconscious has made the changes that you requested). If possible to do so, see it, feel it, smell it, hear it and taste it. Create it as your extremely vivid present reality.

Six:

Suggest and thereafter use in your conversation your post-hypnotic trigger word(s) that reinforces all your suggestions like the words, *great* or *bless you*.

Seven:

State positive affirmations and/or mantras as part of your suggestions. Use the first person pronoun, *I*, when suggesting your affirmations.

AN EIGHT-STEP (WITHOUT REPROGRAMMING) SELF-HYPNOSIS OPTION

One:

Find a comfortable place to sit or recline where you may remain uninterrupted during self-hypnosis. Put phones on silence.

Two:

Look up focusing comfortably on one spot on the ceiling until your eyelids feel heavy. Then close your eyes as you take in two deep breaths in through the nose and slowly exhale through your mouth to the count of eight.

Three:

Imagine as you exhale, you are releasing all the stress, tension, anxiety and negativity that may be anywhere within your entire body and personal energy field.

Four:
   Touch together two of your fingers (your index finger and third finger) lengthwise beside each other on only one hand.

Five:
   Imagine seeing, feeling, hearing, touching or tasting something of your special safe and healing place as you feel yourself just drifting and floating down deeper, down deeper into relaxation.

Six:
   Tell yourself that as you count from *ten* to *one* you are traveling to your safe and healing place and when you reach the number *one*, you find yourself in your safe and healing place and once in your safe and healing place, take yourself deeper into relaxation by repeating the word *deeper* five times.

Seven:
   Reaffirm and reinforce all the suggestions that you have already requested for your subconscious to execute just by saying so out loud or silently to yourself. If desired, at this time add your suggestions phrased in clear, specific and positive language.

Eight:
   Mention that you sleep peacefully and deeply relaxed, tonight or whenever it is your appropriate time to sleep, as soon as your eyes close for sleep. Also mention that after you have counted to *ten*, you are wide awake, alert, and able to drive safely and think so clearly. You feel great, relaxed yet energized, focused and able

to concentrate better than ever. Now bring yourself back to your conscious state (Beta) of total awareness, counting from *one* to *ten*. You are WIDE AWAKE at the count of *ten* and say so as your snap fingers three times in a row.

THE RIGHT FRAME IS EVERYTHING:

GUIDELINES FOR FRAMING REPROGRAMMING HYPNOSIS SUGGESTIONS

THINK POSITIVELY

In framing your Reprogramming Self-hypnosis suggestions, it is very important that all statements and commands conclude with a POSITIVE focus or POSITIVE image form of expression. Direct your mind to what you want rather than what you want to avoid. Your subconscious overlooks the negative commands as in phrases such as: *do not* or *don't, can not* or *can't, will not* or *won't,* and *should not* or *shouldn't.* Those words are much less important than the dominant subject of the command. Your subconscious focuses on what or where those commands are directing its attention. Therefore, when you say, *Don't think of a red barn,* you think of a red barn. And when you say, *Don't raise your voice to me,* you are really saying, *Raise your voice to me.*

This may be an appropriate time to recall a story I heard about a famous pitcher, who shall remain nameless, who pitched in the final game of a World Series. He was pitching with the bases loaded in the ninth inning and there were two outs. His team was ahead by one run. His manager came out to the mound and lifted his finger in a warning, saying, *Don't throw your fastball. Whatever you do, don't throw your fastball!* Of course, the pitcher threw his fastball the very next pitch and the ball game was lost!

Compose your suggestions in positive terms using clarity and easy to follow directions. Instead of saying, *Don't forget,* use *Remember.* Instead of *You can't be late,* use *You have to be on time.*

Instead of *Don't eat food with trans fats,* say *Choose foods that have fats of the healthy variety only.*

If you say the following sentences to your subconscious, you are placing emphasis on the negative aspect that you really do not want:

You can't use generalizations with my dad. He won't receive your generalizations well when you report to him.

Instead put what you really do want into the limelight:

It is important to keep focused on the details when you speak with my dad. When you report to him, he will receive details so much better than anything else when you speak to him.

Remember to direct one's attention and focus to the desired outcome rather than the undesirable one. Nevertheless, sometimes you need to identify and speak about something that is negative, such as:

I have neutralized and released all anxiety that related to my parents' divorce. I am now at peace about the past. The past is past, gone.
I feel calm and maintain my harmony and balance in my relationships with both of my parents.

Although anxiety is mentioned here, it is mentioned only once and the rest of the suggestions are filled with positive feelings that keep your focus and emphasis on the positive.

YOUR GOLD MIND

Your mind is your gold mine of Inner Wisdom offering you all kinds of treasures. But there are steps to follow in seeking the best outcome prospecting within your subconscious mind. Your subconscious mind responds well to imagery, similes and Extended Metaphors called analogies. Just as you might find it easier to remember a person's face rather than his name, your Suggestible Subconscious responds well to what appeals vividly to your sense of sight, sound, smell, taste, touch/feelings and intuitive Inner Knowing sensations. When you make your words vivid, it makes it more real.

DIFFERENT STROKES FOR DIFFERENT FOLKS

In writing hypnotic suggestions and in creating hypnotic guided imagery, utilize all your six senses: sight, sound, taste, smell, touch, and intuition. Intuition is your sensory perception beyond the five senses. Emphasize the use of imagery, similes and analogies in order to have the best outcome for programming and reprogramming purposes. This is because people vary in their learning styles. Some people may be mainly auditory learners. They will comprehend verbal directions much better than reading the written word, remembering pictures or learning through doing. Some people learn mainly from practicing doing what they are supposed to be learning. That type of learner is a kinesthetic (hands-on) learner. Typically people are more often visual learners who learn by seeing or a combination of visual, auditory and kinesthetic cues. Successful teachers know this and present their lessons keeping in mind that students have a variety of learning styles. The lessons are prepared so all types of learners can receive the instruction most appropriate for their learning styles.

If you are already certain of your preferred sensory learning style, use that one predominantly. That means if you are visual, your suggestions will include reference to things that you see.

For instance, in your Induction you might describe the shape, size, color or movement of what you visually observe when walking along a path to your safe place. If you are more auditory, you would mention the birds chirping, the swish of the gentle wind, the crackle of the leaves as you stepped upon them, etc. If you were more kinesthetic, you would mention how warm the sun felt upon your cheeks, how soft the ground was as you walked upon it, how it felt like the ground slightly gave way to your weight, or how you felt the exhilaration of being in the wide open spaces. If you were more sensitive to taste (gustatory), you might taste the sweat running down your forehead and taste the sweet gooeyness of the fudge brownie that you nibbled on as you walked along the path. If smell (olfactory) were your dominant sense you would mention the smell of the fragrant roses that you passed by or mention the hickory scented air of burning logs. If you sense things best intuitively you might describe that Inner Knowing that nature was beckoning you to explore the beauty of that moment, knowing it was a special gift that could never be replicated. Or you might mention that this path was actually leading you to discover how you were united in the oneness of nature and all the blessings it provided you at that moment along your path.

ACCEPT THE GIFT BEFORE IT IS GIVEN

When you create your hypnosis suggestions that communicate what you really want, always refer to each suggested request as though it already is happening or has happened already. When you use the future tense as in *I will be relaxed; I will give calm and confident presentations,* your subconscious understands that what you want will occur in the future sometime, but not now. Remember the famous line of Scarlett O'Hara in *Gone with the Wind?* She will think about it tomorrow! But we all know that for her, tomorrow never comes. If you rephrase the suggestion relating to the presentation as though it is happening now and continues to happen every time, it might sound like this:

Every time I give a presentation it is so easy. My entire body remains relaxed. I relax even more just by twice repeating the word relax and rubbing my thumb against all four fingers. All of my muscles immediately respond to my cue for comfort and relaxation. My mouth always remains moist. My voice is clear. I feel calm and confident about my message.

To embellish the suggestion with a simile and metaphor of being like a pilot, you might add:

It is like I am on automatic pilot. All my practice sessions and all my research have been entered into my memory terminal. I consistently, easily and automatically transmit to my audience all my information using my persuasive language smoothly and effectively. I am confident of a smooth landing each time I give a presentation. I feel so great doing presentations! I am an experienced pilot steering my presentations, always in control, poised with complete confidence.

KEEP IT SIMPLE

Remember, the way your Suggestible Subconscious understands your communications may be compared to how a young child would comprehend your statements. Consequently, choose simplified sentences with easy for you to understand word choices and sentence structure. Avoid overly complicated phrasing. Keep it simple.

DANGLE THE CARROT

Create positive associations with whatever desired outcomes you are requesting. For example, through hypnotic suggestion you may instruct your subconscious to associate your feelings of being hugged and congratulated whenever you refuse to eat other-than-healthy desserts. Thus, the act of making a healthy dessert choice is associated with good feelings of self-empowerment, praise and receiving an affectionate sign of acceptance. When appropriate, compose your suggestions with the qualifier *for my Highest Good*. This will qualify what you have requested to be truly good for you in the long run from the perspective of your Mind/Body/Spirit.

NATURAL, SMOOTH AND PLEASURABLE

Make a suggestion that the changes you have requested feel very natural, normal and pleasurable as if things had always been that way. Suggest also that you have made a smooth and easy transition into new changes. Reiterate how wonderful it feels to have made these changes in such a natural and pleasurable way. Suggest that you remain always aware how valuable hypnosis and your subconscious have been in manifesting what you consciously desire.

GIVE CREDIT WHERE CREDIT IS DUE

Why include a suggestion in your self-hypnosis indicating your awareness of Reprogramming Self-hypnosis helping you? Give hypnosis the credit because in doing so it encourages you to continue using hypnosis techniques since you know that hypnosis is truly working for you. Otherwise you might be unaware of the important role hypnosis and your subconscious played in these shifts. You could suggest:

My suggestions manifest so easily and comfortably; nevertheless, I am aware of the valuable role my subconscious and Reprogramming Self-hypnosis played in manifesting my desired changes.

I recognized the necessity for this suggestion from personal experience. In particular I noticed some clients' reactions when we discussed their accomplishments achieved through hypnosis. In one memorable case my client called me a week after her session and said, *The hypnosis is not working.* I listened to her explain that normally she would not have called to say this. She just felt she had to speak up and tell me. I responded telling her that many times it takes longer than just one week to experience the changes that a person has programmed. However, my question to her was, *Weren't we working on your being more assertive?* She replied, *Yes.* My next question was, *And aren't you telling me now something that asserts your opinion when normally you would not have been able to say it?* There was about a five-second pause and she responded with an enlightened, *Oh!*

NOW YOU SEE IT, NOW YOU DON'T

Everything may happen so easily, naturally and normally that you may not always recognize the alterations you have made without a subconscious suggestion to do so. In the past I would give the suggestion that the transition was so natural and easy that the clients would feel as if they never had the issue. Unfortunately I found the consequence of that suggestion was there were occasions when the clients disregarded hypnosis as a crucial tool for future unforeseen issues. Recognize the power of hypnosis because that will encourage you to keep using it. Did I ever mention that hypnosis ultimately best serves your self-empowerment needs when it is woven into your lifestyle? In any case, it bears repeating.

SINCE X EQUALS ONE AND Y EQUALS TWO, THEN X PLUS Y EQUALS THREE

One hypnosis strategy is to set up a logical progression in reasoning so your subconscious approves and integrates your suggestions. If you state the facts first and then lead up to logical conclusions, the conclusions are more easily accepted by your subconscious. One simple example you may use would be:

Since my subconscious is my friend and advocate, and because it wants really to please me and give me more happiness, it has accepted and downloaded my suggestions that please me and give me happiness. My new and permanent Subconscious Programs give me happiness and feel-good feelings now and forever.

To give you another example that is a bit more complex, consider the following that prepares you for favorably accepting public speaking presentations:

Fact: It is important for me to succeed in my job and I am enthusiastic and positive about succeeding.

Fact: I need to reach out to as many people as possible to effectively to market my product successfully and thus succeed in my job.

Fact: Giving presentations to large audiences is one of the best ways to personally reach as many people as possible to effectively market my product successfully and thus succeed in my job.

Conclusion: Therefore, to enjoy greater success in my job, I choose to give sales presentations to large audiences to effectively market my product successfully.

Conclusion: Thus, I feel very enthusiastic and positive about giving sales presentations because by giving large group sales presentations, I can market my product more successfully and thereby create greater success in my job.

KEEP IN TOUCH

The more vivid the senses you incorporate into your suggestions, the better for communicating to your subconscious. *Ideomotor cues* are based on your sense of touch and may be used to reinforce any or all of your suggestions from your entire session of hypnosis. You might choose one Ideomotor cue for specific situations when you need to relax immediately in times of sudden stress. Typically I suggest employing a Ideomotor cue like the following one that becomes a subconscious association. When you touch your thumb to your index finger on the same hand while taking in two deep breaths, your subconscious knows to release any of your negative reactions to perceptions of stress. Below is a more detailed rendition of how an Ideomotor cue could be nestled into your hypnotic suggestions:

Stress happens as a natural part of life; so at any time I sense stress, either consciously or subconsciously, I respond by immediately touching my thumb to my index finger.

Then I take two deep breaths that instantly relax me further. [Ideomotor cue] I breathe in through my nose and out through my mouth to the count of eight. As I breathe out, I am expelling all the tension, anxiety and stress that may be anywhere within my entire body. [Ideomotor cue] I just let it go easily, comfortably and time efficiently. It is easy to relax at the first sign of stress. It happens for me automatically.

Ideomotor cues may be used for different situations as diverse as using Reprogramming Hypnosis/Self-hypnosis for relieving constipation or for relieving fear about flying. You might make the suggestion that when you rub your thumb against all four fingers on the same hand, your Mind/Body/Spirit immediately elicits your relaxation response. While in self-hypnosis you might suggest an Ideomotor cue for memory recall like this:

Anytime I need to recall information quickly, first I relax and then simply touch my fingertips to the middle of my forehead. I tap with my fingers on the middle of my forehead for seven seconds while focused on receiving the answer I need. Then I focus my thoughts on something else and allow the desired information to come to me automatically. My tapping on my forehead is to signal my subconscious quickly to retrieve that information for my conscious awareness. It does just that within ninety seconds.

STAY REALLY REAL

Choose a suggestion that is basically within your human potential. Hypnosis may be unable to make you run the mile in less than four seconds unless somehow your body is equipped to do so. Also include some suggestions that are easier to achieve amongst other more challenging ones. Once you experience one of your suggestions working, it is easier for you to believe it is possible for all of your suggestions to work. The more you believe it is happening, the more it happens. What your mind believes is your reality, really can become your reality.

TAKE IT EASY!

It is easiest to focus on just a few suggestions at a time when first learning self-hypnosis techniques. Certainly, if you are new to Reprogramming Self-hypnosis, it would be appropriate to start with one, two or maybe even three suggestions. Spend at least thirty days, every day, repeating those same suggestions while in self-hypnosis so they may become a permanent habit, a permanent way of thinking, feeling or behaving. The more advanced your skills become the more suggestions you will be able to handle easily.

ONE AT A TIME

In beginning your Reprogramming Self-hypnosis practice, it also would be helpful if all of your hypnotic suggestions were either directly or indirectly related to the same topic or issue. Thus, if you are changing the way you interact and deal with a difficult co-worker, you might suggest a positive way of your responding to that person. Perhaps you could create a favorable image to associate your interactions with him/her such as imagining someone pinning a medal of honor for your patience, onto your shirt.

While in self-hypnosis give yourself a Post-hypnotic Suggestion that states you wait fifteen seconds before responding to that person when he/she engages you in a dialogue. During those fifteen seconds tell yourself to focus on keeping yourself in a relaxed, positive frame of mind so you have clarity of logic and intuition. Remind yourself that you have predetermined positive responses ready for whatever things he/she might say or do. The following is an assortment of suggestions for your subconscious that you could choose ahead of time for dealing with that difficult person:

One, specifically you refuse to take this person's words and deeds personally. His or her words and deeds leave your High Self-esteem unaffected except in a positive or neutral way.

Two, you might think of this person as a spiritual lesson personified for your spiritual growth. He/she is creating the circumstances that help you learn to overcome whatever was in your past, that was other than positive responses to conflict.

Three, instead of past other than positive automatic responses to conflict, you have chosen to use your logic and intuition while remaining calm and detached from the drama of the situation. You have proven to yourself that you can control yourself and your emotions.

Four, you understand and remember that his/her words and

behaviors are in response to his/her own issues rather than reactions related to you or anyone else. Your Subconscious Program automatically releases all negative emotions and replaces all released negativity with pleasant feelings of well-being and self-empowerment. You retain your peace of mind and inner power.

Five, you may choose to remain silent, saying nothing. The focus then remains on the other person and his/her unacceptable behavior. It is possible that the difficult person gets a positive Emotional Payoff from the feeling of having the power to get you to respond in anger. You actually may discourage the person from repeating their negative behavior by refusing to supply them with the Emotional Payoff of you getting upset.

TAKE TIME FOR A CHANGE

For optimal benefits, designate at least fifteen minutes or more each day for self-hypnosis. However, even two minutes would be beneficial if that is all you have. It is the repetition that is so crucial. You can do Reprogramming Self-hypnosis in bed, sitting at your desk, as a passenger in a car, train, plane or boat ... just about anywhere. Practicing Reprogramming Self-hypnosis at least fifteen minutes every day helps to de-stress you and keep you calmer. It does your Mind/Body/Spirit GOOD!! So be good to yourself.

Perhaps if you equate the importance of practicing hypnosis with the same importance as brushing your teeth or washing your hands, you will include hypnosis as part of your daily regimen. Give yourself a hypnotic suggestion that states how wonderful hypnosis feels. Tell yourself how much you look forward to performing self-hypnosis every day. Remind yourself how it is benefiting your well-being every day. You can program associations of purely happy, positive feelings with the practice of Reprogramming Self-hypnosis and that will motivate your subconscious to keep you regularly practicing it.

HOORAY FOR SHORTCUTS!

After practicing self-hypnosis for even a short while, you will be able to use a shortcut method for getting quickly and comfortably into the Alpha or Theta State of Consciousness that is hypnosis. At times you may be in a situation that only gives you a minute or less to give yourself your hypnotic suggestions. Still, for your self-hypnosis Rapid Induction you need at least three simultaneous signals to initiate your hypnotic state so you avoid accidentally going into hypnosis when it would be an inappropriate time. Choose three subtle signals that would be undetected by others. You could take two deep breaths, touch together two fingers from the same hand and think of your special number or special password that you say silently. There are other gestures I would suggest such as rubbing the fleshy part on your palm under your thumb or wrapping your fingers around one finger on the opposite hand. Be as creative as you would like. Remember though you will want to be able to do it in public. If you have a moment now, you might explore what gestures you would choose.

GIVE IT TO ME NOW OR GIVE IT TO ME LATER

One type of hypnotic suggestion is intended to actualize instantly as your reality at the same time while you are still in the hypnosis experience. It also continues to be in effect indefinitely unless otherwise stated. An illustration of this type of instant response hypnotic suggestion implicating instant action is:

My subconscious has released all guilt regarding my car accident. All guilt that may have been stored anywhere in my Mind/Body/ Spirit completely has easily been neutralized and permanently has left me. Instead, I have replaced those other than feel-good feelings with feelings of complete forgiveness for anything other than positive things that I may have thought, said, felt or done relating to that car accident. It is in the past now where it remains, completely neutralized.

PRE-SET LIKE AN ALARM CLOCK

In contrast there is a specific suggestion that directs or implies how you will be thinking, believing, feeling and/or behaving under certain circumstances at a later time. That later time may begin any time thereafter when you are out of hypnosis or at a designated time specified through hypnotic suggestion. That type of hypnotic suggestion is considered a Post-hypnotic Suggestion. The suggestion manifests at some point in time after the hypnosis session is concluded. Frequently you have to wait for a particular situation to occur before the suggestion is activated. This would apply if you focused suggestions on how you would respond in future times to your mother's insulting behaviors. This would be like the following Post-hypnotic Suggestion example:

My subconscious understands that whenever my mother makes comments that are anything other than positive or neutral about me, my family members and/or friends, I react with a sincere feeling of sympathy for her. I understand she is reacting to her own painful issues and to her Faulty Subconscious Programming. As I perceive her words, I disarm and neutralize them with an X in my mind's eye. I also hear and feel the powerful words, Cancel, Cancel. At this time I realize she is incapable of acting otherwise. Then I focus on feeling past happy moments with my mom or remember happy moments with someone else and instantly forgive my mom. This makes me feel great!

TWO IS BETTER THAN ONE

The way your subconscious mind responds to hypnotic suggestions varies, among other things, depending upon your personality, your approach, your word choice of the suggestions and the degree of difficulty of your issue. For some people, their subconscious mind reacts very favorably to hypnotic suggestions that are direct commands. On the other hand, a person's subconscious mind may have different programming that influences him/her to resist or instantly refuse direct commands. Those rejecting *Direct Suggestions* typically will react more agreeably to *Indirect Suggestions* that allow the subconscious to choose a direction without feeling forced to do so.

Why do so many people react to how the suggestion is presented, whether it is a Direct Suggestion or Indirect Suggestion? The most likely answer that supports the theories advanced in this book, relates to how a person's subconscious previously has been programmed as a result of his/her perceptions and experiences. Thus, how you respond to the way suggestions are posed, depends on what your previously downloaded Subconscious Programs dictate for pleasing or protecting you. If you are a person who overall has reacted adversely to being controlled in your past, you will reject the Direct Suggestion method. Then there are people who subconsciously respond less well to Indirect Suggestion. If you are such a person you probably need or feel more comfortable clearly being directed because you are uncomfortable making decisions on your own. Yet some of us may respond well to both Direct and Indirect Suggestions. Perhaps that means in your past you successfully avoided any such Faulty Subconscious Programming on that issue. For those fortunate people, it does not seem to matter whether Direct or Indirect Suggestions are used; they accept both kinds. To ensure your best outcome, use both types of suggestions during your self-hypnosis sessions to cover all your possibilities.

LET'S BE DIRECT

Direct Suggestion is just as the name implies. You straightforwardly direct your subconscious to accept what you want and often include when, how and where as well as how much of it you want. You describe it as though it is happening now, has completely happened or has already started happening and continues to happen until the goal is reached and permanently established. Some issues just naturally take a longer time such as reducing 100 pounds of weight. Thus, in such a situation you would say the process has started happening now and continues to happen each day, bringing you closer to your goal weight until you have achieved the 100-pound weight reduction. Every day and in every way you are getting better!

TAKE A DIRECT SUGGESTION FOR EXAMPLE:

And now, whenever I hear or see the word great, I feel just great, just like I feel when I am at my happiest moment. There is no subterfuge here. The directions are as plain as can be.

Another example might be:

I have released all the fear I used to have regarding snakes. I now am neutral regarding snakes. They are God's creatures too. They are okay. I react calmly to them using my intelligence just as I react calmly toward other wild, natural creatures like birds or squirrels.

COME THROUGH THE BACK DOOR, INDIRECTLY

In contrast, the Indirect Suggestion is calculated to appeal to those of you who have a Subconscious Resistance to being told directly what to think, believe, feel and/or do. There are many independent type people who fall into this category. That is why Indirect Suggestions are so favored by professionals in hypnosis. Indirect suggestions succeed using innuendo and inference to accomplish goals of change. They are a roundabout way of accomplishing what the Direct Suggestion offers. But Indirect

Suggestions get your subconscious' acceptance by making it appear that you are the one in control directing things, rather than you being controlled. It makes it appear that this is your idea of making the suggested changes. Thus, the Indirect Suggestions leave it up to your subconscious to decide while prompted through inference that gives you an influential, gentle nudge in the right direction.

AN INDIRECT SUGGESTION: FOLLOW THE LEADER

One example of an Indirect Suggestion that works well compares the possibility of one client's success to that of another client who was successful with the same kind of situation. The subconscious inference is that if someone like you succeeded using hypnosis, you will succeed too. This suggestion is for a client with a weight issue:

You remind me of someone else I had as a client. He had a weight issue like you and was in a similar situation because food was the only thing over which he felt he had control. He was going to be the only one to decide what to eat. So even though his choices made him gain weight with unhealthy consequences, he could not seem to change his eating habits until he used hypnosis to communicate to his subconscious mind. His subconscious mind heard his desire for new healthier eating habits and a new way of thinking about food. He asked his subconscious to delete the old program that made his choosing to eat unhealthy food represent his feeling powerful. His subconscious, always wanting to help and please him, did just that.

He asked his subconscious instead to make sure he saw how he could take charge of his health and create his preferred body image by making the healthy choices for food that would support his goals. And his subconscious put that into effect also. Furthermore, he decided to use other areas of self-empowerment to build upon his need for feeling independent and in control. So he emphasized that he was the one who chose his friends, his hobbies, his clothes, when to go to bed at night. He chose whom he would vote for, and so forth. He was amazed at how many decisions in his life he actually controlled. Each week he followed his healthy eating plan and found his weight was reducing, so easily, naturally, effortlessly and automatically. His subconscious was following the program just as he requested. He reached and maintained his goal weight. Meanwhile, he focused his energies upon developing his other interests and enjoying life to its fullest. You know, he does remind me so much of you!

ME, TOO!

The Indirect Suggestions cover exactly what you would like to see happen to you without literally commanding your subconscious to do it. To utilize this type of suggestion in your self-hypnosis, you would simply state that there is someone you know who reminds you of yourself. Continue by explaining to your subconscious what has happened to that person. Be specific and report how the other person embraced new, positive mindsets, feelings and/or behaviors by employing self-hypnosis. This person who is just like you used self-hypnosis to communicate her desires to her subconscious. As a consequence, your friend happily succeeded in reprogramming her subconscious and she achieved her de- sired outcome. She felt so comfortable when making the transition to the new changes. It felt so natural. Besides, it had become a routine part of her. In fact she said that it felt like things had always been that way, although intuitively she knew it was also the hypnosis working. Furthermore, she felt so much better with her new Subconscious Programming than ever before. And she does so much remind you of you!

MILTON ERICKSON AND ERICKSONIAN HYPNOSIS

The indirect style of suggestions is associated with Ericksonian Hypnosis, a style of hypnosis that is named after the famous hypnotherapist/psychiatrist, Dr. Milton Erickson (1901-1980). Erickson is considered a founding father of much of the current thinking regarding hypnosis used for therapeutic purposes. He advocated for the use of Indirect Suggestions using similes, metaphors, analogies and favored an informal conversational manner of approaching his clients.

Erickson is also known for utilizing an indirect method of telling stories that twist and turn so as in theory to confuse the Critical Factor of your conscious mind (see Chapter Two). The theory asserts that these Indirect Suggestions that are part of the confusing story can trick you and thus avoid the watchful, evaluating and censoring eye of your conscious mind. Therefore, the suggestions slip past your conscious mind, into your subconscious mind where they readily are accepted.

A NEW WAY OF LOOKING AT THINGS

A differing viewpoint would credit your ever-vigilant subconscious mind for your resistance to accepting Direct Suggestions, rather than crediting it to a part of your conscious mind. After all, your conscious mind is not dominant or directing you when you are in an Altered Consciousness State of hypnosis. Recall that your conscious mind, when you are in hypnosis, remains behind in your different Beta Consciousness State throughout the time you are in hypnosis. In contrast, your subconscious mind exists and operates in your Alpha, Theta and/ or Delta Altered Consciousness States. There your subconscious is always protecting and enforcing your previously accepted and downloaded Subconscious Programs. Furthermore, in fulfilling its responsibility to you, your subconscious mind protects your already established Subconscious Programs by blocking and refusing any new proposed suggestions that would conflict with the Subconscious Programs currently in operation. Logically speaking, it must be your subconscious, protecting your subconsciously initiated and maintained Subconscious

Programs, that is responsible for your current resistance to being told directly what to think, feel and do.

A BENEFIT FROM SELF-DISCOVERY

The benefit of accepting this second perspective is that it removes blame you may have felt believing that you intentionally were harboring self-sabotaging resistances. It would also explain why your attempts had been blocked trying to change any of those feelings and behaviors. Your subconscious holds the key to why you are the way you are, including how you react adversely to being told directly what to do. If you are this way, you probably were not born with DNA markers that made you fiercely independent, stubborn, oppositional, averse to change, unmovable, rebellious and so forth. These are all personality characteristics that have been crafted by your Subconscious Programs that were created from your life experiences. For those believing in *Past Lives*, perhaps your personality characteristics come from your Past Life experiences too. You are driven by your subconscious when you are feeling/acting in ways you consciously would rather not be feeling/acting. You can sense that you are unable to control it consciously. Regardless of why you respond better to Direct or Indirect Suggestions, these types of confusing stories can bypass whatever is blocking you from the successful downloading of new, beneficial suggestions into your Subconscious Programming. Practically speaking, this indirect method overcomes obstacles to get you what you truly want and has a winning record doing just that.

LISTEN BETWEEN THE LINES

Here is an example of a metaphor nestled into guided imagery that I created to illustrate this type of Indirect Suggestion. It is written in a poetic style and format that attempts to lull your subconscious mind into accepting the suggestions by inference. The comparison of the way water changes the rock implies a message for you. Time actually can improve your life conditions smoothing them and evolving them closer to perfection. Your subconscious is indirectly guided by inference to accept change as a natural, positive and cleansing force that can actually help release your past and improve you especially as time goes by:

TRANSFORMATIONS THROUGH TIME

As you allow yourself to drift and float
down deeper into relaxation
perhaps feeling calmer and calmer,
more peaceful and more relaxed
with each breath you take in
and exhale out, you may notice how
easy it is to relax
deeper and deeper
with each breath you take in and
with each breath you release so easily.
You may feel comforted
just by imagining yourself
nestled into a soft, comfy chair.
You are supported by this chair
that cushions your neck,
your back, your hips and your legs. Your
feet rest upon a cushy footstool.
All the muscles, tendons and
ligaments have released all tension.
So relaxed, it is like you are remembering
what it is like to be supported
completely. You can rest there
with your mind cleared of all
the clutter of the day. All pressures
have been lifted from your shoulders
and perhaps you are feeling so relieved.
Just drift and float upon this gentle feeling
of comfort. Focus upon your breathing as

you inhale and exhale. Feeling more and more
relaxed with each breath you let go …
Now imagine you are on a beautiful beach
Listening to the soothing
waves as they roll up gently upon the shore
with rhythmic regularity. There is a sense of
universal cleansing with these waters
as they wash over the sands and
spray against the rocks. The rocks are
so smooth now, so rounded with the
continuous cleansing by the water.
Each wave takes away
some part of the roughness
of the rock. Over time the rocks that were
jagged have been transformed into rocks
that feel as smooth as polished granite.
Time has a unique ability of changing things,
transforming things into something even more beautiful
than originally they were before. Time has the power
of transforming people too, changing them beautifully
with its gentle, yet persistent cleansing of the past,
leaving them yet closer to their perfection.

EXTEND YOURSELF

Another type of Indirect Suggestion is an Extended Metaphor
with a story that twists and turns, confusing your subconscious
mind so it appears that you are not being ordered to accept its
suggestions. This technique like the one used in *Transformations
through Time*, illustrates another example of Ericksonian style
Indirect Suggestion. This meta- phoric confusion technique aims
the suggestions to bypass whatever your ever-vigilant
subconscious mind's resistances might be to following the story's
underlying meaning and directions.

LET ME CONFUSE INDIRECTLY YOUR STORY

You might consider using a story like *Reddy, the Wonder Dog* that makes frequent shifts and changes in subject matter while it weaves together a message or moral of the story. Similar in theme to *Transformations through Time*, this indirect confusing story prompts your subconscious to be prepared for accepting and adjusting to changes in your life as a natural, easy and a very positive way of living.

REDDY, THE WONDER DOG

(Making Ready for Changes)

You might be interested to know
about a wonder dog I knew.
Her name was Reddy and she really was red.
Although I'm not sure what that had to do
with her disposition which seemed always
kind and even tempered even though
she had to come to the rescue of people
who were trapped up in the mountains
or in a blinding snow
or in a boat bopping up and down on the ocean
in such a way one would think it would be difficult
to navigate or even keep one's balance. But she did.
She did many wonderful things, that dog.
She was ready to jog and do whatever it took and
sometimes it took a lot from her. Yet,
she never complained because she knew
already that life was like that, those ups and downs,
those cold and hot times. Things were always shifting
and she had learned to shift with the times.
And though she grew older and
had been through many tough times,
it did not seem to matter. However, matter was
something she knew little about. It never mattered

whether it was summer or spring, winter or fall.
She was wherever she needed to be,
making whatever changes she needed to make,
and staying on course, too. Because of course,
that's what she found life was all about. Picking
a course and changing it whenever the snow blew
too much and a better path opened up.
She knew how to keep changing when necessary
without losing who she was,
and she was after all,
a full of wonder dog, always Reddy
because she needed no reason to explain.
She just was always ready for a change.
And that may suit you just fine, too.

TAP INTO YOUR CREATIVITY

Ideally the examples of hypnotic suggestions in this chapter will trigger ideas for creating your own imagery for Reprogramming Self-hypnosis. Other professionally crafted examples of Direct and Indirect stories will be available through my website. Perhaps now would be a good time to explore your ideas and any specific content for some of your original self-hypnosis suggestions. Maybe you would enjoy creating your own Extended Metaphor suggestions. Have fun. Use your imagination. Tap into your unlimited creativity especially when you are exploring avenues for Reprogramming Self-hypnosis.

MORE OF WHAT YOU MAY NEED TO KNOW AND REVIEW

1. Ways to induce hypnosis

- relaxation techniques (progressive relaxation)
- eye fixation (staring at same spot to induce an altered state

- post-hypnotic cue
- boredom activity with monotony (e.g. listening to a confusing story that ends up boring you)
- kinesthetic (e.g. focus on breathing)
- shortcut (e.g. simultaneously two fingers on the same hand are touching together as you take two deep breaths while thinking of special number counting from *ten* to *one*)

2. Techniques for communicating with your subconscious

- Positive wording
- Past and present tenses only (has already happened or is happening)
- Vivid imagery, similes, metaphors, analogies
- Clear language, easy to understand
- Use computer analogy when possible.
- Set up logical progression in reasoning (optional).
- Make positive associations with what you desire.
- Appeal to all five senses and to your intuition, your *Sixth Sense*.
- Give some easy to achieve goals as well as others.
- Focus first on a limited number of changes (one-three) for thirty days.
- Repetition is very helpful.
- Be specific and concrete, precise and literal.
- Establish sense of being protected and grounded.
- Use your requests with qualifier *for my Highest Good.*
- Make mention that outside noises only help you go deeper into relaxation. In case of an emergency, however, you instantly come out of hypnosis.
- Establish a safe, healing place for hypnosis.
- Suggest you have heightened awareness of any of the requested changes manifesting for you.
- Use both Direct and Indirect Suggestions.
- Make a suggestion that your desired changes manifest naturally, creating such easy transitions into

the new territory, feeling so normal like they always have been there. Yet, you always are aware of how hypnosis has helped you.

3. Conditions optimal for self-hypnosis

- In a safe environment (e.g. avoid while driving a car)
- Seated or lying down comfortably, neck supported
- When you are feeling unrushed
- Physical needs addressed (thirst, hunger, bathroom break before)
- Where you will be undisturbed during hypnosis
- Able to focus and concentrate without being over-tired

4. Follow-up for your self-hypnosis

- Keep a journal to help your awareness of the changes.
- Ask others who have observed you for their feedback.
- Give thanks to your subconscious for making the changes that you have requested.

CHAPTER 5

YOUR MIND/BODY/SPIRIT BONUS

REPROGRAMMING WITH HYPNOSIS AFFECTS ALL THREE

When I first took classes in hypnosis and spiritual development over thirty years ago, I had no idea how the two would prove to be so important and interrelated, providing a foundation that would continue building throughout my life. Over the years I have greatly benefited from a tremendous accumulation of first-hand experiences involving accessing the Mind/Body/Spirit through hypnosis. Recall the poem *The Blind Men and the Elephant* that was discussed in Chapter One. Just as each blind man perceived the elephant from a different perspective, each man's view was a necessary part to the whole understanding of the nature of the elephant. Yet no single perspective was the complete picture. Just as each of the six blind men perceived just part of the whole elephant, I offer my insights regarding Mind/Body/Spirit as only my part of the total picture. Perhaps my perspective can contribute some light that may help illuminate at least a few steps along your path searching for understanding.

Through my work with hypnosis I have discovered the importance of our Spirit and spirituality as it factors into how we reflect and improve upon the many aspects of our lives. My clients ponder spiritual questions that help me understand their view of the world, their life and also their concept of their Higher Power or spiritual leader such as God, Jesus, Allah, Buddha, Nature, Fate, etc. Their answers help me formulate and co-create their appropriate hypnotic suggestions. Here are some of the questions:

- Who am I and how can I define myself?

- Who do I want to be?

- Who or What controls the rest of what I am unable to control?

- What direction do I want my life to take?

- What greater purpose might my life serve?

- How do I want to be remembered at the end of my life?

Take a moment to reflect on any immediate responses you have to these questions. Allow any answers to come to your conscious mind. It will be advantageous for you to continue formulating and fine-tuning your answers over time, especially while you are in self-hypnosis during which time you enjoy direct access to your subconscious and your Inner Wisdom.

INNER WISDOM

When people come for my hypnosis services, they reflect on what subconscious perspectives would give them peace of mind, harmony, balance, self-empowerment, self-fulfillment and happiness. After all, reprogramming your subconscious requires that you identify something positive that will replace what you have deleted. Of course the answers widely differ per individual. Many people have no clue about these matters as they have not yet begun to contemplate these subjects. Nonetheless when a person searches for these answers while in hypnosis, I have witnessed how their subconsciously perceived answers are insightful and helpful for them. These answers appear to resonate as comfortable truth for each individual. Often people experience something profound bubbling into their awareness when searching for Inner Wisdom. Very often people reach an epiphany and/or relieve intense emotional tensions, a catharsis, through a subconscious revelation of *Inner Truth*.

AN UNEXPECTED BONUS

A special bonus you will receive through practicing self-hypnosis is developing your intuition. By intuition I mean that form of Inner Knowing you possess and call *gut feeling*. Some would call it *Opening the Third Eye* that represents your Sixth Sense, beyond sight, sound, smell, touch and taste. Where does your intuitive knowing come from? One answer may be found in Jungian psychological terms. According to Jungian psychology there is a level of consciousness that is known as the *Collective Unconscious* where all the history of mankind is known and recorded. According to the famous Swiss psychiatrist *Carl Jung*, founder of *Analytical Psychology*, the Collective Unconscious has a more accurate knowledge and understanding of us as our ideal individual selves. This is because the Collective Unconscious allows you to view yourself without the distortions created by your ego or created by the clutter in your conscious mind. According to Jungian psychology, it is the Collective Unconscious level of knowing, once your mind reaches there, that may be responsible for supplying you with information you perceive as intuition. It is like an encyclopedia of all history, philosophy and self-awareness.

Regardless where it originates, what comes to you intuitively supports you throughout all kinds of situations, but especially helps with your life challenges. In other words, the revelations you gain through your intuitive, Inner Knowing come from a source beyond your typical human conscious comprehension and can supply you with valuable information and wisdom that otherwise are unavailable to you. Hypnosis allows you to reach and access a higher plane of existence while you are in the Alpha or Theta Consciousness State. So hypnosis is the vehicle that brings your intuitive knowing into your conscious mind's awareness. If this is other than a comfortable concept for you to contemplate at present, just keep an open mind to all possibilities. Allow your personal experiences accessing your intuition to be your guide.

YOUR INTERNAL AND ETERNAL LINK: QUESTIONS TO PONDER

Perhaps something internal and universal throughout the ages has driven us to seek the meaning and purpose of our lives. Could the driving force that is motivating you to make this quest be within your subconscious mind? Are you born with the programming to eventually embark upon this quest? Perhaps your subconscious mind is your internal and eternal link to your Higher Power? Is your subconscious mind the part that scientists suspect continues after death? Is your subconscious mind what links you to both realities? Look at some of the brow-raising research that came to my attention on the Internet in September of 2008 on AOL.com as it spotlighted *Dr. Sam Parnia* who is the lead doctor and researcher with *The Human Consciousness Project.* Dr. Parnia, a Senior Research Fellow at New York's Weill Cornell Medical Center in New York is one of the world's leading experts on the scientific study of death.

The Human Consciousness Project includes an international consortium of multidisciplinary scientists and physicians who are researching the nature of consciousness as it relates to the relationship between your mind and your brain. Specifically, they are studying what happens to your brain and consciousness when you die. In a recording I discovered online, Dr. Parnia basically stated in his address to the United Nations that the doctors' preliminary scientific studies appear to suggest that the human mind and some kind of consciousness continue to function when the clinical definitions of heart and brain death are fully present and the brain has ceased functioning.

Could that *some kind of your consciousness* that Dr. Parnia acknowledged actually be your subconscious mind? It is your subconscious, your eternal part that exists within a specific range of brain wave frequency, that enables a part of your mind to see, hear, and travel anywhere in or out of this world. Could it be your subconscious mind that intuitively knows and/or experiences an elevated truth of your reality? Scientists from around the world associated with The Human Consciousness Project are building upon their current findings from an eighteen-month pilot study, *AWARE* (*Awareness during Resuscitation*). They are now continuing clinical research of a much greater magnitude that collects controlled data on life after death. Stay tuned.

OF THE SAME ESSENCE

Suppose your mind and your body and your Spirit are not separate entities but rather different manifestations of the same one essence. Just think of the analogy of water. Water may manifest as liquid, ice or steam depending upon the environmental conditions. An outside source determines those environmental conditions that may be man-made (e.g. putting water into ice cube trays in the freezer or boiling water in a pot on a stove) or nature-made (e.g. ice from ice storms and steam from volcanic eruptions). Regardless of how the water is manifested, no matter what different characteristics it may have adopted at times, it is what it is without changing its true essence. Water still is water.

Your Spirit may be merged with your body and your mind for the time you are here on earth. Then upon death, your Spirit is released and freed from your mind and your body, parts of you that no longer exist. But while on earth what may impact one part of your Mind/Body/Spirit, impacts your other parts as well. You, as the whole person, are affected at the same time.

Whatever happens in your mind may be observed as happening in an analogous reflection in your body and your *Spirit*. Note that I am including your subconscious mind as part of your Spirit. The same phenomenon applies for each of the components of your Mind/Body/Spirit as whatever affects your body is reflected or mirrored in your mind and your Spirit. Furthermore all parts participate in the lesson, each according to its own unique structure and characteristics. The rest of this chapter will bear this out with case stories that further demonstrate this point.

DELETE THE OPPOSITION

Louise Hay, a leading pioneer in the Mind/Body/Spirit connection, also addresses these points in her book, *You Can Heal Your Life*. She offers a chart to help her readers understand illness and physical issues as they are represented through the interconnections between your mind – thought pattern and belief — and how your body reacts to those thought patterns. To remediate each physical or emotional suffering, Ms. Hay also suggests a specific new thought pattern or patterns (used in repetition as in a mantra) to be adopted consciously by the ailing person desiring healing.

From my perspective, I would add another powerful dimension for your focus … your Suggestible Subconscious. You also must communicate your desires to your Suggestible Subconscious mind in positively stated terms to create best chances for successful understanding and acceptance of your suggestions by your subconscious. But FIRST, you must delete any contradictory and thus resistant, previously programmed mindsets, belief systems and subconsciously determined associations that contradict, oppose or interfere with your new suggestions and your new programming.

WE ARE LINKED

Your subconscious mind may be viewed as your link to your Spirit. Perhaps your subconscious mind is just one part of your Spirit serving also as an integral part of your mind and your body. Your mantras may be easily downloaded into your Suggestible Subconscious through hypnosis where the mantras are positioned to have a permanent positive effect. Remember, with only minimal hypnosis practice you may achieve the Alpha and/or Theta State of Consciousness within a few minutes or even within a few seconds. Thus Reprogramming Self-Hypnosis is a practical, time efficient method sufficiently powerful for you to achieve the changes that will correct your faulty programming. Hypnosis with proper direction may remediate those Faulty Subconscious Programs that were downloaded by your subconscious without your permission or awareness. What has been programmed subconsciously without your awareness or permission may be responsible for the consequences of negative habits, negative behaviors and even ill-health without it being your fault. But the wonderful news is that it is possible for you to change and reprogram what is in your subconscious mind. Yes, you can delete and/or totally neutralize negative thought patterns, negative beliefs and faulty associations.

Reprogramming Hypnosis/Self-hypnosis empowers you to intentionally keep your Mind/Body/Spirit working on your desired goals operating in sync with your consciously selected, positive programs.

OUR GREAT BLESSING

Could your ability to continue perfecting your Subconscious Programming be one of your greatest blessings? Obviously we were endowed with this power for perfecting ourselves physically, mentally, emotionally and spiritually. Is your path to self-improvement far more achievable than you ever believed was possible? Certainly this process of using Reprogramming Hypnosis/Self-hypnosis for spiritual development exemplifies using your free will to align you with God's (or your Higher Power's) will, if that is your spiritual goal. Can you find your answers literally within you as so many spiritual leaders have suggested? Perhaps it is most challenging to get your body and the ego part of your mind (that part of you that recognizes that you are separate and distinct from other people and other objects and that part of you that maintains your opinion of your own separate self-worth) into compliance for what you would want spiritually. While other roadways exist, could hypnosis provide you with a powerful way of accomplishing the clearing away of the haze, the misperceptions caused by your ego, past traumas, past misinterpretations, and your Faulty Subconscious Programming? Could hypnosis therefore facilitate the elevation of your Mind/Body/Spirit to a more spiritually pure existence? My answer is affirmative to all of these questions.

A POSSIBLE TRANSFORMATION

Ideally your Spirit will lead you to align yourself with the ways of your Higher Power. Could this process of clearing yourself of your Faulty Subconscious Programs help you to experience the light of your Creator? Does reprogramming your Faulty Subconscious Programs allow you to align yourself as one with your Higher Power's goodness, peace, harmony compassion and love? You might consider meditating for a while on those possibilities. Definitely you can improve who you are as a total person through reprogramming your subconscious. Hypnosis affords you the platform from which to seize a true understanding of who you are, why you are this way and how you can change to improve your Mind/ Body/Spirit. And importantly, when you gain knowledge about your own Subconscious Programming, you also gain volumes of understanding regarding how other people's Subconscious Programming directs or rules them as well. Subsequently, your learning and practicing Reprogramming Hypnosis/Self-hypnosis, provide additional spiritual lessons of great compassion and empathy for others as well.

WHERE TO BEGIN?

Although Reprogramming Hypnosis/Self-hypnosis offer almost unlimited options for self-improvement for Mind/Body/Spirit, I have a recommendation where to first begin. After you have learned to secure basic relaxation through practicing self-hypnosis, begin to focus on strengthening your self-esteem. Use hypnosis to solidify your High Self-esteem while deleting all Low Self-esteem programming. High Self-esteem begins with truly loving and accepting your total being just as you are. Some people may have difficulty with this concept. Previous negative Subconscious Programming may take the blame. Yet you are capable of truly and completely loving and accepting your total being just the way you are. It is impossible to overestimate the importance of your having rock solid, permanent, invincible High Self-esteem. Belief in your inner goodness, worthiness, deservingness, preciousness and self-empowerment is your foundation for a successful and happy life. It also affects how you relate to others. Most all issues that clients present in session with few exceptions are tied in some way either directly or indirectly to their self-esteem/self-empowerment issues.

OUR LEARNED TRIBAL MENTALITY

One of the great benefits Reprogramming Hypnosis/Self-hypnosis provides is for your self-empowerment and general self-improvement. Through hypnosis you may focus on what is required for you to feel good about yourself, to feel complete and whole on a subconscious level. Often to your detriment there are belief systems that contradict focusing on yourself. Those belief systems are so ingrained in our native cultures that if you were raised with them, you most assuredly have accepted the beliefs without question. One leading intuitive healer, Carolyn Myss, refers to such beliefs as what constitute our *tribal mentality*. A community, regardless of its ethnicity, race, religion and so forth, may hold its own unique community beliefs. Examples of such beliefs that contradict focusing on you, yourself, are:

- If I show concern for myself, then I am conceited and selfish.

- I should always put myself last.

- I am only good if I sacrifice for others.

But community held beliefs like these are not necessarily truisms nor beneficial for your harmonious balance of your Mind/Body/Spirit. Often you need to re-examine your tribal or community held beliefs and decide if they are accurate truisms that are really beneficial for you. Sometimes they are true to a certain extent but need modification for greater accuracy. When they are other than for your Highest Good, you have the option of disregarding them in part or totally.

"FAMILY-ISMS"

Sometimes you may need to eliminate an instilled familial belief that your parents taught you during childhood as part of your family's tradition. One such *Family-ism* is: *It is impolite to promote yourself to others*. For one client, Stuart, this childhood mindset (Family-ism) was a professional liability. It interfered with his business presentations for prospective customers. He needed to bring his talents and strengths to the attention of those he was soliciting. To his delight, Stuart eliminated his ingrained Family-ism using Reprogramming Hypnosis and won the lucrative contract. Again, Reprogramming Hypnosis affords you the opportunity to revise your erroneous beliefs so you may activate the behaviors that are for your Highest Good.

FAMILY-ISMS IN YOUR SUBCONSCIOUS ATTIC?

Perhaps now might be an appropriate time to review what Family-isms you might be storing subconsciously. Which ones are still serving you well? Which ones need to be revised or eliminated? Can you imagine what hypnosis suggestions can help you reprogram those latter ones?

YOU OWE IT TO YOURSELF

As an adult you are equipped to know your own needs. Moreover, you are the one most responsible for monitoring that your needs are met. It is part of the lesson of loving yourself just as much as you love everyone else. If you continuously give and never have a turn, you are not respecting yourself, loving yourself and taking responsibility for yourself. As individuals each one of us is a precious human being with inherent worth and value. No one is better than you. No one is worse than you. We are all equals; we are all the same only in different earth suits with different trimmings. Yes, there are exterior differences. Yes, there are differences in abilities and talents. Someone might be a better singer than you, but that does not make him a better, more valuable person than you are. Someone might have more money than you and therefore, have more choices of how to use that money. Yet that person is no better than you are. People may try to force the idea on you that you may not be as good because of the way you look, because of your job, lack of job, and because of some things you said, felt, or just thought. But those things are unable to alter or destroy your essence as a precious, valuable person.

YOUR HUMBLE INNER GOODNESS

Your inner goodness, your positive sense of self, just is. It is your center, your guide, your Spirit. It came with you before you were born. The essential point to remember is that acknowledging your inner goodness is central to High Self-esteem and a positive self-image. However, allow me to be clear. Humility accompanies your acknowledging your High Self-esteem. Your having High Self-esteem is not synonymous with your being conceited. Conceit is an exaggeration of your importance and is actually your feeling superior to others. Rather, you need to believe in yourself without needing to compare yourself to others. You are like everyone else, on your own unique path. Your High Self-esteem and your positive self-image are two main ingredients for your life's happiness, success and self-fulfillment. Please trust what I say here. I say it with all my heart. One of the greatest gifts you can give yourself is appreciation for who you are and how you are worthy. Just as great a gift is appreciating the worthiness of others. This allows you to see everyone else in the same terms. Thus, we practice the universal paradigm: I first love, appreciate and accept myself, and thus, I love, appreciate and accept all others as well. Yet, you can love and accept all others as equals, and still maintain your personal right and freedom to choose the people who you want to include in your life.

TELLTALE SIGNS

Oftentimes when people demonstrate a lack of nurturing themselves appropriately, the root cause is an issue of Low Self-esteem. Typically this type of person consistently leaves himself/herself last while opting to always help and nurture others first. The roots of the problem may be secured in the person's erroneous mindsets such as a Family-ism that says *you must always put other peoples' needs ahead of yours, otherwise you are selfish*. Oftentimes people who ignore their own needs have a subconsciously based negative self-image. These people feel they are unworthy, undeserving, not good enough or just less important. Consequently, many people who suffer from Low Self-esteem Subconscious Programs are unable to assert themselves. They are more concerned with what others think of them rather than feeling secure in a positive way about how they view and think of themselves. They may feel tremendous pressure to be perfect in order to avoid suffering any more criticism that would make them feel even worse about themselves.

In some cases, parents or caregivers inadequately nurtured the child's self-esteem, thus leaving the child with feelings that he/she was not lovable or important enough to deserve sufficient attention and loving care. It may not matter how successful you are financially, professionally or socially. If you do not have High Self-esteem and a positive self-image, you may feel like a fraud and that you have just fooled everyone.

A REASON TO REJOICE

Now here is reason for optimism for those who lacked sufficient nurturing. Reprogramming Hypnosis/Self-hypnosis is an extremely effective way for you to compensate for your past lack of nurturing, no matter what your age today may be. Yes, it is possible to experience and maintain emotional nurturing similar to what you wished you had experienced in your childhood or at any time in your life.

Of crucial importance is first to delete the negative messages stored in your Low Self-esteem Subconscious Programming. Then nothing is there to contradict your High Self-esteem program's positive self-esteem suggestions that you want accepted and downloaded successfully. Once that is accomplished you can reprogram your subconscious to create new and improved High Self-esteem programs. You place in that file all those positive messages about yourself that you ever perceived plus any and all the new ones you deem to be constructive. That High Self-esteem program becomes the database for how your subconscious determines its choices regarding your feelings, belief systems and actions. Your self-image is now all based on your positive self-image of attitudes, beliefs and feelings.

There is a caution, however. If your self-esteem has been negatively affected because of physical or emotional abuse or through severe trauma(s) in your life, you likely will need the guidance of a highly trained professional in hypnosis. It is easier to be guided by such a professional who can help you delete the resistant negative belief systems that may be too difficult for you to release on your own without assistance.

A QUICK STUDY: HOW I CAN LOVE MYSELF

The following script explains how you might go about accomplishing your goal of self-nurturing and raising your High Self-esteem. When you are in hypnosis simply refer to the title and say:

All that is in this script, How I Can Love Myself, has been programmed as part of my permanent Subconscious Programming for my Highest Good.

You may record this script for your personal listening use only. Be sure you use it also at bedtime. These affirmations represent life goals that increase your ability to love yourself, to love others and to fortify your High Self-esteem:

SCRIPT: HOW I CAN LOVE MYSELF

First, *Loving Myself* means totally accepting myself just as I am regardless of any flaws, emotional baggage, errors, mistakes or failures from the past. *So it is done now. I believe it is so now and forever.*

Second, *Loving Myself* means letting go of any past guilt, fears, anxieties, sadness, grief, anger, disappointments, regrets, resentments, hatreds, inferiorities, insecurities, and feelings of helplessness. Easily I release all negative emotions, whether they have been mentioned or left unmentioned. Whatever negative emotions are still inside me whether I am aware of them or not, unless they are for my Highest Good, I release them. *So it is done now. I believe it is so now and forever.*

Third, *Loving Myself* means I have adopted an attitude of forgiveness and have forgiven myself and all others who may have hurt me, intentionally or unintentionally. I also have released all Self-punishment Programs if any were ever within me. I have created fertile soil within me for love to flourish and so it does. *So it is done now. I believe it is so now and forever.*

Fourth, *Loving Myself* means I recognize my innate preciousness, great self-worth, strong self-empowerment and my innate ability to give and receive love. *So it is done now. I believe it is so now and forever.*

Fifth, *Loving Myself* means I desire only the best that is for my Highest Good for my own happiness, peace of mind and well-being. *So it is done now. I believe it is so now and forever.*

Sixth, *Loving Myself* means I am also able to love others with the same compassion and precepts as I love myself. This I have enthusiastically chosen to do. *So it is done now. I believe it is so now and forever.*

Seventh, *Loving Myself* means I have internalized the belief that I am just as good as any other person. Yet, I am no better than any other person even though my abilities, talents and history may differ. I, like every person, am precious. I, like every person, have a unique path of challenges and blessings. Everyone is an equal in Spirit. *So it is done now. I believe it is so now and forever.*

NO TIME LIKE THE PRESENT TO SET GOALS

This book presents Reprogramming Hypnosis/Self-hypnosis as your invaluable tool for programming what you want in your life as well as removing the barriers that have been slowing you down or stopping you from getting what you want. Best of all, hypnosis is available to everyone. You come already wired to experience it. So if by now you have yet to come to some decisions about your goals, this may be the moment to make some decisions. *First*, what is it you really want that you are missing at present? *Second*, what do you want to eliminate from your life? Identify as specifically as possible those detrimental thoughts, mindsets, attitudes, belief systems, feelings, habits, and behaviors that you suspect have prevented you from actualizing your desired positive goals. *Third*, determine exactly what thoughts, mindsets, belief systems, attitudes, feelings and habits you want included in your Subconscious Programming as positive replacements for the negative ones. *Fourth*, make notes in your journal or elsewhere about adding other positive programs that you desire but apparently are currently missing from your subconscious. Consider issues under different topics such as health (physical, mental and emotional), finances, relationships, occupation, education, hobbies and spirituality. What ways do you want to think, feel, behave or react? *Fifth*, since you have the power of using hypnosis to increase your happiness quotient, you might as well identify other areas of importance to you that you will address at a later time. Take time to prioritize the specific areas according to the importance each holds for you.

DELETING THE NEGATIVE

Hypnosis allows you to relax into that very suggestible Altered Consciousness State where your subconscious is open to accepting changes. Accepting Reprogramming Hypnosis suggestions into your subconscious is one way you can modify your behaviors. An important part of behavior modifications is deleting or neutralizing and thus nullifying the negative emotional associations that are attached to certain memories. You may remember what happened, yet you can neutralize the emotions that are attached to that memory.

For example, you remember that you fell off a horse, but through hypnotic suggestion, the fears and pain from that experience have been released. The memory has been rendered harmless. Subsequently, you can acknowledge that you fell off a horse without feeling pain or anxiety. You now have released the fear related to that memory. When you think about that experience now, you feel calm even though you can remember what happened. This gives you the option of enjoying horseback riding again and regaining self-confidence, self-empowerment and higher self-esteem. You also have more wisdom next time you horseback ride. You are better able to avoid such a fall again. The following case study exemplifies another circumstance where Reprogramming Hypnosis deleted a man's negative, Low Self-esteem feelings and raised his High Self-esteem.

JIM'S NEW REALITY

Jim came to see me when he was age forty-two. As Jim tells it, he heard throughout his childhood that he was no good. His dad always derided him and had said Jim would amount to nothing. As a child Jim subconsciously took in and accepted his father's denigrating words. As a result, Jim had believed since he was a young child that he was worthless and would amount to nothing. Even though as Jim's life progressed and he experienced successes, he still felt and believed he was really a failure. He expected people would find him out one day. He avoided risks because it would likely mean failure for him. As a part of the Reprogramming Hypnosis approach, Jim created suggestions that he used in session to delete his erroneous mindsets. Since it is always imperative to replace the deletions with positive suggestions, Jim substituted very High Self-esteem statements for suggestions that he much preferred to live by. Subsequently, Jim started to feel better about himself as a worthy and successful man. His confidence grew very significantly as did his happiness.

OUR SUBCONSCIOUS COMPUTER

As previously mentioned, you can liken your subconscious mind to the most magnificent computer that has yet to be invented. Your subconscious mind as a magnificent computer holds all your memories, all data about what you have experienced from all of your senses. It runs vast numbers of programs simultaneously with precision and ease. Your subconscious mind runs your body's autonomic system without your need for conscious thought input. Did you have to remind yourself to pump blood through your heart? That's your subconscious working automatically for you.

DELETE, MERGE, COPY, CUT AND PASTE

Currently we use different computer files labeled with titles or names in just the same way people used the old-fashioned files that they stored in actual file cabinets. You can add information to the files and can delete them entirely whenever you want. Figuratively speaking employing the computer analogy, you can do this very same thing in your subconscious mind, using hypnosis. You can create new files, give those files titles and then delete those obsolete files or files that have misleading or incorrect information.

When you delete old mindsets or harmful emotions, they are really gone, in effect totally neutralized and discarded. They no longer influence your Subconscious Programming. Your subconscious, like a real computer, also has the capability to program e-mail letters to be sent at a later time than when you actually typed them in. This is just like a Post-hypnotic Suggestion. You can merge, copy, cut and paste computer files that hold information. Your Suggestible Subconscious cooperates with your directions just like a real computer responds to the directions you type on your keyboard. While in hypnosis it is possible for you to recall happier times when you felt better about yourself and then direct your subconscious to copy those same happy feelings and paste them into your present emotional state of mind so those feelings remain a permanent part of your reality in the now. Your High Self-esteem image that brings along your positive feelings takes precedence over your most recent Low Self-esteem, bad feelings that you have deleted. Believe it or not, your subconscious can do all of these things and more.

THE RENEGADE

Nevertheless, there is a renegade in your subconscious computer design. A man-made computer is built to function purely on logic and logical progression. Human emotions have no place in present day actual computers. Therefore, present-day computers are incapable of performing emotionally or impulsively when following downloaded programs. Your human subconscious computer, in contrast, does utilize the amygdala part of your brain that does respond impulsively. This is because the amygdala reacts so quickly to your stressors that it bypasses the logical part of your brain, your *neo-cortex*. As described in Daniel Goleman's book, *Emotional Intelligence*, research demonstrates that after just a few milliseconds of your perceiving something, you already perceive what it is. What is more, you know how you feel about it, favorably or unfavorably. It is as if your emotions produce impulsively motivated programs that are instantly downloaded independently of your logical mind. Thus, you are burdened with those logically flawed Faulty Subconscious Programs that influence your physical, mental, emotional and spiritual well-being.

WHAT MAY DRIVE ANXIETY

One illustration of this is what happens when you might pass a car on the highway and nearly miss having an accident. In physiological terms, the *hippocampus* part of your subconscious brain remembers the objective facts while the amygdala retains the memory of the emotions created during that trauma. Next time you are in a similar situation passing a car on the highway, your amygdala will send a surge of anxiety bringing up old feelings associated with the passing of a car on the highway.

To make matters worse, the associations that the amygdala makes seem to broaden and spread with time. It may start with anxiety from that specific highway where the first trauma originated. Then later, it may include other large highways that elicit the same anxious response. Next, you may feel the anxiety on any regular highway when you are passing another car. If nothing is done to resolve this situation, the anxiety may grow to where anytime when you are in the car, you feel tremendous anxiety. Since the amygdala is making choices without the benefit of your logical brain, it makes conclusions based on very loose and often incorrect associations. These spreading and mutation-like changes are characteristic of fears, anxieties and panic attacks. They are like weeds that spread, multiply and take root crowding out the grass that constituted your peaceful lawn.

NO PERMISSION GRANTED

As emphasized before, your subconscious consistently chooses things for you without asking permission and without any of your conscious awareness at all! It is like having a computer system running a program that impacts your entire computer without your knowing anything about the existence of the anonymous program. Theoretically, this program functioned for our primordial ancestors as a benevolent program wanting to please and protect them. So when our caveman ancestors found themselves facing a tiger, the amygdala part of their brain registered it while dipping into past data to conclude that this was a dangerous situation. So the amygdala reminded our ancestors of the fear, their past emotional response, that they experienced from their last tangle with a tiger. They had better fight the tiger or take flight as fast as they could run based upon the memory of past experiences. Thus, the adrenalin necessary for either of those two options started flowing (bodily response) and our ancestors were pumped, ready for action.

REFUSE BLAME FOR THE PAIN

In modern, much more complicated times, however, someone such as your spouse, your boss, or your neighbor may be mistaken for that tiger. Consequently, your amygdala probably responds with fear more often in modern times than it did in caveman's times. So chances have increased tremendously for inappropriate emotional responses from your amygdala. With all that outdated information from which to base its reactions, it is not unusual for your amygdala to program something unwisely and none of that programming is your fault! You are free from responsibility, blame and/or guilt for programming choices that your subconscious made without your consent or even awareness, period.

Remember, when there is a strong, emotionally perceived threat, the part of your brain responsible for clear logic, the neo-cortex, never has a chance to alter the subconscious choices because the amygdala has already activated your response so quickly. It is not surprising that the choices produced this way may have negative consequences for you— like chronic anxiety, fears, racing thoughts, high blood pressure, weight gain, addictions and so forth. Your amygdala may be responsible for creating many of your hot buttons that set you off emotionally, mentally and physically. Every time there is a new stressful incident that your amygdala perceives as even vaguely similar to a previous incident, your reaction to the new stress seems to grow in intensity. It is like somebody poured salt upon your open wound. Think about it. What are your current hot buttons? They represent perfect targets for reprogramming your subconscious mind for your Highest Good.

THE BUCK STOPS HERE ... WITH YOU!

Certainly it is imperative to avoid blaming yourself and feeling guilty about your Faulty Subconscious Programs. The programming was performed outside of your awareness and without your permission. Just like our example of the dad who said that his son would never amount to anything, you are not at fault for feeling inferior or having a damaged self-image or whatever the erroneous programming precipitated. Nevertheless, while you are not responsible for creating the Subconscious Programming mistakes, you have the ultimate responsibility for correcting them whenever possible to the best of your ability, using all the resources available to you. In doing so, you reap the positive benefits and rewards from your improved Subconscious Reprogramming. You achieve more peace of mind, harmony, balance and happiness within your life. You are more capable of being the best you can be using all your abilities, talents and feeling self-confident and self-empowered.

An important consideration to keep in mind is that we are all works in progress. The implication here is for continued personal and spiritual growth as a choice for your lifestyle. Clearly, no one said anything about perfection. But what this does mean is that it behooves you to recognize the manifestations of your Faulty Subconscious Programming and do whatever is possible under your circumstances to reprogram them. That is considered nurturing your Mind/Body/Spirit for your Highest Good. That is ultimately your responsibility to yourself. It is still your choice. You are who you are. Yet who are you when you are free of Faulty Subconscious Programming? Are you who you are because of your faulty programs? Who would you be without those faulty programs directing your life? Who could you be without those faulty programs?

Your *free will* still operates here. You need the strong desire to make the changes for yourself and believe (even if just a tad bit) that is possible. In this poker hand of life, you do not have to settle for the cards you have been dealt. You can choose new ones. However, it requires that you be proactive and ask.

MORE MIND/BODY/SPIRIT INTERPLAY

At this time, it would be helpful to review more real-life stories from my HypnoCounseling sessions. These case studies will increase your ability to recognize and further conceptualize the constant interaction among the parts of your Mind/Body/Spirit. Also these examples are to assist you in identifying Subconscious Programs that may be interfering negatively in your life now.

JULIE'S STORY OF INFERTILITY

Julie, a young woman in her late twenties, came for help because she had two miscarriages and was very distressed. The doctors could find no reason for her miscarriages. However, while in hypnosis Julie remembered her mother admonishing her to never become pregnant. At that time, Julie was only a young teenager, not married. Her mom's words had entered into Julie's Suggestible Subconscious resulting in a Subconscious Program that was permanently affixed, remaining even after Julie's wedding. Even though now, it would be wonderful for Julie, as a married woman, to be pregnant, Julie's subconscious was still operating and defending the old program that kept her from becoming and/or staying pregnant. Even with successful in-vitro fertilization, she had two miscarriages. Several weeks after listening repeatedly to her recording, Julie and her husband attempted in-vitro fertilization again. Once more she became pregnant. But this time there was a happy outcome as Julie's child, a girl, was born. About two years later, Julie became pregnant without any medical intervention; and, now Julie and her husband have their second little girl.

Another client, Jamal, was a senior in high school and had a straight A average. However, when it was almost time for his final exams, he started having terrible anxiety and panic attacks. He got physically sick and consequently missed school. What we learned during his first hypnosis session was that Jamal had a fear of failure. Rather than risk failing to achieve the A's on his exams that he emotionally needed for his self-esteem, his subconscious created a fear-based condition that would prevent him from failing. His Subconscious Program called for anxiety, panic attacks and sickness. After all, if he were too sick to take the exams, he would never be able to fail. Of course in the long term, this logically does not make sense because not ever taking the exams would cause him to fail the class.

Recall that the amygdala part of your subconscious reacts so instantly to strong emotions that it skips over input from the neo-cortex, the logical brain. Your subconscious in those situations is more impulsive, illogical and overlooks long-term consequences. Jamal's impulsive subconscious decision indeed did give Jamal just his bottom line. He literally would not fail the exams because he would never take them in the first place. Fortunately by using hypnosis to communicate his pre-approved positive suggestions to his subconscious, Jamal released his fears, calmed himself and built up new confidence. He also realized it was okay not to be perfect. His grades did not define him — only he defined himself. It came as no surprise to me that once the new positive mindsets were in place, Jamal regained his health, confidence and peace of mind. He passed his exams and was very pleased with his high scores.

HYLAND'S STORY OF REVERSING A MINDSET

Another case study I remember vividly involved Hyland. He had been diagnosed with diabetes but was not compliant with the doctor's orders even though he truly wanted to be compliant. His issue was revealed while in hypnosis when Hyland was able to recall his first response to when he was first told he would have to have dialysis. He very angrily thought to himself, *I would rather die than have to do that!* This high stress anger spurred his Suggestible Subconscious into action. It was as if his subconscious responded and said, *I can do that for Hyland.* Please understand that your subconscious is always trying to please you and fulfill your requests; however, it focuses on giving you your bottom line only, without thought regarding long-term consequences. What it chose for Hyland without his knowledge or permission was to have him behave contrary to his doctor's orders in order to hasten his demise. Hyland's subconscious was giving him the means to die because it believed he really wanted to die. Fortunately, while in the hypnosis, Hyland told his subconscious that he very much wanted to live. What he needed was for his subconscious to help him comply with all the doctor's orders, especially limiting his liquid intake. Hyland's Suggestible Subconscious obviously got the message and programmed it. Within two weeks Hyland's subconscious started directing Hyland to follow all the positive suggestions and Hyland's health improved considerably.

SAL: FIGURATIVELY SPEAKING

So often the subconscious communicates using a variety of figures of speech, literal and double meanings. One client came for weight reduction. While he had considerable weight to reduce all over, the big majority was around his middle torso. Actually he carried the most in his stomach. What was revealed to him when he was relaxed into hypnosis was that when Sal was a young kid, one of his brother's friends had gone into a rage, kicking Sal in the stomach. Sal, like most kids in those days, had never told anyone about it. But it really was hurtful physically, emotionally and spiritually too. What Sal had learned from this trauma was that he was not safe. He could be hurt and hurt badly. His subconscious sensing his pain and anguish chose therefore to keep him protected. How? It insulated him with fat especially around his stomach. In order for him to allow the fat to reduce, Sal had to give the appropriate instructions to his subconscious to delete the fears, release the pain of the past traumatic event of being kicked brutally in the stomach and reprogram that he was safe now. So it was safe to reduce his weight and the fat around his torso.

FORGIVENESS BENEFITS YOU

Sal also had to forgive the bully as well. Forgiveness has a special focus when used in hypnosis. Forgiveness is about you and your well-being. It means that you have given yourself permission to release the anger, the pain and the negative emotions associated with someone or some experience. You have released it from you physically, mentally, emotionally and spiritually. In Sal's case, it does not mean what the bully did to him was okay. Forgiveness was initiated by Sal for Sal. It meant Sal was ready to close that chapter and focus on more positive things in his life. Some people feel at peace when they leave the judgments and any retribution to God or to Whomever they signify as their Higher Power. That is part of personal and spiritual growth as well. To his credit, Sal was successful in understanding the many subliminal, figurative meanings associated with his weight. He also was quite successful in reducing his weight.

DONALD'S STORY: TRANSLATING MIND INTO MATTER

There is one case I feel exemplifies so clearly the body accepting and manifesting the mind's figurative language. This case was about Donald, a sales and marketing manager who was struggling with a cough that would not go away. At times the cough was so ferocious that he could not catch his breath. This would send him into a panic attack. The panic attacks continued to exacerbate his condition. By the time he came to see me for hypnosis, he had run out of options. Frequently this is the case with the people who come for my services. Hypnosis often is considered the last stop after people have tried everything else. I am sure one day soon that will all change. One day we will examine the role of a person's subconscious mind as a top priority alongside other important steps for recovery. In Donald's case, medicine only helped the cough slightly and nothing seemed to help the panic attacks that were growing worse. This condition had persisted for over eight years.

With the help of hypnosis, Donald became aware that his deceased son was connected to this physical issue. About eight years previously, Donald's son had committed suicide by hanging himself in the family garage. Donald quite understandably was overwhelmed and traumatized by this tragedy. He could not forgive himself for not being able to stop his son's death. Before he came to see me for hypnosis Donald had thought his issue about his son's suicide had been resolved. This is often the case with so many people. They have already worked through their issues on the conscious level but unknowingly overlooked the programming that still remained in their subconscious and in *Cellular Memory* throughout their body. In this case, Donald's throat and breathing were affected by the son's tragic death. We can hypothesize that the amygdala reacted so quickly and associated the emotional pain that Donald felt, with the physical part of his body that related to his son's death by strangulation. Specifically, It was the throat of Donald's son that was most affected by the suicide rope. We worked on reprogramming Donald's subconsciously held beliefs, releasing the throat association and worked on forgiveness for everyone concerned. After three weeks of practicing Reprogramming Self-hypnosis and listening to his personalized audio, Donald's cough improved. His panic attacks stopped completely.

JEAN'S CASE STUDY OF TRIUMPH

A retired hairdresser named Jean came for HypnoCounseling seeking to feel better about herself as a person, her marriage and her life in general. Her life had been extremely tragic. She witnessed her mom's murder. She along with her sister grew up in several foster homes. Her sister had been sexually abused by their foster father and he had physically beaten Jean. After several years of psychotherapy, Jean was better but not completely healed. Like so many others who have come for hypnosis, Jean had exhausted every other possibility. Nevertheless Jean responded extremely well to her hypnotic suggestions that focused on her getting the nurturing she had missed as a child. Her abandonment fears that were subconsciously programmed from her traumas were defused, neutralized and released through the visualizations and direct Reprogramming Hypnosis suggestions. She started to see herself in a different, positive light as one who was empowered instead of being the victim. Now what happened next is not always the case for everyone. But for Jean, she made a dramatic improvement within thirty days and with only one session. My intuition tells me that when a person is extremely ready and the right guide for that person appears, the self-healing progresses very quickly.

LEONARD'S VICTORY

Another case involved a man named Leonard. Leonard had grown up with a mom who had severe emotional problems. Since Leonard was seven years old he had been aware that his mom was having affairs with many men. Furthermore, Leonard's mom never hugged or kissed him unless there was company in the home. This was a man who received one abuse after another without a drop of love or nurturing. His self-esteem had suffered horribly. He felt totally unlovable and worthless. Hypnosis benefited Leonard because it allowed Leonard to feel better about himself. He succeeded in releasing negative emotions that resulted from a lack of love and nurturing in his life. For over a month he listened to his recording of Reprogramming Hypnosis suggestions and guided imagery that were formulated to reach his subconscious. The recording was intended to help him understand that he could nurture himself through hypnosis visualizations as well as through Direct and Indirect Reprogramming Hypnosis suggestions. His subconscious having accepted the positive suggestions, did the rest, beginning anew to nurture and heal his self-esteem.

HEAL A PAST LIFE; HEAL YOUR PRESENT LIFE

You may view reprogramming your subconscious as a method of improving yourself also with the goal of perfecting your soul. Taking it one step further, some believe the spiritual process described as perfecting or purifying the soul may actually continue throughout hundreds of lifetimes. This concept of people's Spirits having more than one lifetime is not new. The idea of Past Lives is based upon centuries-old concepts of the eternal soul, soul lessons and *Reincarnation*.

Although some world religions support the idea of Reincarnation, I professionally maintain a neutral position regarding Past Lives since my personal beliefs on this subject are irrelevant. It is only my clients' beliefs that are reflected in the work we do together. As a HypnoCounselor, I employ Past Life hypnosis techniques that allow clients to utilize the information gained from a Past Life hypnosis experience for self-discovery and/or self-healing that otherwise might have been unattainable. Many times people can understand their present circumstances better if they are able to see themselves more objectively as someone else in a Past Life. The theory is that the same issues that affected them in a Past Life are presently affecting them in their current lifetime. Furthermore, when they resolve their Past Life issue, it automatically resolves and releases their current lifetime issue that was really an extension of that Past Life issue. Past life hypnosis can be a very powerful technique used appropriately in Reprogramming Hypnosis.

IF IT WORKS, USE IT

The important point is that Past Life hypnosis techniques are extremely useful for many, many people. Sometimes people just automatically find themselves in a Past Life when we request their subconscious to help us understand how their issue first began. So even when our intentions and focus are on other than Past Life work, if and when Past Life information is relevant, it just appears thanks to the person's helpful subconscious mind.

ERR ON THE SIDE OF CAUTION

Before continuing, I want to repeat a caution about doing Past Life visualizations led by amateurs or in a large group session. The person experiencing a Past Life visualization needs to be carefully monitored, preferably by a professional. I emphasize this because it is possible, although not necessarily likely, that you may find yourself in a Past Life when you are having a difficult moment. The hypnosis professional, under those circumstances, is best able to instantly exit you from such a moment and keep you calm and comfortable.

A TECHNIQUE RATHER THAN A BELIEF

Of course, there are many who cannot wrap their arms around a belief in Past Lives. If the Past Life theory goes against your religious beliefs or outside your acceptable belief parameters or if you simply find the concept too difficult to consider, view it only as a hypnosis technique. View it as an analogy your

Suggestible Subconscious creates in order to improve your understanding of your current situations. People who do not believe in the possibility of Past Lives still benefit from Past Life hypnosis. You may view it as another way your subconscious explains in less threatening, less personalized terms about what issues are blocking you. Be assured that you may release your subconscious blockages also through resolving them in what you perceive as imaginary Past Life situations.

LEARNING FROM PAST LIFE TRAUMAS

MICHAEL'S STINGING STORY

One of the more unusual hypnosis sessions that I can recall illustrates how a Past Life trauma may be affecting a person in this lifetime. Remember if you are not of the persuasion to believe in the existence of Past Lives, you can still gain insight from the interesting story it provides. Michael was deathly afraid of bees. He had been stung once before and had a strong allergic reaction to the bee sting. When Michael relaxed into hypnosis, he received an insight about how this bee allergy first began. He could see himself as a child leaving a village very hurriedly because a volcano was erupting with lava spewing ash all over. He could hear the zinging sounds whistling by his head. He was panicked as he fled for his life. From time to time, he felt the stinging from tiny pieces of hot ash. When I asked him what it felt like, he replied, *It feels like bees are stinging me.* From this he surmised that his subconscious carried the association of that Past Life trauma with the bees stinging. Hence in his present life, Michael experienced a violent bodily reaction to the actual bee sting.

Through hypnosis visualization, Michael released the negative emotions from the trauma and out flew the bee fears as well. In the meantime he still avoided bees so as not to tempt a negative physical response until his doctor could test whether he still was severely allergic to bees. Even though Michael chose to stay clear of bees, he was very thankful that he was able to retain his peace of mind whenever he sighted a bee. Michael's case is an example of releasing and neutralizing the negative emotions of the past while in turn releasing the negative feelings in the present. The extra benefit is retaining the wisdom of the past in the present.

ANNA'S TIDAL WAVE OF TEARS

A Past Life incident surprisingly came to light for Anna when she went for HypnoCounseling. She always would cry profusely and uncontrollably whenever encountering anything sad. Anna would be a constant fountain of tears at a funeral even if personally she did not know the person. She could pick up a newspaper and cry when she read the headline about someone getting killed. It had become an embarrassing problem for her. During hypnosis she saw that her problem originated in a Past Life when she was a young mother named Lulana. As the hypnosis began, Anna was directed to see herself as an objective viewer of what initiated her issue of uncontrollable crying in this scene. Rather than re-experiencing anything negative, she was an objective reporter of the events.

While in hypnosis she saw herself as Lulana who had two young sons and they were living in a Polynesian village. She could see herself wearing a grass skirt. Her favorite flower, a gardenia, was decorating her long black hair. When asked why she was so sad, Anna all of a sudden exclaimed, *There is a tidal wave!* Instantly her HypnoCounselor disconnected her from that scene and brought her to her safe place. It seems that the tidal wave had destroyed the entire village. No wonder Anna was so sensitive to death and tragedy. Her Spirit must have been carrying the burden of tremendous grief since that horrific tragedy.

Anna was helped to neutralize all of those intense emotions that were attached to that memory. Almost immediately after the hypnosis session, Anna regained much greater composure and control when faced with sad news or tragic events. Anna's past propensity for tears may be viewed as a response to grief she was carrying subconsciously in her soul's memories.

ADAM'S PERPETUAL HUNGER

Adam came for hypnosis to reduce his weight by seventy-five pounds. He came for his first session already discouraged, suspecting that nothing would help him lose that weight. But he had never tried hypnosis before. Through the process of hypnosis, Adam discovered that as a child in another lifetime, he had experienced starving to death. His subconscious still carried the trauma and message of needing food desperately. So even though he always had access to food in his present life, his subconscious drove him to eat like there would never be enough food. The subconscious belief was that he was still starving. He released those erroneous belief systems and spoke to his subconscious directly to reprogram his healthy eating habits and to motivate him to continue them throughout his lifetime. Additionally he accepted the suggestion that he always had sufficient food. This allowed Adam to lose his excess weight permanently and with minimal effort.

DAVID'S FEAR OF FAILURE FROM A PAST LIFE

David was a successful writer. However, when a major project was awarded to him and his associates, he went into a panic. He could not force himself even to get started with the commitment. Instead, he escaped to a friend's apartment to hide out. I had successfully assisted David with other troubling issues previously, so he returned for more help for this challenging issue. For the first time since I began working with David, his subconscious offered a Past Life experience to explain his unusual behavior. What had precipitated his panic was a Past Life experience when he was a very poor, young girl who was a servant to a cruel and abusive man. She was beaten mercilessly for any, even insignificant, mistakes she would make. This fear of making any mistake transferred into David's current lifetime imposing the fear of making any mistake regarding his new important project. So David cleared his subconscious of the negativity and neutralized all memory of the abuse and fears of making mistakes from that Past Life. Quickly within a couple of weeks David's entire perspective on his new business opportunity shifted into the positive column. David came out of hiding and moved forward with his assignment feeling confident and in control.

LUCINDA: DRAMATIC ANSWERS

Lucinda called me after learning that I had helped her girlfriend overcome an issue, fear of vomiting, that Lucinda also was struggling to overcome. Actually when I met with Lucinda, she had more fears and panic attacks than almost any client I had ever seen. Like other clients with serious anxiety, she came with the approval of her current therapist. She feared throwing up, being choked, being unable to breathe, being abandoned, being alone in the dark, being given an injection with a needle and being closed in while driving in the car, just to name a few of her fears. Most unusual was her fear of being near buttons. Incredibly, this fear of buttons started when she was three years old. Needless to say, Lucinda lived a very challenging life, always full of tremendous anxiety and almost constant panic attacks. She had been seeing a therapist since she was seven years old. When she came to see me, she was in college.

During our Reprogramming Hypnosis session her subconscious revealed to her a Past Life where her anxieties began. In that Past Life Lucinda felt abandoned after her father's death. She worked to support her ill mother by working as a seamstress in a factory. She could remember a terrible accident when she was sewing buttons onto clothing and the needle went high up into her arm. She also was aware of another trauma that she had suffered in that lifetime. She had been accosted in a dark alley by two men who choked her so badly that she almost died. She used hypnosis techniques to release the negative emotions initiated by the traumas. Consequently, the emotions and all memories of the traumas were neutralized. Lucinda also forgave everyone who had hurt her, no matter whether it was intentionally or unintentionally. Immediately following that session, the most prominent of all the major anxieties and panic attacks were almost completely gone. She could experience completely normal human emotions again because the anxiety was no longer controlling her life. She is continuing her hypnosis work to release still other issues. Reprogramming Hypnosis visualization techniques uprooted and removed anxieties that could be explained by Lucinda only if their origins began in a Past Life.

NURTURING YOURSELF WITH POSITIVES

We are all responsible for taking care of ourselves and getting the nurturing we need. Think for a moment of positive ways you can nurture yourself. While you are in self-hypnosis, imagine some of the activities you have done in the past that have been positive and made you feel loved and/or made your Spirit feel nourished. Perhaps you felt so happy spending time with a special friend or relative. Maybe you performed a kind deed and helped someone in trouble. Imagine how wonderful it felt lying on an inflated raft in the pool or lying on the beach feeling the warm sand between your toes. How wonderful was it skiing down the mountain feeling free as you felt the wind rushing, whipping past your cheeks? Remember that last vacation when it felt so great to be refreshed and energized? How great do you feel when you are working out or taking a refreshing walk? If you have difficulty remembering happy nurturing moments, just invent/create some of your own. Pretend you had some wonderful nurturing times. Imagine what you believe others must have enjoyed and put yourself in their place. Just make up those happy times and fill them full of unconditional love and nurturing. When you imagine with vivid clarity and strong emotions, your brain is unable to differentiate between what is imagined and what is reality. So remember, in cases like these, you easily can use your mind to create your reality.

ESTABLISH A REPERTOIRE

It is important for you to keep your repertoire of happy memories, nurturing positive, feel-good images and highly pleasurable imaginings. Plant the self-hypnosis suggestion that one or two of the positive thoughts/images become an automatic response to stress, any stress that brings up threats of negativity such as Low Self-esteem, anxiety, and feelings of helplessness. This is a recommended goal for you. You are defusing stress within the first couple of milliseconds. That way your mechanism of volatile emotional response, the amygdala, remains inactive or at least less active. By staying calm you are cutting off the ringing of your internal alarm of strong emotion. Thus, you may prevent your subconscious from making faulty, impulsive choices. That means you may also prevent Faulty Subconscious Programs that could cause unintended negative consequences physically, mentally, emotionally and/or spiritually. Personally, I picture my therapy dog, Maggie. She is symbolic of pure, unconditional love. There is nothing bittersweet when I think of Maggie. She is also quite adorable. If I think of her I smile and am able to ignore everything else. Maggie's picture is on my website contact page, www.GaleGlassnerTwersky.com. If this would appeal to you, please take advantage of her picture for a feeling of unconditional love and nurturing. You also may enjoy the many other very peaceful, relaxing, feel-good images placed on the website for your possible use as feel-good images.

SUPER HAPPY THINK TANK

When convenient, find a journal time to add descriptions of your happy images, fond memories, blessings and things for which you are grateful. If you have difficulty remembering them, take happiness inducing moments from feel-good movies or a favorite TV show. Just observing someone else doing a kind deed can raise your endorphins and make you feel really good. So use other people's *happy moment* feelings or picture yourself in wonderful fantasy places if you want to create happy moments outside of your personal experience. Maybe think of how you would feel winning the lottery or saving someone's life. Insert all your feel-good images into your self-hypnosis by mentioning them and identifying them as your feel-good images. Then you may recall them instantaneously when they are needed to overpower any of your negative thoughts. Consider also all the ways you may nurture yourself. The next chapter will spend time focusing on staying positive, an important part of nurturing yourself.

CHAPTER 6

REPROGRAMMING TO LIVE
POSITIVELY BETTER

POSITIVE THINKING AND BELIEVING, SUBCONSCIOUSLY

STAYING POSITIVE REGARDLESS OF NEGATIVITY

Perhaps you believe as many people do that nothing happens by accident. Everything in your life is meaningful, especially life experiences that bring you wisdom that could never be communicated in a more powerful way. This is what happened to me when I accepted an encore speaking engagement for the *Health Information Manager's Association* in Atlantic City, New Jersey. My audience consisted of people in charge of medical records. They are in a field that endures high pressures for extreme accuracy since they are extremely vulnerable to legal ramifications.

The topic I chose to speak about was Staying Positive While Surrounded by Negativity. I had quite a few suggestions to offer as to how that might be possible. But first I asked my audience if they thought it was even remotely possible to remain positive while everyone and everything around them was negative. Most people shook their heads with a side-to-side no! And many others just snickered at the mere thought. In response I conducted a planned demonstration for my audience of over one hundred Health Information Managers.

TESTING WITHOUT A TRUTH SERUM

I began by asking for a volunteer to come forward. Without hesitation I beckoned to Susan, a very petite young woman in the second row. She stepped forward to volunteer. Certainly, she did not appear as if she could take on the Negative Energy of that large audience. I began by explaining my use of a type of Muscle Testing known as Applied Kinesiology, *Energy Balancing* or Acupressure. It is frequently used by chiropractors and dentists as well as by others in health and wellness related fields. I use this technique for my HypnoCounseling purposes to demonstrate how the subconscious mind and body are reacting to a verbal statement or a specific thought initiated by the person who is being tested. After the person verbalizes a statement or signals that he/she is silently focused on that thought, I simply press down with my pinky finger on the wrist section of the person's extended arm. An auditory statement or even a silent thought under these conditions can produce what can be interpreted as either a positive or negative physical response. When I push down on the wrist of the person's extended arm and the muscles holding the arm up remain strong, the statement is validated as a positive response. This means that the person's subconscious is affirming the statement/thought as true. To the contrary, if the arm muscle weakens and the extended arm drops downward as I push on the person's wrist, it indicates that the expressed statement/thought produced a negative response.

A negative response means the statement/thought is not true according to the person's subconscious. Specifically it means that the statement/thought is in conflict with the current beliefs held in the participant's subconscious mind.

Next, I directed the young woman to say her name in a statement, *My name is Susan.* I then pressed down firmly with my pinky finger on the wrist of her outstretched arm. Susan had been instructed to resist my pressure without locking her arm or forcing her arm upwards. Susan's arm responded by resisting all pressure to lower it. Her arm effortlessly stayed straight out in front of her. In terms of Muscle Testing analysis, the strong arm response meant the verbal statement produced Susan's Positive Energy response and therefore, was what Susan subconsciously believed was the truth. Then I instructed her to say, *My name is Gloria.* Again I pressed down on her wrist to measure muscle strength. This time her arm went completely down as if her entire arm had lost its strength. This pattern continued as I asked her to repeat that *two plus two equals four.* Again her arm remained strong. Yet, when she said *two plus two equals seven,* her arm went almost limp.

The next step was to ask Susan to think of something very happy, very positive. As she was focused on something positive, again I pressed down on her wrist to muscle test. She reacted with her outstretched arm remaining strong. When I asked her to think of something negative like something sad or fearful, her muscle strength disappeared again as her arm dropped down instantly. This Muscle Testing provides a wonderful visual of what your invisible, yet still extremely powerful, thoughts can do to you physically. The negative thoughts with their kind of Negative Energy produced actual weakness in her muscles.

Theoretically, when Susan said something untrue according to her subconscious perspective, the negatively charged energy of the falsehood interrupted the positive flow of energy continually circulating around her body. It was a short in her circuitry. Think of it like a lie detector test for your subconsciously held beliefs. It is a sensor of a type of interruptive Negative Energy that affects your body. On one hand, a typical lie detector device electronically records your reactions to statements you say. The changes in the graph lines reveal whether your statements are true or false. On the other hand, with Muscle Testing, your body's muscle strength responds to your statements as true or false by either maintaining or losing muscle strength. Both types of testing rely on the body's electrical circuitry response. While we still do not fully understand electricity, we nevertheless can see its effects. The same is true for Muscle Testing and what we call *Negative Energy, negatively charged energy.*

FRANZ ANTON MESMER REVISITED?

Once your energy is interrupted or blocked, your body's flow of energy is thrown off balance. Your loss of muscle strength therefore reflects a compromised, weakened condition. This is the same perspective that Acupuncture incorporates as a basis for treatments.

Acupuncturists use very slender needles positioned precisely on your body along Acupuncture *Meridians* that are channels through which your body's life energy flows. These needles are placed specifically to unblock and free the circulation of energy and enhance the cells' signaling to each other throughout the body. Acupuncture supports this process as the means for your body to return to good health. The continuous uninterrupted flow of this energy encourages your body to heal itself. You may have heard of the word *Chi* also spelled *Qi* and pronounced *chee* rhyming with *knee*. It is what Eastern medicine uses to describe this universal life energy force circulating throughout your body. This may remind you of Mesmer's concept of Magnetic Fluid in Chapter Two. Personally, I use Muscle Testing extensively and successfully to ascertain the positive flow of a person's energy, yet I do remind my clients that it is an indicator only and I avoid relying upon it as always 100 percent accurate. In the meantime I am in favor of using whatever works as long as it is for the person's Highest Good.

NO ONE LIVES IN A BUBBLE

My talk got even more interesting when I demonstrated the effect other people can have on an individual. I asked the audience to think of a good thought such as how happy they feel thinking about something they loved. I requested them to send that happy feeling to our volunteer at the front of the room. I commenced Muscle Testing Susan. Her muscles remained strong and her arm remained outstretched and stationary. Next I asked the audience to send something negative like a fear or a sad thought to Susan at the front of the room. You guessed it! Her arm went down immediately upon Muscle Testing. So, I experimented to test how she would respond when she did not know whether the audience was sending positive or negative thought energy. I instructed the audience to respond to my signal of the number of fingers I raised behind our volunteer's head. One finger was to send a positive thought and two fingers meant to send the negative thought. Again Susan's muscle strength remained strong when receiving the audience's positive thought *vibrations* and weakened measurably receiving the negative ones. This happened consistently even though I mixed up the order and did it several times. We concluded that those around us could have a positive/strengthening or a negative/weakening influence on us without our even being aware of it.

INSIDE, YOU ARE SUPERMAN OR SUPERWOMAN

How many of you have felt your energy being sucked away from you by an energy vampire? I am speaking of those people who leave you feeling drained and weary. Now you can understand how real that drained, weakened feeling was! At this conference I decided to take a bold new step. It came to me intuitively. I had not tested this theory before, but I was willing to take this risk. I really wanted to know the answer. What would happen if I asked the audience to send their negative thoughts while Susan was focused, thinking of positive thoughts? Would her arm weaken as before when the audience sent the negative vibrations or would it remain strong because what she had going on in her mind was positive? Could her own positive thought protect her and keep her strong despite the assault of negative thought energy from more than 100 people in that room? What would be your guess as to what happened? I suspected the outcome and am personally thrilled to report that her arm remained strong as could be, even with all the audience directing their negative thought energy her way. The meaning for us here is huge. Even in a world that may manifest negative energies such as anxieties, fear, hate, greed, guilt, sadness, anger, loneliness and so forth, it is possible for you to remain strong and able to resist the negativity if you remain positive with your thoughts! How amazing is that? This means you can have more control over your life than you may have thought was possible. Yes, you can have more control over the negativity in your life by rejecting the negativity as you keep your mind focused on the positive ... consistently.

LET YOUR SUBCONSCIOUS DO YOUR CONSCIOUS BIDDING

We are guided most of all by our subconscious mind and its programs of accepted mind-sets, belief systems and stored emotional associations. Your conscious mind can only handle perhaps a maximum of seven things simultaneously. In contrast, it is too difficult to estimate how many thousands of things your subconscious mind can handle simultaneously. There is no contest which one is more powerful. Your subconscious wins that award every time. So what stands to reason here?

Put your focus and concentration on communicating with your subconscious mind. Put into your subconscious computer mind the thoughts, mindsets, beliefs, feelings, behaviors that are positive for you and delete what you find are negative. Do so continuously just like your computer protection program checks for viruses, identifies them and then deletes them forever. Repeat on a daily basis this hypnosis process of scanning and deleting harmful programs from your subconscious. It will support your well-being of Mind/ Body/Spirit. Remember a computer is unable to run a program that has been deleted. It only runs according to what still exists as software programs and saved files. You now have that know-how power through Reprogramming Self-hypnosis or Reprogramming Hypnosis to consciously choose whatever programs you want for your happiness, self-fulfillment and well-being. Nonetheless, it is up to you to download them into your subconscious computer.

ONE SHIFT CAN MOVE MOUNTAINS

You have probably noticed that I am an enthusiastic proponent of people having this knowledge. I know it can be a motivator to facilitate the enactment of positive changes in your life. And yes, its implications are for everyone. A couple years ago I was in the audience watching Carolyn Myss, a medical intuitive, taping a TV show for Oprah Winfrey's Oxygen cable channel. I remember Ms. Myss insisted that if you make just one shift, only ONE shift even though small, you could thereby force a multitude of other things to change. You could even move mountains. If you have been feeling stuck in some capacity, feeling stuck in a relationship, feeling stuck in a job, feeling stuck in how you are living, you need to take the responsibility to make the first move. CHANGE something! Now you have a proven pathway to help you make those changes where it matters the most, inside YOU!

YOUR AMYGDALA CALLED TO ACTION

Remember many of those faulty programs that you want to change are due to a part of your brain, the amygdala that stores your emotional scrapbooks of past events. The amygdala is activated when you are experiencing intense emotional feelings. Such things as traumas, injuries, humiliations and losses all are among what activates the amygdala. The amygdala is also activated when you are experiencing highly pleasurable or euphoric feelings during such events as your graduations from school, the births of your children and experiences of great sex. Now recall Chapter Five, when we discussed in more detail the subconscious mind and the amygdala. Your amygdala chooses its reactions during your high caliber stress without the wisdom of the logical part of your brain, the neo-cortex. The unfortunate consequences of this are that oftentimes it chooses responses that are completely inappropriate for you. Besides its choices contributing positive outcomes, it is responsible for producing unwanted or even harmful results for you even though in the moment your subconscious thought it was protecting or pleasing you.

Unfortunately your amygdala is not equipped to eliminate its mistakes ... no matter how harmful to you they may be. It is just not part of its job description.

SAVE THE DEER!

Reprogramming Hypnosis/Self-hypnosis as explained in this book, however, may intercede on your behalf. You may aim to supersede the impulsive amygdala's responses to your stress by reprogramming your Mind/Body/Spirit to react instantly to your stress by relaxing. Importantly such a Subconscious Program would remove you from the *deer caught in the headlights* frame of stressed mind and allow you to access your logic, intelligence and intuition. If the deer had that advantage, it would know to jump out of the way of the oncoming car. All in all, Reprogramming Hypnosis/Self-hypnosis is ready to serve you very importantly in a preventive care manner.

YOUR AMYGDALA REMEMBERS

Let us look at an illustration of the amygdala in action within the familiar setting with a sibling. Suppose you were playing baseball with your older brother and you dropped the baseball several times instead of catching it. Your brother called you *stupid* and this name-calling hurt your feelings. Without your awareness this insult injured your self-esteem and made you lose self-confidence. Within a split second your hurt feelings were automatically recorded and retained within the database of the amygdala part of your brain. From that time on, every time you played baseball, you might have feared dropping the ball and embarrassing yourself again. You might also have developed a pattern of fear and inferiority regarding your brother. Furthermore, you might have avoided future interactions with him so as to avoid his hurting your feelings again.

BIRTH OF A BAD RELATIONSHIP

Another likely consequence is that you might have associated your brother with your feeling that you were not good enough. You might have started to feel anger towards your brother and it could have gotten worse and worse every time he said anything negative to you. Thus, one can create a negative relationship that continues to spiral down if not addressed and resolved. Does this scenario apply for everyone? No, it does not always happen that way for everyone. It depends upon your personality, your vulnerabilities and your sensitivities. Some people might not feel hurt at all about the *stupid* name-calling. I give this explanation so you may understand how in some people, in some cases, under some circumstances, it may and does happen. One person may not care what you say about his ball playing abilities but if you mention anything about his short stature, his emotions flare up. We all have our *Achilles Heel*, our most vulnerable, sensitive part. What is your Achilles Heel? Just think about that one for a moment. That may represent your next spiritual lesson.

NEUTRAL IS HARMLESS

Now imagine what occurs when you neutralize those highly charged emotional feelings of the past tied to the baseball incident and your brother. If those negative feelings were neutralized, they would be unable to give the amygdala any basis for using that historical emotional pain as a guide for future choices of thoughts and action. What happens if your brother no longer is associated with negative self-esteem emotions? You then have no reason to fear his judgments anymore or to feel angry when you are involved with him or to avoid him.

EMPTY THE EMOTIONAL GARBAGE CAN

The emphasis here is that through Reprogramming Hypnosis/ Self-hypnosis you can help clear past emotional garbage and change associations that were erroneously created (most likely by the amygdala's reactions) by giving appropriate and effective instructions to your subconscious. Really, it is possible. Be sure to emphasize all the positives you already possess and create new positive attitudes, beliefs, feelings and behaviors that you truly want. In that way you are directing your life in such a positive mode. Some of the changes may be unbelievably easy to initiate while others will take more concentrated effort. But be persistent and remember that your subconscious wants to please you. What relationships would you like to improve? How could Reprogramming Hypnosis/Self-hypnosis help you accomplish improving your relationships?

LEARN FROM OTHERS' STRUGGLES

The following case studies illustrate Subconscious Resistances that have occurred for some clients. Their examples will assist your understanding of why there may be a Subconscious Resistance to your Reprogramming Hypnosis suggestions. Also you will be encouraged to know how the power of reprogramming your subconscious through Reprogramming Hypnosis/Self-hypnosis can overcome those resistances.

ANGELA'S WEIGHT LOSS FREEZE

I was assisting a fifty-two-year-old homemaker, Angela, reduce her weight. She was doing beautifully and had already lost fifteen pounds when she abruptly stopped losing weight. Even though she had stayed on her healthy eating plan, the scale just would not budge. After two and a half weeks of remaining on a plateau weight, we knew something was resisting. So I did Muscle Testing for Angela. Her outstretched arm remained strong when we tested with the statement that there was an emotional issue preventing her from continuing to reduce her weight. We tried several possibilities of central emotional issues and out of the process of elimination came upon her self-empowerment as a general reason.

She finally zeroed in on her husband as the specific cause. This immediately made sense to Angela because her husband had started to get involved with monitoring her eating decisions and she resented it tremendously. While consciously she wanted to reduce by another forty pounds, her subconscious perceived her angry feelings about her husband's interference. In order to protect her from being controlled, she subconsciously was being directed to stop doing what he wanted her to do ... lose more weight! With this new knowledge Angela was able to take care of that resistance. Through new hypnotic suggestion, Angela easily released her anger and resentment toward her husband and forgave him. This re-established Angela back on her track of successfully reducing her weight to meet her goal. And she did, just in time for her daughter's wedding.

JOHN'S STORY: A FAMILY-ISM

John was also challenged by a Subconscious Resistance. John was forty-eight years old and an engineer, methodical, analytical and very scientific. He had an anxiety issue and had come for HypnoCounseling to learn how to stop worrying and to relax more. I told him he was in the right place. We did hypnosis with guided imagery and I read to him the suggestions that he had pre-approved. He was able to go into the relaxed state of hypnosis. Yet even though he had requested those specific suggestions, he had difficulty imagining and accepting that he was actually talking to his subconscious. It just was not logical enough for him. Consequently, he had unintentionally and subconsciously put up a resistance to accepting his desired self-improvements. After two weeks he showed no improvement regardless of all the suggestions he received in session.

At his next visit I decided to do a technique called *Subconscious Conference*. It illuminated the mindset responsible for the problem. In this technique his subconscious parts that all were related to this resistance agreed, when John requested, to participate in a round-table visualization of a conference with John during hypnosis. Under those circumstances John gained insights by talking directly to those subconscious parts and then listening to their replies. His subconscious parts revealed that John's father had told John that he should always go by logic rather than the emotional, intuitive stuff. In effect, John was predisposed to disregard anything that went outside the boundaries of conventional, logical, concrete facts. Once John acknowledged that it was that mindset stopping him from going forward, he decided on the appropriate Reprogramming Hypnosis suggestions to eliminate the Faulty Subconscious Program. Thus, he deleted what was directing him to use the logical part of his brain only. With only one more session he was successful in overcoming that resistance. Furthermore, he continued to practice hypnosis that empowered him to have consistent control over anxiety.

DIANA'S CASE OF SMOKE AND MIRRORS

One young client, Diana, did not have as favorable an outcome. She had terrible anxiety and fear regarding driving a car. Yet she needed her car for the family business. When she started to make headway during hypnosis, she would push herself back to her conscious state. What we later learned was that the anxiety was not her main issue. The anxiety was rather a smokescreen, a diversion from her core issue that was actually a fear of failure. If Diana got over her driving fears, she would have to take on more family business responsibility. Eventually, she would have to take over her entire family interior design business. Her anxiety was in effect fiercely protecting her from exposing herself to any possibility of failing as manager of her family business. So by keeping her anxiety, she eliminated her chances of failure. And rather than face that core issue that was so terribly frightening, she simply stopped the hypnosis sessions.

You cannot force someone to do what they are not yet ready to do. Furthermore, there are people who have not been able to resolve all their issues from our work. Sometimes I am unsure why. I just know there is a reason and I have faith that I did my part in one way or another. I have come to understand that sometimes my role is limited to assisting my clients to heal a part of their Spirit only. Sometimes the hypnosis work is merely one stepping-stone creating the readiness stage so people can begin to let go of their pain, their imbalance and/or their fears, even if it means doing so at a later date. I just feel blessed to be part of the process.

PROGRAM A POSITIVE PERSPECTIVE

Being positive is a point of view, a perspective that you consciously and subconsciously may subscribe to. But you have to really want it—consciously as well as subconsciously. Maintaining a positive outlook does, as the demonstration for the Health Information Managers may have indicated to you, keep you strong physically, mentally, emotionally and spiritually. Perhaps you have heard that optimists may live longer. Even scientific research supports that happiness keeps healthy people healthy. Happiness may not prolong life, but it helps you to better cope with your stresses. Reacting in a more positive way to your stressors can keep your immune system from being overworked. That means you support a stronger immune system and are better equipped to stay healthy. Perhaps the key issue then is keeping a positive frame of mind that helps you defuse the very unhealthy effects of stress. The faster and more often we can stop ourselves from having a *fight or flight* stress reaction, the better for our health on all levels. Does this sound logical to you too? This is where hypnosis brings critical help.

You actually can reprogram your subconscious mind by downloading all the directions necessary for having a positive perspective on things. You really can choose to be an optimist and live your life with a positive attitude. Positive thoughts manifest Positive Energy. Positive Energy and positive thinking are contagious just as Negative Energy can be contagious. You also have the ability to program your attitude of being in the state of happiness. Why search for happiness? You simply manifest it in your mind and accept it as your reality. Happiness is a choice that is yours every day; just accept it as yours. Allow your thoughts to use your happiness as your home base. Regardless of everything happening around you, you can program yourself to enjoy being in a state of happiness daily. If you find yourself avoiding this choice of happiness, seek out and delete the Faulty Subconscious Programs that are stopping you.

SURROUND YOURSELF WITH POSITIVE PEOPLE

You may recall how you feel when you are with negative people who draw you into their negativity. Remember feeling pulled down by that negative thinking? It does not feel good. Actually it can affect you physically in a negative way, really draining your energy. That was another idea the HIMA demonstration clarified. Recall when our volunteer Susan physically responded with losing muscle strength due to receiving the audience's negative thoughts? The moral of the lesson is to surround yourself with others who are very positive, and reduce your exposure as much as possible to people who are negative. To a large degree you can be selective regarding friends, acquaintances, people you hire and what job you select. However, you do not always have the option to surround yourself only with positive people. Sometimes you are left with no other alternative but to deal with negative people. They may be your relatives, your colleagues or supervisors and you may not have the option to walk away. But you still have the option to limit the amount of time you are exposed to them. It is particularly important to keep a positive outlook and refuse to permit their negative thoughts to stay with you. Again, keeping a very strong, self-empowering, positive view is essential. Of course, hypnosis is invaluable here too.

REACTIONS TO <u>POSITIVE</u> PEOPLE

Take a moment now and think about the positive people in your life. They may have any of the following characteristics: They are the ones who make you feel so comfortable, are so supportive and non-judgmental. You can be honest with them and trust them. They have compassion and are empathic. They see you as an equal even though you are younger or less well off, or less beautiful or less handsome, or less successful or whatever. Perhaps they keep you laughing too. You just feel you can be yourself around them. I will stop for a moment while you sense the perceptions you experience when you are around people like these.

REACTIONS TO <u>NEGATIVE</u> PEOPLE

Now take a moment and think about the people who send you Negative Energy. They may have any of the following characteristics: These people may be very critical, never happy with what they have for they never have enough. They may frequently take advantage of your kindness and depend on you rather than take care of themselves. They may lay guilt and blame upon you to manipulate you into taking care of their needs. You may suspect them of talking badly about you behind your back even though they pretend to be your friend or caring relative. They are far too competitive and enjoy making themselves feel superior. You may feel like you are walking on eggshells around these people. Take another moment now and allow yourself to safely sense the perceptions you experience when you are around people like this.

THE COMPARISON TEST

Now how would you compare how your body and emotions responded to each category? What physical reactions did you experience with each? Most probably your body tensed or your heart rate may have increased slightly just thinking about the negative people. Maybe it was another type of reaction. Most likely it was not very pleasant. Now how did you react to the positive people? Most probably you smiled? Most probably your heart felt warmed and comforted? Maybe you felt your muscles relax? These descriptions are typical reactions to negative and positive stimuli which these different folks represent for you.

WHAT DO YOU SEE IN THE MIRROR?

Ask yourself what negativity you may be projecting that the negative people may be reflecting back at you. What gift, that is, what understanding of an aspect of yourself does the negative person offer to you? Often we are most disturbed by a characteristic in others that is within ourselves that we dislike and keep hidden in our shadow, the uncomplimentary side of our personality. It may be that this negative person is stirring up one of your negative characteristics or something about yourself that you dislike. Perhaps by their bringing it into your awareness, you may acknowledge your ownership of the characteristic. Your goal then might be to feel, think and behave without that negative aspect.

BUBBLE VISUALIZATION FOR DISTANCING NEGATIVITY

The *Bubble Visualization* may be used in Reprogramming Self-hypnosis as a technique that can help you send away the negative influences of negative people. Read these instructions through and then follow on your own step by step:

You begin by closing your eyes for a moment and imagining the negative person standing alone inside a giant plastic bubble. The person is completely sealed within this bubble. It is impossible for his/her voice to be heard. Now visualize this bubble lifting off the ground with the person enclosed. It is going higher and higher up into the sky. As the bubble travels further and further away, the bubble, this person, and this person's influence are getting smaller and smaller. They are getting even smaller and smaller, so very small and smaller. Soon they are just a tiny speck in the sky. Now the person is out of sight, quite non-threatening and far removed from your perceptions. Feel the immense relief. Feel the relaxation as the person is removed from your view and is out of your body's energy field.

Perhaps you have heard the saying, *out of sight, out of mind?* It has some truth to it. It is within you and your mind's power to keep negative people out of your thoughts and place them outside of your mind.

THE CLOUD EXPRESS

Another visualization to release specific, painful emotions imagines a gigantic cloud that is waiting in front of you to receive your negative emotions, thoughts and experiences. Push out into the cloud your negative feelings, thoughts and associations carrying painful memories. When you have emptied yourself of all the negativity, send the cloud up to the sun. When the cloud gets close to the sun's atmosphere, the cloud explodes leaving all the negativity and Negative Energy trapped within the sun's proximity. There the negativity is transformed into Positive Energy by the sun's magnificent healing light. You feel free and relieved. You then accept the sun's healing Positive Energy symbolized by colored lights that fill you up with everything positive that is for your Highest Good. Allow the positive lights to conduct whatever healing is necessary for your Highest Good in that moment. Furthermore, the effect of these healing lights is cumulative. Thus, every time you accept more Positive Energy, healing lights during your hypnosis session, you are strengthened, supported and motivated for your Highest Good.

SOME ARE JUST TOO TOXIC

You can decide to gather the positive people in your life around you and let go of the negative ones if at all possible. If someone frequently creates a negative response in your Mind/Body/ Spirit, it is time to consider detaching from that person's effect in your life. If conditions permit and it is at all possible, you might first let the person know how you are feeling and what it is they do that is making you feel badly. Allow them the opportunity to be considerate of your feelings. You might allow them to tell you how you may be more sensitive to their feelings. If you are unable to resolve these issues, that person is probably too toxic to keep near you at the present time. It is up to you how near to these kinds of people you can afford to stay. After all, you are the person most in charge of nurturing and taking care of you. If you are unable to release the toxic person from your life, consider establishing safeguard limits of influence and clearly communicate your boundaries. You may insist that your boundaries are respected. It is your right to do so. Remember you are your own best friend.

SHEILA'S LESSON FOR YOU

Speaking of the influence of toxic people, this reminds me of Sheila's story. Sheila was sick with diabetes and had a foot wound that would not heal. She had tried everything to heal her foot such as medicines, water therapy, special bandages and specially designed medical boots. Sorrowfully nothing had worked. Her brother, who had been a client of mine, called me on a Friday night and was desperate for me to see his sister. The medicines were not working. Now as a last resort the doctors planned to amputate her foot on Monday. After being granted special permission from her doctors, I went to see Sheila in the hospital the next day. She had agreed to a hypnosis session at her bedside. We found that Sheila's subconscious had set up a roadblock in her healing. Sheila was seething with anger at her doctor's associate who she had felt was not taking her complaints seriously. According to Sheila this doctor doubted her foot was worsening. Anger festered in her subconscious and kept her foot festering as well and unable to heal. Her subconscious had also heard Sheila repeat in anger that her foot was not healing. Remember that whatever you say, think, or believe, when it is attached to very strong emotions, is communicated directly to your Suggestible Subconscious and may be accepted as your reality.

During the session I guided Sheila to reverse the mindset and instead believe her foot was now healing. She also released the anger toward her doctor's associate and replaced it with complete forgiveness. Before the scheduled amputation on Monday, the doctors began to see some signs of healing and postponed the surgery. Sheila remained in the hospital as her doctors supervised her recovery now that her subconscious had cleared the way. She did in fact make a good recovery and averted the amputation. I saw her one more time at her home while she was recuperating nicely.

About three years later, Sheila's brother called regarding another matter and I inquired about Sheila. Sadly, Sheila had passed away. I learned that Sheila had a very demanding spouse who was emotionally abusive and bombarded her with constant negativity in her home situation. While hypnosis had self-empowered Sheila to allow her foot to heal, she was never able to take control of the external pressures at home that daily tormented her. Sheila's tragic story reminds us is that maintaining one's positive attitude and Positive Energy is really a two step process. First, you work on yourself. Second, you work to protect your positive self from outside negative influences — people, places and things that are just as threatening and potent. In both steps, you can effectively use hypnosis and reprogramming to overcome negativity. But it takes consistent practice and dedication to do so. This case confirms why Reprogramming Hypnosis best serves you as an ongoing process, part of your lifestyle. Euphemistically speaking, stuff happens and we need to address it on a continuous basis.

THE "COINCIDENTAL" BIRTH

One possible way for you to surround yourself with very positive, nurturing people is to intentionally create such a group. This came about for me *coincidentally.* I offer my experience and my hope that you may be able to join or create such a group on your own. Ever since the book *The Celestine Prophesies* by James Redfield became popular, many people became convinced that there is no such thing as a coincidence. Rather coincidences are reminders that God (or your Higher Power) is still involved in your universe. It was one of those coincidences that began for me over seventeen years ago when one of my new friends confided that people did not understand or accept her as an intuitive, spiritual person. She was highly intuitive but could not discuss it with anyone in our area because she felt she would be ostracized. I suggested that I gather a group of my friends together to whom she could relate. While I had a diverse group of friends, many who had not even met each other before this meeting, I knew they were open-minded. They all had a willingness to go beneath the superficial layers of daily living to reach into very meaningful discussion.

Thus, our group began one night with ten of my women friends. It was spontaneous combustion. We electrified each other with our excitement that we had found a forum where we could talk about our thoughts, questions, philosophies and share with other kind souls without fear of being judged. Our personal growth and spiritual development group, later named *Soul Sisters*, was born instantly because everyone at the first meeting refused to allow it to stop.

TREASURED TIMES

I asked one of the original members to write something about our Soul Sisters so I could explain it to others interested in starting their own group. Joyce Lantzman summed it up well:

I have been fortunate enough to be part of this group from its beginning. You may wonder what would keep a person involved in monthly meetings for such a long time. Simply, it is the invaluable experience of being with people who share a common goal — nurturing each other to reach our highest potential, personally and spiritually, in an authentic environment.

A SAFE HAVEN

To my delight I have discovered that others have found this type of group to be most beneficial and have already written about it. Belleruth Naparstek is one such writer. Another example of a synchronicity is that my husband had worked with Belleruth's late husband, Art, a kind and considerate man who personally gifted me one of Belleruth's books. It promoted support groups like Soul Sisters as especially meaningful for those upon a spiritual path. I absolutely agree. Our group provided a safe haven for our thoughts and personal discoveries. Personally, I found each member of our group had a little different take on the issues that we discussed so we each contributed something unique and interesting. Each woman had her own style. No one was allowed to dominate. We insisted upon total confidentiality. Soon we created a format of organizing our hour and a half to two-hour meetings on Sunday nights. We had time to share, reflect and if requested, receive feedback. We had an educational segment when we shared a book, an audio, an essay, a meditation exercise or a guest speaker. There also were times that we opened meetings up to our spouses or interested friends.

At the end of each meeting, we held hands or put our arms around each others' shoulders while standing in a circle. One person led us as we envisioned our projected positive light energy encircling each of us. Then we imagined sending it out to the next person on our left while simultaneously accepting the Positive Energy from the person on our right. We would imagine the circling of the Positive Energy speeding up incredibly at which time again, using our imaginations, we would throw the white light energy into the middle of the circle. Next we would say out loud names of people who needed healing on any or all levels. Putting names into the healing circle gave each of us a sense of doing something positive for those who were in need. When I would tell acquaintances, friends or relatives who were ill that I was putting their names into my healing circle at the Soul Sisters' meeting, they were deeply grateful.

I will always be incredibly appreciative and indebted to my Soul Sisters for helping me feel so validated, for helping me gain greater self-confidence and achieve a heightened awareness of who I truly am. As an aside, there actually has been scientific validation for the positive effects on our well-being resulting from such social groups. Check out the article listed in the bibliography, *Happiness Is Infectious in Network of Friends: Collective — Not Just Individual — Phenomenon.*

STICKS AND STONES AND WORDS CAN REALLY HURT ME

When speaking about the importance of being positive, remember the power of the spoken and silently chosen words. Recall the old saying, *Sticks and Stones will break my bones, but words can never hurt me!* WRONG!! Read the article, *Humiliation is Harmful* in Appendix One, for more discussion on this topic. Indeed, our words are immeasurably powerful. Already through the previous Muscle Testing discussion in this chapter, you can appreciate that thoughts have power to affect your muscle strength. Furthermore, when the thoughts are negative, the words may throw your energy balance off at least temporarily. The cumulative effect of your thoughts could alter a temporary effect into a permanent one. Words can create a stress reaction in another person such as has been referenced earlier with the brother and the baseball catcher mistakes. Also words can be heard and misinterpreted by your subconscious to your detriment. So if you are talking consistently in a repetitive manner with strong feeling about someone else and saying something like: *That guy is a pain in the neck* or *He is a pain in my behind*, guess who may well get those pains in those specific places? Yes, you may get them thanks to the generalized, literal and sometimes faulty, interpretation by your subconscious!

NEGATIVE WORDS EQUAL NEGATIVE ENERGY

In terms of energy, one theory says that when you say something negative about another person, your negative words are forms of Negative Energy that are received by that person subconsciously. Your words reinforce and strengthen that other person's negativity. You are in effect making that person without their awareness, subconsciously even more negative. Besides, with your negative affirmations you are certainly reinforcing that person as even more negative to you! If someone is acting like a jerk and you somehow keep thinking/saying it is so, remember you may be subconsciously encouraging that person to act like a jerk more often.

Words and thoughts are energy forms. They travel instantly like emails can travel, covering the globe and beyond. Subsequently what negative words you say about that person subconsciously feed his/her tendency for more jerk-like behaviors. So what is the solution? See the best in people and support that good part with your positive thoughts. Take the view that they are the way they are only because of their experiences or personality tendencies. You can bet that the difficult person in your life has suffered his/her own traumas and assaults to self-esteem regardless of how successful, wealthy, handsome or talented the person appears to be. Consider remaining neutral, compassionate and non-judgmental about people. Yet, clearly reject their unacceptable behaviors and unacceptable values. Keep the attitude that they are just being who they are in their current human development and for the moment, they are unable to change. They are doing the best they can under their circumstances. This is especially important when you are in hypnosis and referring to other people. Focus on positive words or else neutral words to describe negative people and negative events.

YOU ARE AN ENERGY STOREHOUSE

Negative Energy can be stored within a person's Mind/Body/ Spirit even after the person believes he/she has worked through a specific issue at an earlier time. Candace Pert, PhD, a neuroscientist and formerly a research professor in the Dept. of Physiology and Biophysics at Georgetown University Medical Center, has done research on issues related to this. She is perhaps best known for her discovery of the opiate receptors in the brain and how our minds and feelings influence health and well-being. Candace Pert wrote *Your Body is Your Subconscious Mind* published by Sounds True. *Your Body is Your Subconscious Mind* explains that the mind is not just in the brain; it is also in every muscle, organ, gland, every cell in the body and it is signaling, sending messages back and forth. Each cell in effect has a brain and thus, has a memory also. This corresponds with my findings related to when clients are in hypnosis speaking to their different body parts and gain subconscious information held in their Cellular Memory.

SONDRA'S STORY OF CELLULAR MEMORY

Sondra, age thirty-three, had been a tap dancer as a young child and teen. She planned to become a professional dancer until unfortunately she fell during an audition. She injured her ankle. Humiliated, she never returned to dancing. During a hypnosis technique to remove negativity, Sondra found a large, negative spot on her ankle. I instructed Sondra to address her ankle as she would a person and ask her ankle why the negativity was there. Sondra heard her ankle's response intuitively, *I am here to remind you of the pain and embarrassment of the moment when you failed as a dancer.* After we finished a resolution regarding that trauma, we asked the negativity to leave Sondra's ankle and return with the angels to be eternally in God's light and love. This imagery was chosen because of Sondra's belief in God and God's angels. According to Sondra, the negativity agreed to leave. After the session, Sondra felt much better and her ankle was not as sore or tender as before. When she thought about that audition, she remembered it but did not feel the humiliation that had been associated with that fall. Her trauma was transformed into a neutral memory. Within days the soreness that had been characteristic of that ankle was completely gone.

SPENCER'S STORY OF A PAINFUL REMINDER

Spencer, age twenty-five, had a different kind of experience that may enlighten you further regarding how the Mind/Body/Spirit works. Spencer had a severe pain in his left side. For about two years, doctors had tried but failed to find any cause of the pain. The pain refused to respond to medicines. Spencer actually came for help for smoking cessation. During the hypnotic *Negativity Cleansing Technique,* Spencer found a big gray spot on his side where his pain was located. He spoke to the spot as if it were a person and inquired as to why it was there. The answer that popped into his mind was that it was there to remind him to stop abusing his body with alcohol. In addition to cigarette smoking, he also overindulged with alcohol. Spencer acknowledged his body's wisdom and pledged to stop those behaviors. After pledging to do so, Spencer confirmed that the gray area had left. Once back to his conscious state, he was astonished that the terrible pain in his side had disappeared. Even years later Spencer verified that the pain had never returned.

NEEDED: ONE POSITIVE PHILOSOPHY

In Appendix Two, you will find three Hypnotic Guided Imagery (with Affirmations) Audio Scripts revised from the original Series, Reprogram Your Subconscious. Important revisions to the scripts have improved upon the original version. Within each script please note that the hypnotic guided imagery consistently offers a form of Negative Energy cleansing since harboring negative emotions and negative thought forms is detrimental to your Mind/Body/Spirit. It represents your holding on to the negative effects of stress.

In maintaining a positive attitude, positive perspective, you are advised to have a positive philosophy consistently supporting you. If you are searching for a philosophy, one of the most powerful spiritual philosophies I have encountered is the one that believes everything is happening as it should. In other words, everything that is happening is meant to happen and it has special meaning for you. We learn from all experiences, good and bad. This philosophy eliminates tremendous worry and concern about what may happen to you. You are in the hands of God or whatever Higher Power you believe in. No matter what, you are not alone. You are always connected. It is okay to ask for help at any moment. It is also okay to ask as many times as you need because God (or your Higher Power) does not run out of favors.

If this philosophy is acceptable to you, you will benefit from developing a deep faith to sustain this philosophy. The rewards are immense. You simply release all need to worry anymore. The result is a consistently peaceful state of mind. It also focuses your attention on each present moment as it is unfolding. Additionally a very important component of your positive philosophy recognizes the important value of giving and receiving love perhaps as one of your highest purposes for being here. In the bestselling book, *Tuesdays with Morrie,* by Mitch Albom, Morrie communicated this philosophy beautifully even through his most challenging time struggling with a fatal disease. At the end of his life he said that love is what all of life is about. Certainly that does make sense. Einstein has proven that it is impossible to destroy energy. Love is eternal. Everything else about you is transitory except for your energy, your Spirit and the love that you have given to others as well as the love that you have received from others. Love is the epitome of Positive Energy. Do you practice this priority of both giving and receiving love? Both are equally necessary for your personal and spiritual growth as well as for your Mind/Body/Spirit well-being.

YOUR LIFE PHILOSOPHY IS YOUR BLUEPRINT

Now this is just one philosophy. You may have a different, positive one and that is, of course, wonderful. What is important is that you do have a philosophy that guides your choices and helps you consistently lead the life you truly want to have. This will answer the provocative question: *You may be doing things right, but are you doing the right things? This emphasizes the significant part of knowing what to program for your subconscious computer so the end result is you are congruent with who you really want and are proud to be.*

Science supports the fact that spirituality helps people to live longer and more happily. In an article in *AARP* magazine November/December 2008, p. 32, psychiatrist Dr. Harold G. Koenig, professor of psychiatry and behavioral sciences at Duke University Medical Center who studied this issue extensively, made some impressive observations. He described people who believe their lives are part of a Higher Power's plan and who follow the guidelines created by their Higher Power, as those people who reap many health benefits. They actually have stronger immune systems, lower risks of major illnesses such as heart attacks and cancer, plus they heal faster from illness and actually live longer. In the same article, Deepak Chopra, MD, a well-known spiritual leader, summarily concluded that a sense of purpose provides a sense of living your destiny that brings you the joy of peaceful contentment and happiness.

YOUR LIFE AS A JIGSAW PUZZLE

As an exercise to continue in this line of thought, review your life thus far and see if you can conceive of your life as a big picture and all the contents of your life as pieces of a jigsaw puzzle creating that big picture. How did you get to where you are today? Remember the coincidences in your life that introduced you to the people, places or things that made a difference in directing your life? Remember the times when what you thought was an awful stroke of bad luck turned out to make other positive things possible? Remember the synchronicities? What choices made the most differences to get you where you are now? What did you learn from those pivotal life choices? What is your life's dream? What have you been focusing upon? How much attention do you pay to each person who enters your life even if it is a brief encounter? Which people have really mattered to you in a positive way? What changes do you believe are necessary to put the way you live your life each day into sync with your philosophy of life?

ONE ZAP FOR POSITIVE CHANGE

I want to share with you an exceptionally positive day I spent in New York City when I was so in the moment. After a successful meeting with my client, I found a cab to return to the bus terminal and start my travel back to New Jersey. To my surprise, I had the most fascinating discussion about spirituality with my cab driver. Ironically, I had this same cab driver just a few days earlier when I had visited a client. Can you imagine the odds of getting the same cab driver in New York City? But remember this was a magical day. Anyway, I had to exit the cab in a rush as my cab and I were stopping traffic. But first I had to retrieve my briefcase from the backseat. Behind us was a huge truck and the impatient truck driver started honking his horn as if he were sitting on it. Once my briefcase was in hand, I flung the taxi door shut and turned to look up at the truck driver who was obviously upset about waiting an extra minute. I automatically responded with my smile and waved to him with a sincere, *Have a nice day!* The man froze in disbelief. He was speechless. He looked at me as if something in his world just did not compute. His face softened and not a word did the man utter, certainly no typical expletives. Somehow he had been stopped in his tracks, transformed in that split second. He was calm and returned my smile. I imagined he was probably dazed by the zap of kindness. Talk about the power of Positive Energy!

NOW IT IS YOUR TURN

You may want to experiment with this realizing that you also have that power to share your Positive Energy with others. Next time you are waiting in a checkout line at the grocery store and someone lets you know how impatient they are getting, send them a blast of Positive Energy with your smile or a Positive Energy zap with your thoughts. Let them subconsciously understand that you recognize their pain. Experiment when you are sitting in traffic. Do something positive instead of attacking your horn or swearing. Consider these moments reflective moments. Your mind is a powerful, Positive Energy transmitter. Really, your positive thought energy can be received subconsciously. Take advantage of those moments when all you can do is use your mind. It is a gift of time, honest. Imagine what positive things you can do with it.

BE YOUR OWN GOAL KEEPER

One way to focus daily on positive ways of thinking is to repeat affirmations in your mind. Besides hearing and/or thinking about the affirmations when you are in hypnosis, you will find it reinforcing to read the affirmations out loud as well silently to yourself during your regular waking hours. They help you focus on what you believe and want to attract for yourself. Many of the following examples of affirmations are included in our guided hypnotic imagery scripts in Appendix Two. Use them as a guide for creating your own.

AFFIRMATIONS:

- I appreciate and accept with love every part of my entire being, my mind, body and Spirit. I love and accept myself totally and unconditionally.

- I remain aware of each present moment. Life flows easily for me as I experience joy in here and now. All is going well.

- I release all that is outside of my Highest Good. I focus on the positives in my life and celebrate them daily.

- I have released all the negativity from my past. I consider my past only as my guide-post. I live in the present moment experiencing happiness.

- I refuse to take personally anything another person may think, say or do. I acknowledge that other people's reactions are based in their own issues.

- I am doing the best I can under my circumstances. I accept that all people are doing the best they can do under their circumstances.

- I am just as precious as everyone else. No one is better than I am and no one is worse than I am. We are all equals. We are all of the same energy.

- I am self-empowered. I have choices that allow me the control I have over my life. I am powerful in many ways.

- I am safe. It is safe to be me. It is safe to love and be loved. It is safe to lead my life in a fulfilling way.

- It is safe to be on my own and be my own unique person. I am capable and competent.

- I am grateful for all my blessings.

- I am continuously attracting an abundance of good things. I have all I need.

REFLECT ON YOUR PERSONAL AFFIRMATIONS

Take this time now to reflect on other personal affirmations you have been using or those you would like to follow. Also browse through affirmations in Appendix Two for possible affirmations you would like to adopt. Be sure to review the affirmations/ hypnotic suggestions that appear at the top of your journal pages at the end of this book.

CHAPTER 7

GET READY, GET SET, GO!

TO ENSURE YOUR REPROGRAMMING SUCCESS NOW AND BEYOND

The keys to your success are now in your hands. Yes, you have the keys and have opened the door to the kingdom of your subconscious mind. You are well on your way towards attaining your goals. You have the information, the tools for reprogramming your subconscious using Reprogramming Self-hypnosis. You possess the understanding of how to use hypnosis to get what you really want. Yet, the most challenging last leg of your journey resides within you — in your will, your persistence, your determination, your perseverance, and your dedication. Do it because YOU WANT IT enthusiastically. Do it because you want to believe in yourself with all your heart, Mind/Body/Spirit and believe: YES, I CAN DO IT! I AM DOING IT! Remember you have your powerful subconscious on your side. In addition you have the opportunity to use Reprogramming Self-hypnosis every day to encourage and support your determination. You also can take advantage of the Glassner Associates Group Hypnosis Meetings online that will support your Reprogramming Self-hypnosis efforts. Every day congratulate yourself. You are taking responsibility for your Mind/Body/ Spirit nurturing and growth.

DOWNLOAD FOR YOUR SUCCESS

One:

Practice patience and perseverance. Although Reprogramming Hypnosis and Reprogramming Self-hypnosis may bring positive results relatively quickly, for some people, it may take considerably longer. Keep in mind that your Faulty Subconscious Programs may have been initiated a long time ago. Consequently, they may require more time for you to adjust comfortably to thinking, believing and behaving differently. Your subconscious may need more time to integrate the new information while letting go of the old habitual ways of thinking, believing, feeling and behaving. Meanwhile, have you heard of the saying, *Fake it until you make it?* Translated into hypnosis terms this means continue to believe that your hypnosis suggestions are working even if you have to pretend it to be so. Keep persevering and experiment with new approaches as need be.

At the first sign of a delay in the manifestation of your hypnosis suggestions, it is possible you may feel discouraged. This is a normal reaction. Still it is something that your strong emotions of determination will help you to squelch. Sometimes people have given up quickly and declared themselves a failure. That reaction could come from a subconsciously held belief that is one that you can reprogram. So recognize that response and avoid that pitfall on your way to success. As you know, you only fail when you give up. Instead look for the subconscious reasons behind the delay. Believe with great happiness that your hypnosis suggestions are working. Your subconscious will agree with you and make them work! What you believe and feel with strong emotions, after deleting contradictory Faulty Subconscious Programs to your belief, become your reality.

Psychiatrist Judith Davis supports this concept and brings another interesting perspective. She asserts in her book, *Emotional Comfort, The Gift of Your Inner Guide,* that your subconscious is uncomfortable with the disparity between what is your actual current reality and what you think/feel/believe/ say is your reality. Since your subconscious is unable to reconcile those two conflicting views of reality, it feels compelled to create a comfortable harmony by generating the specifics that you claim are your reality. Yes, your subconscious then makes the changes that are necessary for you to actualize your suggestions. Keep thanking your subconscious for already having produced what you requested through your suggestions. Imagine the establishment of all your suggestions with all the most vivid details coupled with your feelings of heightened gratitude as well as happiness. After all, your subconscious wants to please you and provide you with what will make you even happier.

Two:
Record in your journal all the changes large and small that you are experiencing as a result of planting your Reprogramming Self-hypnosis suggestions. The more you validate that your hypnosis is working, the more it works. Ask the positive, supportive people close to you for their feedback regarding their observations of your positive changes. Often they can discern more accurately the fine nuances of what you may be unable to observe about yourself because the changes seem so natural. One client had confessed to me that she observed no new changes since her hypnosis session a week before. Ironically, earlier in the day her friend and co-worker who had referred her to me, had just told me how happy he was that his friend was saying *good morning* to him when she arrived at work — something she never did before.

Three:
Be sure to sprinkle some easy-to-manifest suggestions along with the more challenging ones so you can build upon your successes right away. Begin with baby steps. Success breeds more success. Make it easy to succeed.

Four:
Continue daily Reprogramming Self-hypnosis practice for thirty to sixty days. Consider extending this daily practice ritual to six months

to ensure its permanent addition to your lifestyle. Continue to use the word *great* or another favorite key word to keep reminding your subconscious to maintain your positive changes permanently. Your key word then automatically reinforces all of your positive suggestions.

Another way to reinforce your subconscious compliance is to tell yourself during your self-hypnosis that every time you read your Reprogramming Self-hypnosis script, and/or when you listen to *Relax, Release and Dream On*, it reinforces all of the suggestions you have requested to be downloaded into your subconscious. There is evidence that suggests that whatever you study right before sleep is reinforced even stronger when you are sleeping. So whenever possible listen to your hypnotic guided imagery audio just before bedtime and again just as you are going to sleep at night.

Five:
Avoid sharing your hypnosis experiences with detractors or even bringing up the subject of hypnosis with anyone who may be other than definitely positive and supportive of you and the hypnosis process. Share your excitement with those people who are truly supportive of you and the hypnosis process. Unfortunately there are many people who have Faulty Subconscious Programs that make them unable to even imagine hypnosis being successful for you. You need to proceed with total belief and conviction that your hypnosis is working. If someone makes you question your using hypnosis, he or she could plant the sabotaging seeds of doubt. This may shock you so that you accept their strong disbelief. I have seen it happen unintentionally. So simply avoid telling those potential disbelievers and potential saboteurs. Instead, share your excitement with your positive enthusiastic supporters. They will be a wonderful support system for you. If negative people were to attempt to pressure you to share information you would rather not share, simply tell them to respect your need for privacy. You need to please and protect

yourself first, especially now. Your needs in this situation are more important than others' need to know your personal business.

Six:

Strategize, target and then remove any resistances obstructing the total acceptance of your hypnosis suggestions. Resistances that persist indicate the presence of at least one contradictory Faulty Subconscious Program that is still protecting faulty mindsets, erroneous belief systems, invalid associations or any combination thereof. Consequently, you will need to focus on other underlying issues that are preventing your progress and then proceed to delete them. Reread the sections in Chapter Three and Chapter Four that explain how to avoid resistances and how to overcome them. More ideas to help you are below:

STRATEGIES FOR RESISTANCES

IF IT RESISTS, PERSIST

If after two weeks of practicing your hypnosis, there are no signs of even slight changes, conduct an investigation during your Reprogramming Self-hypnosis and query your subconscious parts responsible for delaying the enactment of any of your suggestions. Ask yourself if all is proceeding well. You might ask your subconscious if it just needs additional time in order to process your requests. You may receive your answers in symbols, images, memories, sounds, feelings and/or intuitive knowing. Do your best to trace what these answers mean to you. Ask for a specific sign to let you know your subconscious is working on your request. For instance, you may direct your subconscious to have you hum a few bars of a happy tune or whistle a tune for a few seconds within an hour after you awaken from your regular sleep time. When you find yourself happily humming or whistling, this would indicate that all is going well with your subconscious processing your hypnosis suggestions.

YOUR BODY REVEALS THE TRUTH

You might use an exercise used by *shamans*, who are traditional medicine men, to uncover your subconscious reactions to the accuracy of specific thoughts or spoken statements. First establish how your body reacts when you close your eyes and think of something simple that you absolutely love, like a favorite flower or animal. Note how these positive feelings physically are affecting you. Then distract yourself for a minute or two. Next, focus on something simple that is negative for you like an unappealing insect or a food you really dislike. Note how your body physically responds to these negative feelings. Next distract yourself again. Then you are ready to test your body's reactions to statements. For instance, you might make a declarative statement like, *I am hooked on sweets because I still have an emotional association with sweets.* If that statement produces a similar feeling like you had for something you loved, this feeling in your body indicates that the statement is true subconsciously. In contrast, if you respond with a feeling like you had when thinking of the negative subject, your statement subconsciously resonates as not true for you.

POINT TO THE TRUTH

Another method of discovering your Inner Truth while practicing self-hypnosis is to utilize your body's Ideomotor Responses. One common Ideomotor Response technique uses three of your fingers. Each finger signifies a possible answer to the question that you pose. So whenever the finger (predetermined to mean *yes* or *no* or *unclear*), lifts up on its own, you have the answer to your question. Typically you would select an index finger on one hand to represent *yes*, the index finger on the other hand to represent *no* and the pinky finger on one hand to mean *unclear* at this time. Verify each statement with Ideomotor Responses while in self-hypnosis that: one, *I feel that I am worthy* (test your response after each statement); two, *I feel that I deserve good things*; and three, *I feel that I am sufficiently safe*. Another statement you could make while in hypnosis and using the Ideomotor Response is: four, *The changes I have requested are for my Highest Good*. Sometimes your path is being blocked for a truly benevolent reason. Remember the intention of your subconscious basically is to protect and/or please you. Sometimes if it is blocking you, it does have your best interests at heart.

NIX NEGATIVE SELF-FULFILLING PROPHESIES

Oftentimes people with difficult issues come to the conclusion that no matter how hard they have tried to resolve their issues, they have failed and it is hopeless. Sometimes past failures initiate their subconscious belief that becomes a *self-fulfilling prophesy* that says: *Nothing I can ever do will help me to resolve my issues. I am doomed to failure.* If this is your case, you need to delete that faulty mindset before downloading the new Reprogramming Self-hypnosis suggestions. Another mindset that causes self-sabotage and needs to be eliminated is: *Since I know that I will fail, when I fail, I will not be disappointed or hurt. I knew it was coming. No surprise.* Your subconscious may be protecting you from further painful disappointment by anticipating and setting you up for failure. If that is your situation, it means you are being protected from disappointment and the pain that it brings. Fortunately this is a subconscious mindset that you can eliminate through Reprogramming Self-hypnosis suggestions. Focus on High Self-esteem suggestions first. Yes, it is possible to delete such subconsciously programmed self-fulfilling prophesies.

PEELING THE ONION

You need to consider the possibility of having resistant, underlying issues that need to be addressed before you can move forward to your goal. That is illustrated by eight coworkers who came for a group hypnosis session for smoking cessation. After the first hypnosis session lasting two and a half hours, one man exited the building and threw his cigarettes in the garbage and was a non-smoker from that moment on. Another four participants dabbled with one or two cigarettes for a few days and then, by the end of the first week, automatically and effortlessly completely stopped smoking cigarettes.

However the remaining three co-workers were still actively smoking at the end of the first week even though they had reduced the number of cigarettes considerably. So I initiated a private phone hypnosis session for each of the three smokers. As a result it became clear that each of the remaining smokers had specific issues previously unknown to them that were creating resistances to their smoking cessation suggestions. During the phone hypnosis session we addressed the new stress issues. Then after another week, two of these smokers had quit smoking entirely. That left one who was still actively a smoker. During a second phone hypnosis session for this person, it surfaced that she had yet another mind-set that made it unsafe for her to stop smoking. Multi-layers of blocking issues are possible. You could compare it to peeling that onion. Finally after the third hypnosis session, she deleted her last obstacle to stopping the awful cigarette habit. So after another week, this last smoker, the last of the original eight coworkers, stopped smoking. Nonetheless, be aware that although it is fairly common to have resistances, not everyone experiences them. Approach your hypnosis with a positive attitude that one way or another, hypnosis is a tool that gets you what you want.

CHECK FOR SMOKESCREENS

Always check your most obvious presenting issue for any submerged positive gains it may be providing you. Those positive gains may actually be related to another issue that really is your primary issue. Thus, what seems to be a resistant issue for you could be your subconscious in reality creating a smokescreen (represented on the surface by the presenting issue) that diverts your attention away from your primary issue. The presenting issue resists change in order to protect and sustain the underlying primary issue that is supplying you with strong benefits. We have already discussed how this played out for Diana, the interior designer, mentioned in Chapter Six. Another example of a smokescreen occurs when people who are lonely and feeling abandoned develop an illness that resists any remediation. As a result others, including their doctors, offer them sympathy and attention. Having this issue of poor health subsequently attracts feel-good attention. This positive payoff of attention then may subconsciously stop the ill people from improving their health. Why? Because when their ill-health issue ends, so ends the strong benefit, the feel-good attention that assuages their loneliness and abandonment feelings, the primary root issue. Of course if you have a smokescreen, it almost always resides outside your conscious awareness. Fortunately you can search your subconscious and use Reprogramming Self-hypnosis suggestions to dismiss the smokescreen.

RESISTANCES: CAUSE, EFFECT AND FAITH

Remember we are all so individualized because of our life experiences, our physiology, our environment and our belief systems. Consequently, we all respond to the hypnosis process in varied ways. *Nevertheless, your mind works in cause and effect dimensions.* It is unlikely that things just happen in a vacuum or out of nowhere without any cause. Unfortunately it is our current human understanding that is narrow. The entire body of knowledge that we humans claim to know is clearly very limited. The body of knowledge that is presently unknown to us is of far greater proportions. And there is an entire body of knowledge so far beyond our human comprehension that we do not even know that we do not know it. To us, it does not even exist. That body of knowledge goes beyond our human comprehension; therefore, it does not even appear on our radar screen. When and if you hit a roadblock on your road to self-discoveries and are unable to comprehend the reason, that is an especially appropriate time to focus on your spiritual explanations and continue walking in faith. Look for the lessons and wisdom to be gained through your experiences. Look at the illogical roadblock as an opportunity for your spiritual side to carry you where you need to be for your Highest Good.

ALWAYS AN OPTION

After doing all you can to correct your issue by yourself, you always have the option to seek professional hypnosis services to assist you in seeking what you really want. If no one suitable for your hypnosis needs is available in your area, you may opt for telephone hypnosis or hypnosis through video conferencing. Check my website for professionals who have completed Reprogramming Hypnosis certification. I will only recommend those professionals whom I would recommend to my family members and friends. Training, experience and fees vary widely depending on the individual professional.

CONCLUDING WORDS AND A REQUEST

Words only inadequately express my feelings of happiness when I am a participant in your attainment of personal growth, spiritual development and well-being. If I have been of service to you on your life's path, I am very grateful to you. Thank you for giving me the opportunity to share my vision and my life's passion. For the time being, I have a request if you are comfortably agreeable to it. Please keep me informed through comments on my Contact page, GaleGlassner.com, of your progress, your challenges and your achievements. My office phone# also is found on my website. In essence, you will assist me in accumulating additional data supporting the substantial benefits hypnosis provides. One goal that I have had in mind for many years is to establish a hypnosis foundation. It would guarantee that those who have the greatest need for professional hypnosis services would have a financial resource through which to receive them. I know in my heart it is possible. Whatever we can imagine and keep focused on with our strong emotions, we can create! Together we can inspire others to join us, share our vision and make an incredibly positive difference in people's lives.

[Please continue reading Appendix One that reprints my published articles on hypnosis that offer additional perspectives. Also, in Appendix Two, review the newly revised and extensive scripts from my 2005 Nightingale-Conant program. The scripts will provide you with examples that will assist with writing your own material. Furthermore, you will be able to record the scripts or any part for your personal self-hypnosis use.]

APPENDIX ONE

PUBLISHED ARTICLES ON HYPNOSIS BY GALE GLASSNER TWERSKY, A.C.H.

Between 2001 and 2008, these articles appeared in the *Montclair Life and Leisure* newspaper. I wrote them to promote understanding about the nature of hypnosis and how hypnosis that is partnered with HypnoCounseling promotes Mind/Body/Spirit well-being. (revised 2010)

YOUR SILENT, INVISIBLE PARTNER

Have you ever wondered why you keep repeating the same foolish behaviors when you already have learned your lesson and know better? Think about the mistakes you make in relationships like being attracted to the same kind of partner who is verbally or physically abusive to you. Or think about your spending choices that keep you in debt when you desperately are committed to getting out of debt. Even fervent decisions to resist any desserts can evaporate from memory when you see that hot fudge sundae on the menu.

Would you feel less guilty and totally relieved to learn that the reasons you believe, feel and act the way you do, are found in your Silent, Invisible Partner? Your Silent, Invisible Partner is operating outside your awareness and making choices for you. These choices can affect your life for a very long time. In fact, often your Silent, Invisible Partner's choices may determine your thoughts, feelings and behaviors for your entire lifetime without you ever finding out the truth. Unless, that is, you find a way to reprogram your silent partner's decisions by reprogramming that part of your mind we call your *subconscious mind*. Actually, that is a simplified explanation of exactly what we do in HypnoCounseling. We help you reprogram negative thoughts, erroneous belief systems and self-sabotaging behaviors/habits that are adversely affecting your happiness and peace of mind. We help empower you to eliminate the obstacles and blockades that have stymied your good health, success in life and your sense of self-fulfillment.

As a HypnoCounselor I specialize in using hypnosis to help you specifically to address issues as they exist on your subconscious levels. That is because your subconscious mind is responsible for creating and downloading your problematic mindsets, belief systems and behaviors without your knowledge or permission. Now your subconscious did not mean to harm you. It just does not see long term consequences of its choices for you. By employing hypnosis as your tool, however, you are able to target for deletion what you have identified as other than for your Highest Good. You focus on your desired changes and reinforce them by listening to your personalized audio as well as following other techniques that reinforce your changes. HypnoCounseling is also used in conjunction with psychologists, social workers, marriage counselors and medical doctors. Massage therapists, nutritionists, life coaches, tutors, priests, ministers, rabbis and, of course, parents also partner with HypnoCounselors for very effective team efforts.

Finally, more research is revealing that hypnosis is one of your best tools for personal growth and wellness. Just scan the Internet to view recent findings. It is time for hypnosis and HypnoCounseling to be among the first places that you seek in your quest for self-knowledge and self-healing.

HYPNOSIS AND THE RIGHT BRAIN DOMINANT CHILD

You've heard of how difficult it is to put a square peg into a round hole? That comparison can explain how a child who is right brain dominant feels living in and being educated in a school environment that is more appropriate for left brain dominant or brain balanced children. Can you imagine how it feels when all the time you just think and learn differently from your peers? Imagine how it feels when your peers as well as your teachers have difficulty understanding you and vice versa?

Typically the left brain dominant children are attracted to math and science. Later they are attracted to such professions as accounting, engineering and other very concrete, logical studies. In contrast, right brain dominant children are attracted to music, drawing, drama, inventing, writing and occupations that necessitate creativity.

Many right brain dominant children are very sensitive. They have a highly developed sensitivity to nature and beauty. They may also be extremely sensitive souls whose feelings get injured easily. They accept your words into their hearts and feel them deeply. These are the children who are most adversely affected by scary movies and violent TV shows, frightening amusement park rides and listening to the news reports of tragedies.

Perhaps you can recognize this type of child as the one who is often daydreaming, easily distracted and has difficulty concentrating for long periods of time. Many of these children are categorized as ADD and ADHD as well. What you may be surprised to know is that these children can do extremely well when they use hypnosis to help them adjust to their world and to practice focused concentration for the tasks at hand.

How is that so? Well, where do you think these children go when they seem to be in outer space? Most likely they are in the altered state of Alpha or Theta rather than in the usual Beta State of Consciousness. In fact, they feel much more comfortable being in Alpha/Theta than in Beta Consciousness. Besides offering the right brain dominant children an escape from left brain activities that present either considerable boredom or overwhelmingly uncomfortable challenges, it is more natural and comfortable for the right brain dominant children to be in the Alpha and or Theta Consciousness States. Being in Alpha/Theta is very relaxing and mind expanding. It is an adventure. Alpha is one of the states you enter when you begin sleeping. Many of our greatest artists, inventors and political leaders received their inspiration when in that altered state of Alpha, Theta and Delta. In fact when your conscious mind is unable to find a solution, you often use that Alpha/Theta state to find successful solutions. You also purposefully may access your intuition while you are in the Alpha/Theta states.

But allow me to return to how hypnosis can help the right brain dominant child adjust better to demands of our left brain dominant society. Hypnosis utilizes the child's Alpha/Theta Consciousness States to present suggestions about changing attitudes, feelings and behaviors. A child thus can learn to identify when the circumstances require him/her staying anchored appropriately in the Beta state and when circumstances are best for soaring into the adventurous realms of Alpha/Theta. Actually, the ideal is to have a balanced brain, equally able to use left and right sides of one's brain power in an integrated approach to living well. The exciting news is hypnosis helps children as well as adults do just that and without changing their personalities or diminishing any of their abilities.

SURVIVING THE VERY CONTROLLING PARENT

Do you have trouble saying no? Do you put everyone else's needs ahead of your own so you are most often last? Are you afraid of hurting other people's feelings? Are you self-conscious about what other people are thinking? Do you feel lost or feel lack of control over your life? If you answered *yes* to any of these questions, you may be manifesting the effects of being raised by a very controlling parent or by another very controlling caregiver.

If you are one of those people who suffered through the effects of having a controlling parent, you probably as a result have to deal with lack of self-confidence, lack of High Self-esteem and lack of belief and trust in the good person you are. You most likely have been indoctrinated to trust everyone else more than yourself. You depend upon others rather than recognize and trust your own capabilities. You may tend to procrastinate, to be a perfectionist and you know the fine art of pleasing others. I would bet you are a delightful person but often other people take advantage of you.

And why are you so easily victimized? One answer is that since childhood you have opted (usually out of fear after having been intimidated as a child) to give up your power to a very controlling parent or caregiver. In giving up your power, you have given up your sense of self and a part of your Spirit as well. What is left may seem empty and confusing.

Now the very controlling parent most probably had good intentions of raising obedient, well-behaved children. Perhaps these folks were raised in a similar environment where their parent or parents were very strict and demanding. Maybe having high expectations was a matter of culture. Whatever the reason, the purpose of this article is to alert rather than chastise, educate rather than assess blame. Controlling parents did the best they could under their circumstances. So if you were one of these controlling parents, please avoid the negative outcome of guilt or blame. Instead, seek positive change. Give your children (even as adults) the sense that their opinions are valid and can be important too. Teach children how to make judgments and give them a chance to learn from mistakes and improve upon their judgments the next time around. Teach children that they have the right to discern their feelings and the right to acknowledge what their intuition is telling them. That way you will be encouraging your children to develop High Self-esteem and high self-empowerment while eliminating the subconscious acceptance of victimhood.

If you are a child who was raised by a controlling parent or caregiver, you may be encouraged to know that HypnoCounseling is an effective way to directly reach your subconscious levels where you may reprogram Low Self-esteem into High Self-esteem and Low Self-confidence into High Self-confidence. You can become self-empowered through hypnosis techniques and reclaim your self-worth, self-identity and happiness.

CAUTION: MOVIES AND YOUR SUBCONSCIOUS

Anytime someone says to me, *It's only a movie. What's the harm in seeing a movie?* I think of the Alfred Hitchcock movie, *Psycho*, and how it affected those who saw it and even those who did not see it but rather, merely heard about it. That movie planted such fear of being violated (brutally murdered actually) while taking a shower, that people (including people I personally know) to this day check the shower first upon entering their hotel room. These frightened folks still have thoughts that while they are taking a shower, they are vulnerable to being surprised by a murderous villain. Yes, it was only a movie. It was just actors and fake blood. But it got into our psyche, specifically into our subconscious. And that fear, regardless of all logic, span of time, or conscious efforts to remove it, remains today for many people. Even though that murder occurred in an imaginary place, Bates Motel, people subconsciously responded powerfully to that terror and brutality that lasted only minutes on the screen. Without conscious awareness, their subconscious initiated behaviors that would protect them from ever personally experiencing anything like that horrific scene. In fact, someone I know openly admits that because of that movie, she takes only baths so as to be able to hear if someone were to break in.

Now think of another violent movie example, *Jaws*. How many people were so frightened by that movie, that they even gave up swimming in the ocean for fear of sharks? If you are like me, you will know quite a few people who did. Fortunately, avoiding taking a shower and avoiding swimming in the ocean are not severe life-altering behaviors. Yet, there are movies that actually have the potential for consequences of great harm to people. But that is for another time, another article. Did everyone who saw *Psycho* and/or *Jaws* react that same way? Of course not everyone reacted in the same way. Yet, these scary movies still produced negative, life-altering effects in many, many people.

As a HypnoCounselor who has helped individuals release fears that specifically resulted from watching upsetting movies, I want you, the reader, to be aware of these possible consequences. When you see a movie and you are deeply, emotionally moved especially by fear, anger or grief, the subconscious part of your mind may spring into action, putting you into an altered state. It is where the suggestible part of your subconscious will process what you are emotionally experiencing. Subsequently, your subconscious oftentimes will initiate new mindsets, belief systems and behaviors to help you feel safer or feel better. Therefore, when you are watching a brutal movie, you unintentionally may adopt negative attitudes, fear-based mindsets and prejudices relating to who is doing the brutalizing; that is, who is seen as the *enemy*.

Important to note is that this subconscious process is completed without your awareness or permission. The final outcome reached outside your awareness is that you have downloaded fears and prejudices against the villain. These Subconscious Programs then dictate your future responses to that same villain or any people who just remind you of that villain.

Fortunately, the movie industry regulations prevent young children from viewing violent movies at the movie theaters so young children are protected to some degree. However, how many times do children gain access to watch these violent movies in their home or at the home of friends? Furthermore, we adults are not immune.

Your logical mind is bypassed when your subconscious takes over in such emotional cases and establishes a mindset in what appears to be a genuine effort on the part of your subconscious to protect or help you in some manner. While the intentions of your subconscious are always good, the outcome of those choices may be devastating to you or devastating to the recipients of your actions. The surest way to prevent this subconscious negative imprinting is to avoid seeing those kinds of violent movies, especially if you are a very empathic, sensitive type of person. Trying to convince yourself to dismiss a fear or prejudice after the fact, that is, once the negative mindset has been firmly planted in your subconscious, is like you trying to talk yourself out of having a panic attack, while you are having one. It is like you trying to talk yourself out of having diarrhea while you already are experiencing it. Therefore, consider yourself forewarned. The decision of which movies to avoid, for yourself as well as for your children is ultimately yours. The consequences of what may follow are also yours.

HYPNOSIS AND LOVE

Hypnosis and love? There is a connection. I frequently challenge my clients to focus intently on two very strong but opposite emotions at the same time. Just imagine experiencing a strong fear like the fear of dying while simultaneously feeling the strong emotion of love (romantic love or love for a parent or child). Go ahead, try it now. Can you do it? Actually, it is virtually impossible to focus on and feel the strong intensity of both at the same time. It just refuses to compute. You have to make a choice which one to focus upon and which one to let go. Hint: The strongest one stays and the weaker one is overlooked. This Valentine's Day, and in fact every day, may I make a suggestion for you, my reader? Let go of all your negative emotions and embrace LOVE multiplied to the nth degree. In HypnoCounseling, our clients frequently choose hypnotic suggestions that focus on positive improvements in their attitudes. This is one technique that leads to your habit of positive thinking that in turn eliminates your negative thinking, worrying and obsessing over all the horrible things you could imagine that might happen. You see, you have the power to choose what to focus upon and what to discard. If you want to choose happiness in your life, focus your thoughts on LOVE, GRATITUDE, COMPASSION, FORGIVENESS and other such important healing emotions. And continue choosing to focus on other positive emotions as well as on positive people, places and things. As a consequence, you reject the negative emotions like fear, grief, humiliation, insecurity, regret, anger, anxiety and so on. In effect, you defuse all negative emotions plus thoughts of terrible things that before may have dominated you or even worse, caused harmful reactions of stress in your Mind/Body/ Spirit.

When you focus on the positives like LOVE, your body responds in a favorable, healthy way by physically relaxing, feeling safe and feeling connected to someone or something else meaningful. After all, love is our greatest endorphin, our greatest companion. Its Positive Energy is self-healing. We come into this world pre-wired for love. We all were born with the ability to love, to give and receive love. When you focus upon love when you are in hypnosis, it also may magnify and intensify those feelings of love with a concentration perhaps unobtainable in your conscious state. Now just imagine expressing your love to your partner while you both are in self-hypnosis ... What a LOVELY thought!

HAVING SURGERY? HOW ABOUT A HYPNOSIS COACH?

One of the most frightening situations a person faces all alone is going into the hospital or medical center for a surgical procedure. Yes, your family and friends may surround you up to a point. But you are the one alone who faces the procedure and must deal with its requirements pre-surgery and post-surgery. It can be very difficult to cope with all that stress, anxiety and fear of the unknown. But it does not have to be all that difficult if you employ the help of hypnosis and a HypnoCounselor/hypnosis coach. How does a hypnosis coach help you or your child facing a medical or dental procedure? Just peruse the following list and just imagine ...

One:
Hypnosis effectively reduces the fear factor. You release all fear and negativity about the procedure. You also instruct your body how you want it to respond in a relaxed way regarding whatever takes place during the procedure.

Two:
Since you caution your body ahead of time regarding what will be taking place and programmed it how to react, you preclude the shock or surprise factor. So your emotions and your Mind/Body/Spirit are pre-warned and ready.

Three:
Research has shown that hypnosis helps the following:

reduces bleeding, regulates blood pressure, reduces the perception of pain and discomfort and promotes faster bone healing, aids in enlisting the body's natural healing responses for better-than-average recovery and shorter hospital stays. Hypnosis gives the person a sense of self-empowerment when typically a person would feel totally helpless and at the mercy of others.

Four:
Hypnosis helps to create a positive attitude regarding the medical or dental procedure so the Mind/Body/Spirit understands how beneficial the end result of the procedure will be. This keeps the person's focus on receiving what he/she needs as well as feeling good about the results.

To give you an idea of how one might respond to a surgery coach, I quote a letter with permission from one of my clients:

No one could alleviate my extreme terror and concerns. The reality was that I was alone in dealing with my feelings. That is when I called for help ... Gale individualized my sessions to meet my objectives. Through hypnosis I feel I was recreated. I actually became calm and serene, sleeping like a baby every night before the surgery so that I was fully rested going into the operating room. In addition, my recovery period was pain-free and uneventful. Even my surgeon was amazed ... I continue to listen to my after-surgery hypnosis recording prepared for me so that I continue to get strong, heal completely and stay healthy. Thanks, Gale

As a hypnosis client for medical procedures, you would begin listening to your customized surgery audio at least two weeks before the procedure. You may choose one audio that covers before, during and after the procedure or choose a separate, customized audio for each phase. After you receive permission from your doctor or the person in charge during the procedure, you may listen to the recording during the procedure and in the recovery room too. Hypnosis helps reduce your perception of pain so you awaken after the procedure feeling considerably more comfortable than if you had not used hypnosis.

In addition to sending flowers to your loved one before their surgery/procedure, you may want to send your loved one to your favorite HypnoCounselor/hypnosis coach for the best outcome. Come to think of it, if you are headed toward surgery, what better gift for you to give to yourself?

COPING WITH THE STRESS OF DIFFICULT PEOPLE

You can recover from serious stresses like moving, job loss, floods and stock market losses. However one of the potentially serious stresses that may damage your physical well-being as much as any of the above is a difficult person issue that continues long term. That kind of stress has no conclusion. It is a no-win situation. It may be impossible to please (for any appreciable amount of time) a difficult person because such people get an Emotional Payoff by eliciting your anger, fear, guilt and all those kinds of negative emotions. It is almost as if they enjoy their power to inflict suffering upon you. Maybe misery loves company.

As a HypnoCounselor, I suggest at the core of most difficult people is usually a Low Self-esteem issue. When people feel that their self-esteem is being attacked, they may take their bat and ball and go home. Or they may turn that bat on the unsuspecting person who said or did something to push their Low Self-esteem hot button. Additionally, difficult people are often stymied in their personal development. Consequently they often resort to very childlike behaviors. They may adopt a vengeful attitude like: *I'll get back at you for hurting me.* When you attempt to deal with a difficult person, it often becomes apparent that there is no reasoning with them. One explanation may be the difficult person has an attitude that their view of the world is the only right way and others are just wrong. They are unwilling to see that others may differ from their perspective yet still have a view just as valid as theirs. With more rational people, you are more likely to strike a compromise, but not so with the difficult person.

The difficult person is unlikely to agree just to disagree and leave it at that. No, they are right and according to them, *nine out of ten people surely would agree with them and share their view.*

Unfortunately many of you find yourselves in a job with a supervisor or co-worker who belongs to this difficult people category. No matter what you do, it seems you are unable to please this person. Often extreme stress grips you and you may experience ulcers, heart problems, colitis, headaches, acid reflux, etc. How do you cope with this type of stress so as to avoid the negative physical consequences?

During HypnoCounseling sessions I employ hypnotic suggestions enabling you to first relax totally and then avoid all tension, anxiety or physical, mental, emotional and spiritual manifestations of stress. Other hypnotic suggestions guide you to problem solve using your logic and intuition. What is beyond your control, you direct your subconscious to let it go. You also need to alter your attitude toward the difficult person, recognizing that the difficult person is reacting to his/her own issues rather than to you personally. The difficult person is almost like a two-year-old having a tantrum. Would you take the behavior of a two-year-old personally? Thus, from that perspective you avoid getting drawn into the negativity.

Ultimately, you have the choice of how much you are able to tolerate from difficult people. You need to create boundaries and limits with difficult family members. Sometimes you must leave the job, transfer departments or even divorce. Nevertheless, HypnoCounseling can help you with stress management. It can assist you in deciding when you have had enough and must take other action. Remember the answers are within you.

HUMILIATION IS HARMFUL

It still haunts me ... the pathetic picture on AOL.com of the twelve-year-old girl hanging her head in shame while standing on a street corner close to her home and holding up a huge poster that read something like this: *I don't keep my room picked up and I act out in class ... Willing to work for money.* The mother, who forced her daughter to stand there, was smugly grinning probably because she imagined she had won the battle to make her child behave even though it took deep humiliation to do it. Her premise most likely was, *I'll do whatever it takes to make her toe the line.* Maybe this response sounds reasonable to you. Nonetheless, as a HypnoCounselor, I have a different and hopefully enlightening perspective on this controversy to share with you. If you agree, please pass this article to those who may benefit from it.

Children need clear limits and parents need to be consistent so the child knows where he/she stands with the parent. However, there are devastating repercussions to teaching a child or anyone a lesson using humiliation. Yes, the parent may win the initial struggle but significantly damage the most precious part of his/her child, the child's High Self-esteem. In fact, teaching with humiliation always does teach a lesson but probably one that parents, teachers and others may not be able to perceive. Actually, it is the lesson the child's subconscious mind perceives when there are feelings of humiliation and shame. Specifically in that moment, the child's subconscious perceives the child's view of his self-worth in the worst possible light and then, without anyone knowing it, downloads those perceptions as the truth. The perceived response to humiliation may be any of the following or even worse: *I am a bad person. I am not good enough. I will never succeed. I do not deserve respect. I am not lovable. I hate myself. I should punish myself. I do not deserve anything good. Everyone hates me. No one understands me. I am such a disappointment.*

Once such negative self-image messages are installed in the child's subconscious mind, they exert a permanent influence on how the child perceives himself/herself. Therefore, these negative self-esteem messages can create self-fulfilling prophesies that potentially follow the child throughout a lifetime. You become who you subconsciously believe who you are. Your subconscious follows your internal instructions and directs you there.

Frequently during HypnoCounseling I encounter clients who are struggling with stress directly traced to their past humiliations. Following the act of being humiliated, it is very possible for your subconscious to adopt a consistent Low Self-esteem programming associated with that humiliation. Unknowingly you manifest the negative belief systems you adopted about yourself subconsciously even if it started in very early childhood or even in infancy. Fortunately, HypnoCounseling has proven very effective in reversing such devastating negative mindsets. Hypnosis empowers you to revise and improve attitudes and belief systems to comfortably transform Low Self-esteem into High Self-esteem.

Of course, it is always best to avoid using humiliation to control anyone, of any age in any circumstance, ever. The short-term payoff of using humiliation never justifies the possible long-term adverse effects. Now, could I be more emphatic!?

APPENDIX TWO

SCRIPTS REPRINTED FROM REPROGRAM YOUR SUBCONSCIOUS, NINE-CD SERIES (REVISED 2010)

Scripts Reprinted From Reprogram Your Subconscious: How to Use Hypnosis To Get What You Really Want (revised 2010)

Some of the options these scripts offer you:

One, when you are performing self-hypnosis, refer to one or more of these scripts in part or in total to identify desirable suggestions that you want downloaded and reinforced by your subconscious for your Highest Good.

Two, you have permission to record these revised scripts in Appendix Two only if using your own voice and used only for your own personal and private recording/listening use.

Three, use the scripts as examples and guides for creating your own unique guided imagery suggestions and affirmations.

INNER PEACE MAINTAINS HARMONY AND BALANCE SCRIPT

INTRODUCTION

This recording relaxes you and involves your attention and focus. Consequently, no one should listen to this recording while driving a car, as a passenger in a car without a head set or ear buds or while operating any machinery that requires concentration and/or decision-making.

This recording is not a substitute for medical treatment. Rather it is an exercise enlisting the support of your Mind/Body/ Spirit response to help you maintain well-being. It explores the natural self-healing powers of your mind using guided imagery while in a relaxed, altered state of hypnosis. It targets your stresses and suggests approaches to disarm them. While you may not be able to totally eliminate your stresses, you may choose improved ways to respond to them. This recording offers a safe, noninvasive method for creating positive changes in your life and in your perspectives about your life. What your mind focuses upon, your body reacts to just as if it were a reality. This explains why guided imagery is so effective. Additionally the relaxation exercises relax you and allow your subconscious to absorb and integrate new positive ways of thinking, feeling and behaving. Be assured though your subconscious automatically rejects anything that is against your morals, ethics or religious beliefs. This is (put your name here), your guide and facilitator for this gentle, safe journey that offers for a mainstay in your inner life, relaxation, peace, harmony and balance. This is a time dedicated to you and your well-being. You are worth this time. You deserve this time. Whatever you hear when my voice guides you through the imagery, take only the positive parts that apply to you and leave the rest. Revise any statements that need changes in order to be acceptable to you personally. You are the master of this journey. I am your guide.

BEGINNING OF GENERAL MAIN SCRIPT

Begin now by taking two deep breaths, breathing in through your nose and exhaling through your mouth to the count of eight. As you are slowly exhaling, imagine you are releasing all the stress, tension and anxiety that may have settled anywhere within your entire body. Just let it go! Continue to breathe normally and now each time you exhale, relax every muscle within your entire body more and more. Each muscle, each tendon, each ligament, all internal organs respond to your desire to let go. It is safe. It is okay. It feels so good to let go of all the stress, tension and tightness throughout your entire body. Just as a candle melts from the heat of its flickering flame, the tightness softens and releases. See tension just melting away. Feel the subtle warmth as your muscles relax feeling so loose, so heavy, and so relaxed. From the top of your head to the tips of your toes, you may begin to notice stress and taut muscles are releasing their hold on you. Comfortably, gently, steadily just let any tightness go. Releasing the muscle tightness is like easily loosening a knot or letting go of the strings attached to helium balloons. Stress and tension leave so easily, naturally as you exhale them with each breath. Almost magically, you find yourself starting to feel so calm, so peaceful, so comfortably relaxed as you remain focused on your breathing.

Every thought that was running through your mind, slows, slows, and slows down. All thoughts now gently depart as you exhale. The only thought that remains is of total relaxation. Any thought or distractions, simply escort them out with your breath. Focus again on your regular breathing. Notice that with every regular breath you release, your body feels more and more and more relaxed. Your arms and hands may feel so heavy now, so relaxed that you may be barely able to lift them at all. The relaxation has smoothed your forehead, softly spread over your eyes, your nose, your mouth, your jaw. You open your mouth slightly to relax your jaw as this is a place where tension often settles. Good.

Now the relaxation goes down your neck and across your shoulders and as you imagine the muscles relaxing, they do relax. You may feel them relaxing. Next perhaps you feel the relaxation traveling down your back, down, down, down to the lowest part of your back and then returning up again. Again the tension just melts away. The relaxation continues down your chest, your stomach, your abdomen, your hips, your thighs, your legs, your knees, your shins, your ankles and your feet. The tops and bottoms of your feet relax and let go. You focus now on a peaceful scene that you have placed in the middle of your forehead, in your mind's eye. Perhaps your scene is a small pond without a ripple in the clear water. Or perhaps it is a single candle's flame, steadily glowing sending forth soft light. Whatever represents peace and calm to you, even if it is a sound, scent, taste or feeling rather than a picture, is what you bring to the center of your forehead, your mind's eye. Now everything is so peaceful, calm and so relaxing. You continue enjoying this sense of complete peace, calm and relaxation ... Yet in a few moments you may be drawn to deepen your feelings of relaxation by visiting your safe and healing place that lies yonder.

Your special safe and healing place is just for you. It can be any place you choose — on a beach, in the woods, in the mountains, in a special room. Wherever you choose as your safe place is perfectly fine. Whatever comes to your mind first, you can trust is a wonderful choice for you. Besides, you can always change your safe place if you so desire. Now that you feel ready to go deeper into relaxation, you may stay where you are or travel to another safe and healing place. If you are ready to travel, you may see and feel your body walking down a simple dirt path. It is a beautiful day with a deep blue sky and little birds are cheerfully chirping. There is a gentle, fresh breeze and it is just warm enough for you. It is absolutely a delightful day. As you are enjoying your walk, you come upon a stairway which in another moment or two is right in front of you. It has ten shallow steps with a handrail on either side. In another moment, you will be stepping down upon those stairs. As you go from the tenth step down to the first step, you easily allow yourself to become more relaxed than before. Any thoughts that would try to disturb your concentration are immediately cancelled when you stamp a big *X* upon them in your mind's eye. You maintain your focus guided by my voice. We are ready to begin the stairs now. Remember, these shallow steps are easy to maneuver. Imagine yourself in a strong state of body where you comfortably can walk on your own. Begin with the tenth step and end with the first.

Now that you are ready, here we go now … *Ten*, feeling more relaxed now, so calm and peaceful … *Nine*, relaxing more and more … *Eight* … more deeply relaxed than before, so deeply relaxed … *Seven*, the deeper relaxed you go, the more intensely wonderful the feeling … *Six* … deeper, way down now. You may sense how heavy your entire body feels, so heavy, so relaxed … *Five*, way, way, down into your deepest relaxation … *Four*, deeper than ever before … *Three*, even deeper relaxed, feeling so comfortable with such harmony and balance … *Two*, almost there now, so very, very deeply relaxed and so calm, so peaceful … and *One*, feeling so, so, deeply, deeply, deeply relaxed, oh, so, so deeply relaxed. Regardless of the stresses in your life, you may find yourself so deeply, deeply relaxed and feeling so calm and supported that you look so forward to repeating this journey each and every day. And each time you repeat this journey you may find it easier and easier to relax even deeper and deeper.

Notice now you can sense your new surroundings … sense the peace and the calm. You are in your safe place. Perhaps you can touch it, smell it, taste it, hear it, see it. You are in your safe, special healing place and no one can disturb you here. Imagine yourself in your safe place. Perceive it with all of your senses. Amazingly your feet feel as if they are growing roots that dig into the soft ground and secure you now to the earth, grounding you and centering you. You can see the roots, feel them and even detect their fresh, outdoors scent. Perhaps immediately you also perceive an energy that you are receiving through the crown of your head. It is as if you have plugged yourself into the unlimited energy of the universe, of nature, of creation. This is perfect harmony and balance. Feel that harmony and balance, the perfect alignment and attunement to the energy of the universe and your connection with your Creator. It feels so great! In fact, its description is beyond words. You are so grateful to have this amazing acceptance of peace and tranquility. It includes the feeling of belonging, the feeling of unconditional love. Soak up the power of this incredible, safe and healing place. It is there for you always.

Whenever you wish to return to this safe and healing place, first find a comfortable position, either sitting or lying down with your head supported, where you will be undisturbed for the desired time you have allotted for this relaxation. Just gently close your eyes. Next, take in two deep breaths, in through your nose and exhale through your mouth to the count of eight as you imagine the stress, tension and anxiety leaving your body each time you exhale. Using two fingers on your right hand, your index finger and third finger, place them together by touching them lengthwise next to each other. Then think of your special number from *one* to *ten* or any special number you like. As soon as you think of that special number, you may feel yourself relaxing deeper and deeper. It is as if a wave of relaxation draws you steadily like a magnet into relaxation. Then you find yourself facing your special stairway with the ten steps. Or you may use another entrance of your choosing into your safe and healing place. Now allow yourself to experience the deepening process going so deeply into relaxation as you count to yourself from *ten* to *one*. As you reach the count of *one*, you are in your safe place again. Remember to sense your feet growing roots into the earth, grounding you and centering you. Visualize or sense again the white light that gently touches you and returns each cell to its healthiest status. Notice the cord that plugs you into the universal outlet for love, light and energy. Also repeat that the sun is beaming down beautiful, healing lights of Positive Energy that heal wherever healing is needed. Remember to reinforce and reaffirm all the suggestions you desire to keep.

At this time you may sense an even deeper relaxation as if you were floating and drifting lulled with very gentle movement, drifting and floating more and more relaxed. You have agreed that you are worthwhile and you deserve this time. Focus on your breathing. Notice how rich and full each breath is, bringing new serenity into your Mind/Body/Spirit. You are on cruise control now enjoying each pleasurable moment. Your relaxed muscles may feel so heavy, so heavy they are content to just be still. You are protected in this very safe environment of your safe place. Anyone you invite here needs your permission in order to return.

Very conveniently there is a designated Subconscious Programming area in your safe place that is here just for you. Fortunately, everything that is possible for you to know is stored here for you to access through your subconscious computer. Surprisingly, even if in the past you were unable to operate computers, this computer was made to respond to your thoughts as well as your pressing the keys of the keyboard. So you are very intuitively adept at this computer. In fact, we have multiplied your intuitive knowing so it is 100 times more powerful than before. This computer also listens to you and you simply tell it what to do. It is really a spectacular computer. To make this even easier, I will be your guide.

CORE OF INNER PEACE SCRIPT

You have indicated to me that you are desirous of having abundant inner peace. You want to maintain harmony and balance in your life. This can be done through reprogramming your subconscious computer.

Now sometime in your past, you may have suffered from hurtful words and/or from actions of others. Additionally, you may have said or thought negative things about yourself. Maybe you called yourself other than positive names or reinforced a belief that you were other than capable of succeeding at something. You may have found your life was treating you other than as you thought it should. You may have experienced negative emotional reactions like feeling anger, rage, grudges and revenge. Perhaps you reacted in other than peaceful and respectful verbal and/or physical behaviors. Perhaps you had only some or none of these strong emotions. Nevertheless, if you did experience any such negative emotions, maybe it just happened so automatically it seemed beyond your control.

Your subconscious computer works like magic though and can correct these undesirable things. You may communicate to your subconscious and inform it regarding what you want to keep and what you want to discard. For your subconscious is like a computer. It has the capacity to delete undesirable programming and add different, very desirable programming. It can create programs in your computer-like mind that store the information just like storing it in a filing cabinet. Once this is done, your subconscious continues to store those approved programs and files using them to direct your life, your attitudes, beliefs, feelings and actions automatically just as you requested. Thus, your subconscious keeps you following your accepted and already downloaded computer programs. As you have requested, your subconscious computer has been programmed by you to comfortably maintain your abundant inner peace, harmony and balance for now and forever. Relax now as it is easy to get started.

You are in the subconscious computer work area designed to make you completely comfortable. You have come because you are desirous of eliminating anger, rage, revenge and other related negative emotions from your Mind/Body/Spirit. You understand that your subconscious computer, as your advocate, wants to please you. So it supports your happiness by eliminating all Faulty Subconscious Programs that in your past served to create any faulty programming of anger, rage, revenge and other related negative feelings and behaviors that you experienced that were other than for your Highest Good. The Faulty Subconscious Programs are deleted automatically, effortlessly and replaced instead with wonderfully positive Subconscious Programs. These programs are designed to keep you consistently calm connected to your intelligent reasoning and intuition, especially when responding to any stressors. Therefore, these replacement Subconscious Programs maintain your peace of mind, harmony and balance. Let's begin. Now when you touch the delete key that is right in front of you, all the negative messages that you ever received or perceived that adversely affected your self-esteem are instantly deleted. It is your choice to press that delete key or use your thoughts to do so. Do so now … Good. Good. It is done.

Next focus on deleting all negative emotions from the past that were other than for your Highest Good and were downloaded into your subconscious. They either directly or indirectly may have caused negative emotional responses responsible for disturbing your desired inner peace, harmony and balance. You are targeting all files that have anything to do with your stored negative emotional memories of anything in your entire past that were anything other than your Highest Good. These negative emotional memories may have caused you to experience anger, rage, revenge, grudges, vindictiveness, inferiorities, helplessness or any other related negative emotional reactions. In a split second you will have deleted those files.

Ready? …Yes… Good, it is done now. That's right. Those negative emotions have been neutralized and are deleted from your subconscious now and forever. All past negative emotions that gave you feelings of anger about people, situations and/or circumstances that were other than your Highest Good are gone now. Those feelings were from your past and your past is gone.

That's right. You are living in your present moment. You have separated yourself from the negativity of the past. You sent it to the sun where it was transformed into Positive Energy. That's right. Now you are filled with abundant peace of mind, harmony and balance that you maintain as your natural, comfortable way of being. You have sent up to the sun all remnants and all traces of negative programming that were other than supporting your peace of mind, harmony and balance. The sun has transformed the Negative Energy into Positive Energy and you are free, really free.

You are truly self-empowered. Whatever was said or done to you that precipitated those past negative emotions is forever neutralized and deleted. It is all gone, gone just as easily as pressing down on your delete key of your keyboard. The memory of those emotional situations is completely neutralized. Of course, you may remember the memories. However, all the attached negative emotions have been neutralized and what remains is peace of mind. Your reaction to those memories now may be, *I know it happened but so what? I have retained the wisdom from it. That's what I value.* At last, it feels like a huge weight has been lifted off your shoulders ... because it has. It feels so freeing, so exhilarating! In fact, you may notice how much lighter you feel.

Gratefully you have carefully replaced all negative programming with very positive, wonderful programs. One new and positive file is entitled: Inner Peace, Harmony and Balance. In this file is your unwavering belief that you are a precious, valuable, deserving, lovable, capable, and compassionate human being who is worthy, and good enough. Your goodness, your essence and your value are intrinsic. Thus, they are unaffected by what others may think, say or do. It is unaffected by any mistakes you have made or mistakes you may make. It is unaffected by mistakes that took place in past events or other events that may take place. This file also contains the message that you love and accept yourself unconditionally. Thus, you easily, automatically maintain your state of harmony and balance with peace of Mind/Body/Spirit. Your positive self-esteem is invincible. This file supports your calm demeanor, your peacefully effective ways of dealing with your life stresses and dealing with other people. Consequently you refuse to take personally anything negative others may think, say and do related to you. You recognize their strong negativity is about their issues rather than being about you. You let all the negativity go, sending it up to the sun to be transformed into Positive Energy. Now only the wisdom of it remains.

This file also includes the following instructions: *At any time you perceive stress, internally or externally, consciously or unconsciously, you touch your index finger to your thumb on the same hand. This reminds you to take two deep breaths that immediately relax and calm you. If possible, the logical and intuitive parts of your brain problem solve the causes of the stress. Whatever is left unresolved, you leave it in the hands of your Creator, your Higher Power or to Nature to resolve. You have done your best under your circumstances. No one could be expected to do more. So you have just let any remaining other than positive or neutral thoughts go. And that feels great!*

Next are affirmations that many have found so helpful in maintaining Inner Peace, Harmony and Balance:

- I have learned to love and to accept me, just as I am. I have learned to accept others' loving and accepting me. I am able to give and receive love as a natural part of my living. It is as natural as inhaling and exhaling my breath.

- I allow myself to go with the natural flow of my life happenings, finding joy in each moment. I trust the way my life unfolds. Good things are always happening for me. All is going well.

- I release all that is outside of my Highest Good. I have programmed my subconscious to make choices that are automatically consistent with my Highest Good.

- I focus on the positives in my life and celebrate them daily. I perceive deep gratitude for the positives in my life. In fact I understand the positive aspects in all of my experiences.

- My past is my guidepost. I have integrated the wisdom of my life lessons. I have released all negativity from the past. I live in the present experiencing happiness right now.

- I refuse to take personally anything negative a person thinks, says or does. I acknowledge that their strong reactions are based in their own issues. I easily let their negativity go and bring in positive thoughts instead. I imagine the person surrounded with healing energy.

- My being alive means being able to learn and to improve. I embrace with joy and gratitude my opportunities for positive improvement. I embrace change with courage and confidence.

- I avoid making assumptions. I avoid making assumptions about what someone might be thinking or feeling. Instead, whenever possible I ask people to clarify what they are thinking and feeling.

- I trust my Inner Knowing and my connection to my

Creator to guide me always toward my Highest Good. My connection is always there. It is a given. I am doing the best I can under my circumstances. I view others as if they are doing the best they can do under their circumstances. They just are being who they are.

- I am just as precious as everyone else. No one is better than I am and no one is worse than I am. We are all equals. We are all of the same energy. We are all good enough.

- I am self-empowered. I have choices that allow me to have control over my life. And so I do. I also recognize that others need to have control over their lives as well. I acknowledge and respect their right to make their own choices and follow their own path.

- I am responsible for my choices and I learn from them. Others learn from their choices as well.

- I am safe. It is safe to be me. It is safe to love and be loved. It is safe to lead my life in a fulfilling way. It is safe to be happy. It is safe to be an adult and be on my own and to be my own person.

- I lovingly allow happiness to express itself throughout my Mind/Body/Spirit.

- I am at peace, in perfect alignment and harmony and balance with my universe, my Creator, family, friends, any and all coworkers, all acquaintances and with everything in my life. All is going well.

CONCLUSION OF GENERAL SCRIPT

Very importantly, your subconscious computer file contains your commitment to forgiveness. To assist your going forward with your life, you have forgiven all those who have ever hurt you whether it was done intentionally or unintentionally. You have forgiven them all as well as you have forgiven yourself completely. Yes, you have forgiven yourself for anything you said, thought and did that was wrong, inappropriate or hurtful. This way you have a clean slate. You remain always free, unburdened by the negative emotions that were other than for your Highest Good. You also recognize that no one is better than you and no one is worse than you. We are all equals even though we may have different abilities and talents and different appearances. We are all of the same energy.

All that was previously other than positive or neutral energy within you has been completely healed and cleansed, remaining in the eternal light of the sun and stars. And you bask in the brilliance of the light and love, feeling your loving connection to your Creator. You know deep within you, all is calm, all is peaceful and all is well.

As a sign of your accomplishment a magnificent rainbow appears reflecting the most beautiful colors imaginable. These colors are also there for you as they offer powerful healing so you maintain peace of mind, harmony and balance within your life. Select now the colors that you personally need for reinforcing the desired positives you have brought into your life and for releasing any future Negative Energy that is other than supportive of your well-being. The name or names of the colors instantly are within your knowing. This is part of your intuitive knowing. Summon them now from the sun. Immediately you may perceive your entire body is blanketed with comforting, soothing, gentle lights. You feel them on the surface of your body with their healing, gentle, warm glow. Next, they enter your body through your feet and travel up to the top of your head continuously cleansing and healing, cleansing and healing from the darkness that you have already expelled. Feel those lights as they lovingly supply your body with healing energy for every atom within every cell.

Imagine the beautiful color or colors. Notice how bright or soft they are, how clear or how muted. Imagine them quietly flowing throughout your organs like miniature, soft waves that wash over your cells, your thoughts, your dreams. Fortunately you have the power to request reinforcements of these colors at any time. Request more and they return and replenish, cleanse and make whole all areas within your complete body that are in need of their magnificent energies.

Remember answers may be found within you. You are self-empowered. So you are positive as you approach each day with courage and confidence. What a wonderful journey this has been! In essence you have transformed yourself and you continue processing the desired changes over the rest of this day and evening in a very comfortable, non-invasive, easy and time efficient way. Whatever positive changes you have programmed, they are part of you now and feel just as comfortable as if they have been part of you always. Yet you are aware of your hypnosis tool and its power to make these comfortable changes. Your subconscious computer has been cleansed and updated. You are truly renewed!

And now if it is your appropriately selected time to sleep, begin sleeping ... NOW. If you already have begun sleeping, and it is your appropriate time to sleep, continue sleeping. Sleep peacefully, deeply and uninterrupted while of course you are always able to awaken instantly if there were an emergency. Sleep wonderfully all the selected hours until it is your appropriate time to awaken. Process gently, comfortably, compassionately and time efficiently all that these words have done to serve you. If anything were to attempt to interfere with your sleep, simply put it in a big soup pot and put the lid on it. Put it on the back burner until your normal waking hours when you have appropriate time to process it. When you arise from your sleep, you are totally refreshed and feel like your batteries have been recharged. You feel absolutely great! Continue sleeping now and if it is your appropriate time to sleep, disregard the end of this recording that would bring you to your conscious state. For these instructions then only help you to sleep more deeply and peacefully in the most relaxed sleep. Enjoy your nourishing, peaceful, relaxing sleep ...

However, if it is your time to return to your conscious state, continue following the instructions as you listen to my voice and I do bring you back to your conscious state as I count from one to five. Remember that when you return to your normal State of Consciousness, you are completely alert, able to think clearly, focus and concentrate extremely well. You are able to drive safely and easily. Remember though, tonight or whenever it is your time for sleep, as soon as your head touches the pillow and your eyes close for sleep, you enjoy a deep, peaceful, relaxed, and wonderful sleep. During your sleep time, you process easily anything resulting from this recording. You continue sleeping uninterrupted just as I described previously until it is your selected time to awaken.

Only if now is your time to return to your conscious state, do you follow my instructions to bring you out of deep relaxation by counting from one to five, the same way you bring yourself out of self-hypnosis ... However, if it is your appropriate time to sleep, the following instructions and suggestions only help you to sleep more deeply, more relaxed and more peacefully ... Now if it is truly your appropriate time to come back to your natural, normal State of Consciousness, then begin with: *One*, it is time now to come back to your normal Beta Consciousness State, coming out of deep, deep relaxation ... *Two*, your entire body feels great. It has been cleansed and healed, revitalized and re-energized ... *Three*, your mind feels great! It has been cleansed and healed, revitalized and re-energized. It has gently, easily, comfortably, compassionately and time efficiently processed everything ... *Four*, your eyelashes are starting to gently flutter open as you are returning to your totally aware, alert, conscious state feeling so refreshed, able to drive easily and safely ... *Five, Six, Seven, Eight, Nine* and *Ten* your eyes are now open wide, comfortably focusing. Your eyes are now wide open. You are back to your completely normal conscious state, alert, clear headed, able to focus and concentrate better than before, remembering everything from this recording and feeling absolutely great!! Totally ALERT, AWAKE NOW!

INNER SECURITY MAINTAINS FAITH THAT ALL IS WELL

INTRODUCTION

This recording relaxes you and involves your attention and focus. Consequently, no one should listen to this recording while driving a car, as a passenger in a car without a head set or ear buds or while operating any machinery that requires concentration and/or decision-making.

This recording is not a substitute for medical treatment. Rather it is an exercise enlisting the support of your Mind/Body/Spirit response to help you maintain well-being. It explores the natural self-healing powers of your mind using guided imagery while in a relaxed, altered state of hypnosis. It targets your stresses and suggests approaches to disarm them. While you may not be able to totally eliminate your stresses, you may choose improved ways to respond to them. This recording offers a safe, noninvasive method for creating positive changes in your life and in your perspectives about your life. What your mind focuses upon, your body reacts to just as if it were a reality. This explains why guided imagery is so effective. Additionally the relaxation exercises relax you and allow your subconscious to absorb and integrate new positive ways of thinking, feeling and behaving. Be assured though your subconscious automatically rejects anything that is against your morals, ethics or religious beliefs. This is (put your name here), your guide and facilitator for this gentle, safe journey that offers for a mainstay in your inner life, relaxation, peace, harmony and balance. This is a time dedicated to you and your well-being. You are worth this time. You deserve this time. Whatever you hear when my voice guides you through the imagery, take only the positive parts that apply to you and leave the rest. Revise any statements that need changes in order to be acceptable to you personally. You are the master of this journey. I am your guide.

BEGINNING OF MAIN SCRIPT

Begin now by taking two deep breaths, breathing in through your nose and exhaling through your mouth to the count of eight. As you are slowly exhaling, imagine you are releasing all the stress, tension and anxiety that may have settled anywhere within your entire body. Just let it go! Continue to breathe normally and now each time you exhale, relax every muscle within your entire body more and more. Each muscle, each tendon, each ligament, all internal organs respond to your desire to let go. It is safe. It is okay. It feels so good to let go of all the stress, tension and tightness throughout your entire body. Just as a candle melts from the heat of its flickering flame, the tightness softens and releases. See tension just melting away. Feel the subtle warmth as your muscles relax feeling so loose, so heavy, and so relaxed. From the top of your head to the tips of your toes, you may begin to notice stress and taut muscles are releasing their hold on you. Comfortably, gently, steadily just let any tightness go. Releasing the muscle tightness is like easily loosening a knot or letting go of the strings attached to helium balloons. Stress and tension leave so easily, naturally as you exhale them with each breath. Almost magically, you find yourself starting to feel so calm, so peaceful, so comfortably relaxed as you remain focused on your breathing.

Every thought that was running through your mind, slows, slows, and slows down. All thoughts now gently depart as you exhale. The only thought that remains is of total relaxation. Any thought or distractions, simply escort them out with your breath. Focus again on your regular breathing. Notice that with every regular breath you release, your body feels more and more and more relaxed. Your arms and hands may feel so heavy now, so relaxed that you may be barely able to lift them at all. The relaxation has smoothed your forehead, softly spread over your eyes, your nose, your mouth, your jaw. You open your mouth slightly to relax your jaw as this is a place where tension often settles. Good.

Now the relaxation goes down your neck and across your shoulders and as you imagine the muscles relaxing, they do relax. You may feel them relaxing. Next perhaps you feel the relaxation traveling down your back, down, down, down to the lowest part of your back and then returning up again. Again the tension just melts away. The relaxation continues down your chest, your stomach, your abdomen, your hips, your thighs, your legs, your knees, your shins, your ankles and your feet. The tops and bottoms of your feet relax and let go. You focus now on a peaceful scene that you have placed in the middle of your forehead, in your mind's eye. Perhaps your scene is a small pond without a ripple in the clear water. Or perhaps it is a single candle's flame, steadily glowing sending forth soft light. Whatever represents peace and calm to you, even if it is a sound, scent, taste or feeling rather than a picture, is what you bring to the center of your forehead, your mind's eye. Now everything is so peaceful, calm and so relaxing. You continue enjoying this sense of complete peace, calm and relaxation ... Yet in a few moments you may be drawn to deepen your feelings of relaxation by visiting your safe and healing place that lies yonder.

Your special safe and healing place is just for you. It can be any place you choose — on a beach, in the woods, in the mountains, in a special room. Wherever you choose as your safe place is perfectly fine. Whatever comes to your mind first, you can trust is a wonderful choice for you. Besides, you can always change your safe place if you so desire. Now that you feel ready to go deeper into relaxation, you may stay where you are or travel to another safe and healing place. If you are ready to travel, you may see and feel your body walking down a simple dirt path. It is a beautiful day with a deep blue sky and little birds are cheerfully chirping. There is a gentle, fresh breeze and it is just warm enough for you. It is absolutely a delightful day. As you are enjoying your walk, you come upon a stairway which in another moment or two is right in front of you. It has ten shallow steps with a handrail on either side. In another moment, you will be stepping down upon those stairs. As you go from the tenth step down to the first step, you easily allow yourself to become more relaxed than before. Any thoughts that would try to disturb your concentration are immediately cancelled when you stamp a big *X* upon them in your mind's eye. You maintain your focus guided by my voice. We are ready to begin the stairs now. Remember, these shallow steps are easy to maneuver. Imagine yourself in a strong state of body where you comfortably can walk on your own. Begin with the tenth step and end with the first.

Now that you are ready, here we go now ... *Ten*, feeling more relaxed now, so calm and peaceful ... *Nine*, relaxing more and more ... *Eight* ... more deeply relaxed than before, so deeply relaxed ... *Seven*, the deeper relaxed you go, the more intensely wonderful the feeling ... *Six* ... deeper, way down now. You may sense how heavy your entire body feels, so heavy, so relaxed ... *Five*, way, way, down into your deepest relaxation ... *Four*, deeper than ever before ... *Three*, even deeper relaxed, feeling so comfortable with such harmony and balance ... *Two*, almost there now, so very, very deeply relaxed and so calm, so peaceful ... and *One*, feeling so, so, deeply, deeply, deeply relaxed, oh, so, so deeply relaxed. Regardless of the stresses in your life, you may find yourself so deeply, deeply relaxed and feeling so calm and supported that you look so forward to repeating this journey each and every day. And each time you repeat this journey you may find it easier and easier to relax even deeper and deeper.

Notice now you can sense your new surroundings ... sense the peace and the calm. You are in your safe place. Perhaps you can touch it, smell it, taste it, hear it, see it. You are in your safe, special healing place and no one can disturb you here. Imagine yourself in your safe place. Perceive it with all of your senses. Amazingly your feet feel as if they are growing roots that dig into the soft ground and secure you now to the earth, grounding you and centering you. You can see the roots, feel them and even detect their fresh, outdoors scent. Perhaps immediately you also perceive an energy that you are receiving through the crown of your head. It is as if you have plugged yourself into the unlimited energy of the universe, of nature, of creation. This is perfect harmony and balance. Feel that har- mony and balance, the perfect alignment and attunement to the energy of the universe and your connection with your Creator. It feels so great! In fact, its description is beyond words. You are so grateful to have this amazing acceptance of peace and tranquility. It includes the feeling of belonging, the feeling of unconditional love. Soak up the power of this incredible, safe and healing place. It is there for you always.

Whenever you wish to return to this safe and healing place, first find a comfortable position, either sitting or lying down with your head supported, where you will be undisturbed for the desired time you have allotted for this relaxation. Just gently close your eyes. Next, take in two deep breaths, in through your nose and exhale through your mouth to the count of eight as you imagine the stress, tension and anxiety leaving your body each time you exhale. Using two fingers on your right hand, your index finger and third finger, place them together by touching them lengthwise next to each other. Then think of your special number from *one* to *ten* or any special number you like. As soon as you think of that special number, you may feel yourself relaxing deeper and deeper. It is as if a wave of relaxation draws you steadily like a magnet into relaxation. Then you find yourself facing your special stairway with the ten steps. Or you may use another entrance of your choosing into your safe and healing place. Now allow yourself to experience the deepening process going so deeply into relaxation as you count to yourself from *ten* to *one*. As you reach the count of *one*, you are in your safe place again. Remember to sense your feet growing roots into the earth, grounding you and centering you. Visualize or sense again the white light that gently touches you and returns each cell to its healthiest status. Notice the cord that plugs you into the universal outlet for love, light and energy. Also repeat that the sun is beaming down beautiful, healing lights of Positive Energy that heal wherever healing is needed. Remember to reinforce and reaffirm all the suggestions you desire to keep.

At this time you may sense an even deeper relaxation as if you were floating and drifting lulled with very gentle movement, drifting and floating more and more relaxed. You have agreed that you are worthwhile and you deserve this time. Focus on your breathing. Notice how rich and full each breath is, bringing new serenity into your Mind/Body/Spirit. You are on cruise control now enjoying each pleasurable moment. Your relaxed muscles may feel so heavy, so heavy they are content to just be still. You are protected in this very safe environment of your safe place. Anyone you invite here needs your permission in order to return.

Very conveniently there is a designated Subconscious Programming area in your safe place that is here just for you. Fortunately, everything that is possible for you to know is stored here for you to access through your subconscious computer. Surprisingly, even if in the past you were unable to operate computers, this computer was made to respond to your thoughts as well as your pressing the keys of the keyboard. So you are very intuitively adept at this computer. In fact, we have multiplied your intuitive knowing so it is 100 times more powerful than before. This computer also listens to you and you simply tell it what to do. It is really a spectacular computer. To make this even easier, I will be your guide.

CORE OF INNER SECURITY MAINTAINS FAITH THAT ALL IS WELL SCRIPT

You have indicated that you are desirous of having more inner security, peace of mind and faith that all is well. That can be done easily and comfortably through reprogramming your subconscious computer. You simply delete your Anxiety files and replace them with complete Inner Security, Peace of Mind and Faith That All Is Well. I will guide you so you easily may accomplish these goals. Relax even deeper than before, allow yourself to just let go, going way deeper into relaxation. Good. It feels so good to relax. Now imagine or feel yourself in the Subconscious Reprogramming computer area where all is designed to make you completely comfortable. So perhaps you sense it already. You are surrounded by your favorite color and the temperature is so pleasant. Your favorite calming scent is in the air. A wonderful chair that conforms to your body shape gives you support as you are seated now in front of this magnificent subconscious computer feeling calm and in control.

When you touch the key directly in front of you, labeled delete, you automatically delete all your *Anxiety Files* that contain all the negative messages from your entire past. These messages may have given you the impression that you had to be always on alert because perhaps something opposite from good might happen. Perhaps you felt something opposite from feeling safe. So you may choose now to push the delete key on your keyboard or use your thoughts to delete that file in your subconscious computer. Excellent, it is done. That feels great! You have released all the useless worry, all the unnecessary concentration on things beyond your control and other than positive in your life. All erroneous messages have been deleted and are gone, completely. Compassionately, carefully and safely you extracted them from your subconscious computer. You sent them to the sun where they were transformed into Positive Energy. Also in those Anxiety Files were all the fear inducing thoughts, feelings and beliefs that have been other than positive for you. Those were fears that interfered with you pursuing and enjoying your life with the trust, faith and belief in yourself that all is well and continues being okay.

Instead you have created a new, wonderful file entitled Trust and Faith in Me and my Mind/Body/Spirit. In that file you have put all the positive revisions of false or erroneous mindsets that you used to have. The new revisions say *all is well. Just as you have faith that the sun will rise tomorrow, you have faith that you are and always will be okay. You are able to deal with whatever comes your way and be fine. Whatever misperceptions, erroneous mindsets, and detrimental belief systems that may have been created in your subconscious from anything in your past, easily have been deleted along with all Anxiety files. Congratulations!* It is all done. You are free of those faulty fears and useless worries! You easily have replaced them with faith and belief that all is well. You have taken back your power and freedom. You have chosen freedom and eliminated useless worry and anxiety. You trust and believe in yourself. You are powerful, capable, intelligent and wise.

You know, it reminds me of the story of how baby elephants are trained for the circus. The circus owner begins the process by tying a rope around the baby elephant's one front foot and then ties the other end of the rope around a stake that is hammered into the ground. The baby elephant thrashes and wails trying to get free. But, finally after perhaps many days, the baby elephant accepts the conclusion that regardless of anything it can ever do, it will never be able to get that stake out of the ground and be free. So the baby elephant stops trying. Even when the baby elephant grows up and becomes an adult elephant it does not try to get free. Actually as an adult elephant it easily could lift that foot up and jerk the stake out of the ground. Yet the elephant does not even try to get free simply because it is trapped by its faulty, limited belief.

A person in the same way can get trapped by his or her own limited belief. It is called an erroneous, invalid, limited belief. That belief now is incorrect and no longer valid. In many cases, your erroneous belief was never valid but merely based on your faulty perceptions.

Fortunately you have deleted all faulty perceptions and invalid, erroneous beliefs known as Faulty Subconscious Programs that were stored in your subconscious computer. Those Faulty Subconscious Programs are gone forever. Yes, they are all gone. You sent them up into the sun's atmosphere. They are stuck there transformed into Positive Energy. At last you are getting what you want. And all is for your Highest Good. It is done. It has happened effortlessly. And it feels so great!

Instantly, you have added a powerful positive Subconscious Program that permanently has programmed your inner security, peace of mind and faith all is well. In this file are all the positive beliefs that emphasize that you have the power to cope with all your life's challenges, get through them just fine and grow in wisdom and enlightenment. You have attained peace of mind. It is your normal state of being. Whatever comes your way, you make the best of it. You have faith that you are connected to universal love, light and energy. Your faith perpetually reaffirms that all is well.

Next are affirmations that many find so helpful in maintaining Inner Security, Your Trust and Belief in You, Yourself:

- I have choices that allow me to have control over my life. And so I do. Whatever I am unable to control, I turn it over to my Creator or Nature's Forces. I live my life with peace of mind, trust and faith that I can cope with whatever comes my way and I am fine.

- I openly and gratefully accept my Higher Power's Guidance. I am safe.

- I allow myself to flow naturally with the happenings of my life, finding happiness in each moment. I trust the way my life flows. All is going well.

- I am safe and secure. It is safe to be me. It is safe to love and be loved. It is safe to lead my life in a fulfilling way. It is safe to be an adult and on my own and to be my own person.

- It is safe to let go of all that is other than for my Highest Good. All that is other than for my Highest Good, I easily, safely and continuously release from my Mind/Body/Spirit.

- Everything that is happening is happening for a greater purpose. Although I may not be always aware of the meaning, I trust and believe that I benefit from the positive in every outcome.

- It is the oak tree although big and strong that is rigid and easily blown over by the strong winds. I am as the willow tree, able to bend and lean with the wind. I am adaptable. I keep my mind flexible and open to new ideas for my consideration.

- I appreciate and accept with love every part of my being. I love and accept myself totally and unconditionally. I am deserving of all of life's blessings and I accept them eagerly with deep appreciation. Good things always are happening to and for me.

- I release all that is outside of my Highest Good. I have programmed my subconscious to make choices that are automatically consistent with my Highest Good and for my inner peace and security. I have trust and belief in my goodness and my self-empowerment.

- I am at peace and maintain harmony with my Creator, family, friends, any coworkers, acquaintances and all within my life.

- My past is my guidepost. I am learning from my life lessons with ease. I continuously release all that is other than positive from my past while retaining the wisdom from my experiences. I live in the present moment finding happiness here and now.

- I refuse to take personally anything negative people think, say or do. I acknowledge that their reactions are based in their own issues. I simply let their negativity go and replace it with a positive thought or image such as surrounding the person with healing light.

- I love being able to learn and to improve. Joyfully and gratefully I embrace my opportunities for positive improvement. I embrace whatever changes I must face with courage and confidence trusting it is a gift of wisdom for my Spirit.

- I trust my Inner Knowing and connection to my Creator to guide me always toward my Highest Good. I am always able to sense my connection. It is a given.

- I am doing best I can under my circumstances. Also, I view others as if they are doing the best they can do under their circumstances.

CONCLUSION OF MAIN SCRIPT

Very importantly, your subconscious computer file contains your commitment to forgiveness. To assist your going forward with your life, you have forgiven all those who have ever hurt you whether it was done intentionally or unintentionally. You have forgiven them all as well as you have forgiven yourself completely. Yes, you have forgiven yourself for anything you said, thought and did that was wrong, inappropriate or hurtful. This way you have a clean slate. You remain always free, unburdened by the negative emotions that were other than for your Highest Good. You also recognize that no one is better than you and no one is worse than you. We are all equals even though we may have different abilities and talents and different appearances. We are all of the same energy.

All that was previously other than positive or neutral energy within you has been completely healed and cleansed, remaining in the eternal light of the sun and stars. And you bask in the brilliance of the light and love, feeling your loving connection to your Creator. You know deep within you, all is calm, all is peaceful and all is well.

As a sign of your accomplishment a magnificent rainbow appears reflecting the most beautiful colors imaginable. These colors are also there for you as they offer powerful healing so you maintain peace of mind, harmony and balance within your life. Select now the colors that you personally need for reinforcing the desired positives you have brought into your life and for releasing any future Negative Energy that is other than supportive of your well-being. The name or names of the colors instantly are within your knowing. This is part of your intuitive knowing. Summon them now from the sun. Immediately you may perceive your entire body is blanketed with comforting, soothing, gentle lights. You feel them on the surface of your body with their healing, gentle, warm glow. Next, they enter your body through your feet and travel up to the top of your head continuously cleansing and healing, cleansing and healing from the darkness that you have already expelled. Feel those lights as they lovingly supply your body with healing energy for every atom within every cell.

Imagine the beautiful color or colors. Notice how bright or soft they are, how clear or how muted. Imagine them quietly flowing throughout your organs like miniature, soft waves that wash over your cells, your thoughts, your dreams. Fortunately you have the power to request reinforcements of these colors at any time. Request more and they return and replenish, cleanse and make whole all areas within your complete body that are in need of their magnificent energies.

Remember answers may be found within you. You are self-empowered. So you are positive as you approach each day with courage and confidence. What a wonderful journey this has been! In essence you have transformed yourself and you continue processing the desired changes over the rest of this day and evening in a very comfortable, non-invasive, easy and time efficient way. Whatever positive changes you have programmed, they are part of you now and feel just as comfortable as if they have been part of you always. Yet you are aware of your hypnosis tool and its power to make these comfortable changes. Your subconscious computer has been cleansed and updated. You are truly renewed!

And now if it is your appropriately selected time to sleep, begin sleeping ... NOW. If you already have begun sleeping, and it is your appropriate time to sleep, continue sleeping. Sleep peacefully, deeply and uninterrupted while of course you are always able to awaken instantly if there were an emergency. Sleep wonderfully all the selected hours until it is your appropriate time to awaken. Process gently, comfortably, compassionately and time efficiently all that these words have done to serve you. If anything were to attempt to interfere with your sleep, simply put it in a big soup pot and put the lid on it. Put it on the back burner until your normal waking hours when you have appropriate time to process it. When you arise from your sleep, you are totally refreshed and feel like your batteries have been recharged. You feel absolutely great! Continue sleeping now and if it is your appropriate time to sleep, disregard the end of this recording that would bring you to your conscious state. For these instructions then only help you to sleep more deeply and peacefully in the most relaxed sleep. Enjoy your nourishing, peaceful, relaxing sleep ...

However, if it is your time to return to your conscious state, continue following the instructions as you listen to my voice and I do bring you back to your conscious state as I count from one to five. Remember that when you return to your normal State of Consciousness, you are completely alert, able to think clearly, focus and concentrate extremely well. You are able to drive safely and easily. Remember though, tonight or whenever it is your time for sleep, as soon as your head touches the pillow and your eyes close for sleep, you enjoy a deep, peaceful, relaxed, and wonderful sleep. During your sleep time, you process easily anything resulting from this recording. You continue sleeping uninterrupted just as I described previously until it is your selected time to awaken.

Only if now is your time to return to your conscious state, do you follow my instructions to bring you out of deep relaxation by counting from one to five, the same way you bring yourself out of self-hypnosis ... However, if it is your appropriate time to sleep, the following instructions and suggestions only help you to sleep more deeply, more relaxed and more peacefully ... Now if it is truly your appropriate time to come back to your natural, normal State of Consciousness, then begin with: *One*, it is time now to come back to your normal Beta Consciousness State, coming out of deep, deep relaxation ... *Two*, your entire body feels great. It has been cleansed and healed, revitalized and re-energized ... *Three*, your mind feels great! It has been cleansed and healed, revitalized and re-energized. It has gently, easily, comfortably, compassionately and time efficiently processed everything ... *Four*, your eyelashes are starting to gently flutter open as you are returning to your totally aware, alert, conscious state feeling so refreshed, able to drive easily and safely ... *Five, Six, Seven, Eight, Nine* and *Ten* your eyes are now open wide, comfortably focusing. Your eyes are now wide open. You are back to your completely normal conscious state, alert, clear headed, able to focus and concentrate better than before, remembering everything from this recording and feeling absolutely great!! Totally ALERT, AWAKE NOW!

INNER NURTURING MAINTAINS SELF-ESTEEM AND SELF-EMPOWERMENT

INTRODUCTION

This recording relaxes you and involves your attention and focus. Consequently, no one should listen to this recording while driving a car, as a passenger in a car without a head set or ear buds or while operating any machinery that requires concentration and/or decision-making.

This recording is not a substitute for medical treatment. Rather it is an exercise enlisting the support of your Mind/Body/ Spirit response to help you maintain well-being. It explores the natural self-healing powers of your mind using guided imagery while in a relaxed, altered state of hypnosis. It targets your stresses and suggests approaches to disarm them. While you may not be able to totally eliminate your stresses, you may choose improved ways to respond to them. This recording offers a safe, noninvasive method for creating positive changes in your life and in your perspectives about your life. What your mind focuses upon, your body reacts to just as if it were a reality. This explains why guided imagery is so effective. Additionally the relaxation exercises relax you and allow your subconscious to absorb and integrate new positive ways of thinking, feeling and behaving. Be assured though your subconscious automatically rejects anything that is against your morals, ethics or religious beliefs. This is (put your name here), your guide and facilitator for this gentle, safe journey that offers for a mainstay in your inner life, relaxation, peace, harmony and balance. This is a time dedicated to you and your well-being. You are worth this time. You deserve this time. Whatever you hear when my voice guides you through the imagery, take only the positive parts that apply to you and leave the rest. Revise any statements that need changes in order to be acceptable to you personally. You are the master of this journey. I am your guide.

BEGINNING OF MAIN SCRIPT

Begin now by taking two deep breaths, breathing in through your nose and exhaling through your mouth to the count of eight. As you are slowly exhaling, imagine you are releasing all the stress, tension and anxiety that may have settled anywhere within your entire body. Just let it go! Continue to breathe normally and now each time you exhale, relax every muscle within your entire body more and more. Each muscle, each tendon, each ligament, all internal organs respond to your desire to let go. It is safe. It is okay. It feels so good to let go of all the stress, tension and tightness throughout your entire body. Just as a candle melts from the heat of its flickering flame, the tightness softens and releases. See tension just melting away. Feel the subtle warmth as your muscles relax feeling so loose, so heavy, and so relaxed. From the top of your head to the tips of your toes, you may begin to notice stress and taut muscles are releasing their hold on you. Comfortably, gently, steadily just let any tightness go. Releasing the muscle tightness is like easily loosening a knot or letting go of the strings attached to helium balloons. Stress and tension leave so easily, naturally as you exhale them with each breath. Almost magically, you find yourself starting to feel so calm, so peaceful, so comfortably relaxed as you remain focused on your breathing.

Every thought that was running through your mind, slows, slows, and slows down. All thoughts now gently depart as you exhale. The only thought that remains is of total relaxation. Any thought or distractions, simply escort them out with your breath. Focus again on your regular breathing. Notice that with every regular breath you release, your body feels more and more and more relaxed. Your arms and hands may feel so heavy now, so relaxed that you may be barely able to lift them at all. The relaxation has smoothed your forehead, softly spread over your eyes, your nose, your mouth, your jaw. You open your mouth slightly to relax your jaw as this is a place where tension often settles. Good.

Now the relaxation goes down your neck and across your shoulders and as you imagine the muscles relaxing, they do relax. You may feel them relaxing. Next perhaps you feel the relaxation traveling down your back, down, down, down to the lowest part of your back and then returning up again. Again the tension just melts away. The relaxation continues down your chest, your stomach, your abdomen, your hips, your thighs, your legs, your knees, your shins, your ankles and your feet. The tops and bottoms of your feet relax and let go. You focus now on a peaceful scene that you have placed in the middle of your forehead, in your mind's eye. Perhaps your scene is a small pond without a ripple in the clear water. Or perhaps it is a single candle's flame, steadily glowing sending forth soft light. Whatever represents peace and calm to you, even if it is a sound, scent, taste or feeling rather than a picture, is what you bring to the center of your forehead, your mind's eye. Now everything is so peaceful, calm and so relaxing. You continue enjoying this sense of complete peace, calm and relaxation ... Yet in a few moments you may be drawn to deepen your feelings of relaxation by visiting your safe and healing place that lies yonder.

Your special safe and healing place is just for you. It can be any place you choose — on a beach, in the woods, in the mountains, in a special room. Wherever you choose as your safe place is perfectly fine. Whatever comes to your mind first, you can trust is a wonderful choice for you. Besides, you can always change your safe place if you so desire. Now that you feel ready to go deeper into relaxation, you may stay where you are or travel to another safe and healing place. If you are ready to travel, you may see and feel your body walking down a simple dirt path. It is a beautiful day with a deep blue sky and little birds are cheerfully chirping. There is a gentle, fresh breeze and it is just warm enough for you. It is absolutely a delightful day. As you are enjoying your walk, you come upon a stairway which in another moment or two is right in front of you. It has ten shallow steps with a handrail on either side. In another moment, you will be stepping down upon those stairs. As you go from the tenth step down to the first step, you easily allow yourself to become more relaxed than before. Any thoughts that would try to disturb your concentration are immediately cancelled when you stamp a big X upon them in your mind's eye. You maintain your focus guided by my voice. We are ready to begin the stairs now. Remember, these shallow steps are easy to maneuver. Imagine yourself in a strong state of body where you comfortably can walk on your own. Begin with the tenth step and end with the first.

Now that you are ready, here we go now ... *Ten*, feeling more relaxed now, so calm and peaceful ... *Nine*, relaxing more and more ... *Eight* ... more deeply relaxed than before, so deeply relaxed ... *Seven*, the deeper relaxed you go, the more intensely wonderful the feeling ... *Six* ... deeper, way down now. You may sense how heavy your entire body feels, so heavy, so relaxed ... *Five*, way, way, down into your deepest relaxation ... *Four*, deeper than ever before ... *Three*, even deeper relaxed, feeling so comfortable with such harmony and balance ... *Two*, almost there now, so very, very deeply relaxed and so calm, so peaceful ... and *One*, feeling so, so, deeply, deeply, deeply relaxed, oh, so, so deeply relaxed. Regardless of the stresses in your life, you may find yourself so deeply, deeply relaxed and feeling so calm and supported that you look so forward to repeating this journey each and every day. And each time you repeat this journey you may find it easier and easier to relax even deeper and deeper.

Notice now you can sense your new surroundings ... sense the peace and the calm. You are in your safe place. Perhaps you can touch it, smell it, taste it, hear it, see it. You are in your safe, special healing place and no one can disturb you here. Imagine yourself in your safe place. Perceive it with all of your senses. Amazingly your feet feel as if they are growing roots that dig into the soft ground and secure you now to the earth, grounding you and centering you. You can see the roots, feel them and even detect their fresh, outdoors scent. Perhaps immediately you also perceive an energy that you are receiving through the crown of your head. It is as if you have plugged yourself into the unlimited energy of the universe, of nature, of creation. This is perfect harmony and balance. Feel that har- mony and balance, the perfect alignment and attunement to the energy of the universe and your connection with your Creator. It feels so great! In fact, its description is beyond words. You are so grateful to have this amazing acceptance of peace and tranquility. It includes the feeling of belonging, the feeling of unconditional love. Soak up the power of this incredible, safe and healing place. It is there for you always.

Whenever you wish to return to this safe and healing place, first find a comfortable position, either sitting or lying down with your head supported, where you will be undisturbed for the desired time you have allotted for this relaxation. Just gently close your eyes. Next, take in two deep breaths, in through your nose and exhale through your mouth to the count of eight as you imagine the stress, tension and anxiety leaving your body each time you exhale. Using two fingers on your right hand, your index finger and third finger, place them together by touching them lengthwise next to each other. Then think of your special number from *one* to *ten* or any special number you like. As soon as you think of that special number, you may feel yourself relaxing deeper and deeper. It is as if a wave of relaxation draws you steadily like a magnet into relaxation. Then you find yourself facing your special stairway with the ten steps. Or you may use another entrance of your choosing into your safe and healing place. Now allow yourself to experience the deepening process going so deeply into relaxation as you count to yourself from *ten* to *one*. As you reach the count of *one*, you are in your safe place again. Remember to sense your feet growing roots into the earth, grounding you and centering you. Visualize or sense again the white light that gently touches you and returns each cell to its healthiest status. Notice the cord that plugs you into the universal outlet for love, light and energy. Also repeat that the sun is beaming down beautiful, healing lights of Positive Energy that heal wherever healing is needed. Remember to reinforce and reaffirm all the suggestions you desire to keep.

At this time you may sense an even deeper relaxation as if you were floating and drifting lulled with very gentle movement, drifting and floating more and more relaxed. You have agreed that you are worthwhile and you deserve this time. Focus on your breathing. Notice how rich and full each breath is, bringing new serenity into your Mind/Body/Spirit. You are on cruise control now enjoying each pleasurable moment. Your relaxed muscles may feel so heavy, so heavy they are content to just be still. You are protected in this very safe environment of your safe place. Anyone you invite here needs your permission in order to return.

Very conveniently there is a designated Subconscious Programming area in your safe place that is here just for you. Fortunately, everything that is possible for you to know is stored here for you to access through your subconscious computer. Surprisingly, even if in the past you were unable to operate computers, this computer was made to respond to your thoughts as well as your pressing the keys of the keyboard. So you are very intuitively adept at this computer. In fact, we have multiplied your intuitive knowing so it is 100 times more powerful than before. This computer also listens to you and you simply tell it what to do. It is really a spectacular computer. To make this even easier, I will be your guide.

CORE OF INNER NURTURING MAINTAINS SELF-ESTEEM AND SELF-EMPOWERMENT SCRIPT

You have indicated your desire to feel and maintain High Self-esteem and strong self-empowerment. So that is what you have programmed into your subconscious computer.

You have created a new file entitled: My High Self-esteem. You copied from all your previous files that had messages and proof that formulated your High Self-esteem and put them all in. All the beliefs, feelings and mindsets asserting your positive self-worth; how lovable you are; how valuable you are; how valuable your thoughts are; how you trust and believe in yourself completely are in your High Self-esteem file. Additionally all validation of you and all your abilities and talents, the genuine good person you are, and your positive self-image internal and external, complete your new High Self-esteem file. This is the only self-esteem file that resides in your subconscious and is operable. In fact, you have deleted the file that was entitled: Other than High Self-esteem. All negative messages, negative mindsets, negative impressions, indeed, anything and everything that were other than positive about your self-esteem, have been deleted. They are all gone, healed and unable to affect you or influence you in any way other than in a positive way, for a positive gain of wisdom or in a neutral way.

You have also created another file entitled, *My Very Strong Self-empowerment.* In this file are all the positive messages, beliefs, mindsets, and positive feelings supporting your Inner Knowing and belief that you are highly self-empowered. You have power in the choices you make every moment of every day. You can choose to accept, challenge, adopt, adapt, reject, compromise or any number of options regarding the decisions you make daily. You recognize that your power is over you and only you unless you are also a legal guardian. In that case you also have considerable power in decisions for your ward. Otherwise, you acknowledge that each person is in charge of himself/herself. You might make suggestions, debate, give guidance, encourage, and inform other adults. However, the only person you truly can control is you.

Now everyone knows that each of us has the responsibility to take care of ourselves and you too, have the power to do so. You are empowered to nurture yourself and take responsibility for yourself. Maybe your caregivers may have been unable to nurture you or to nurture you sufficiently. However you have learned how to nurture yourself. And so you do. Sometimes people I know put their hands over their hearts and tell themselves: *I love and accept you unconditionally* as a reminder that they are nurturing themselves. I do not know when but at some time within thirty days from your first hearing this guided imagery, you may feel more nurtured than before, more complete and more whole than you may ever recall from times past. Consequently, you speak up for yourself, take good care of your physical being, your mental, emotional, spiritual and general health needs including healthy food choices. And that feels great. You truly care about yourself and take whatever measures are necessary to nurture yourself in a positive manner. It is like you are your own best friend. In fact you are your own best friend. You are worthy, valuable, deserving, lovable, good enough, attractive enough, smart enough, capable enough, intuitive enough, lucky enough and very precious.

Next are affirmations that many find so helpful in maintaining Inner Nurturing, Self-esteem and Self-empowerment:

- I appreciate and accept with love every part of my being. I easily love and accept myself totally and unconditionally. I am worthy; I am lovable and I am deserving of all good things.

- My past is my guidepost. My past is past, never to return. I live in the present moment living in happiness here and now. I have released all that is other than for my Highest Good.

- I refuse to take personally anything negative people think, say or do. I acknowledge that their strong reactions are based in their own issues. I release their negativity and focus on a positive thought or image like sensing they are surrounded by healing light.

- I am doing the best I can under my circumstances and all other people are doing the best they can do under their circumstances.

- I am just as precious as everyone else. No one is better than I am and no one is worse than I am. We are all equals. We are all of the same energy.

- I am self-empowered. I have choices allowing me to have control over my life. And so I do.

- I am deserving of all of life's blessings. I accept them with open arms. Good things consistently happen to me. I am aware of all my blessings. I am deeply grateful for all my blessings.

- I am safe. It is safe to be me. It is safe to love and be loved. It is safe to give and receive love. It is safe to lead my life in a fulfilling way. It is safe to be on my own and be my own person. It is safe for me to continue self-improvements.

- I support myself in loving and caring ways. I am worth it. I am lovable. I am good enough.

- I respect myself and I respect others as well. I am responsible for making sure my needs are met. My needs are just as important as everyone else's needs.

- I am able to tell other people what I need and what my

limits are. This is part of my self-respect. This is part of taking care of me.

- Nothing anyone may think, say or do is able to affect my positive self-image and *High Self-esteem* in any other than a positive or neutral way.

- I learn and improve upon any mistakes. I view whatever mistakes I may have made as stepping-stones to greater successes.

- I have goodness in the core of my being. I have confidence about who I am. I trust and believe in myself. I know that I know. My self-confidence is a natural part of who I am.

- I like who I am. I like the good person I am. I forgive those who were supposed to nurture me but who were unavailable to me emotionally, physically, and/or spiritually. Forgiving those people has allowed me to go on with my life in a positive way.

- I forgive myself for anything I believed I did that was wrong, inappropriate or brought anything other than good fortune to myself. I take responsibility for my actions and I do so with integrity.

- I have learned valuable life lessons from my mistakes.

Thus, I have grown in character, wisdom and spiritual enlightenment.

- I take full responsibility for nurturing myself. I do sufficiently nurture myself. It makes me feel so happy to feel nurtured. I am self-empowered and it feels so great!

- I am supported by the love that eternally surrounds me. I am always connected. I am always in the good company of love, light and Positive Energy from my Higher Power.

CONCLUSION OF MAIN SCRIPT

Very importantly, your subconscious computer file contains your commitment to forgiveness. To assist your going forward with your life, you have forgiven all those who have ever hurt you whether it was done intentionally or unintentionally. You have forgiven them all as well as you have forgiven yourself completely. Yes, you have forgiven yourself for anything you said, thought and did that was wrong, inappropriate or hurtful. This way you have a clean slate. You remain always free, unburdened by the negative emotions that were other than for your Highest Good. You also recognize that no one is better than you and no one is worse than you. We are all equals even though we may have different abilities and talents and different appearances. We are all of the same energy.

All that was previously other than positive or neutral energy within you has been completely healed and cleansed, remaining in the eternal light of the sun and stars. And you bask in the brilliance of the light and love, feeling your loving connection to your Creator. You know deep within you, all is calm, all is peaceful and all is well.

As a sign of your accomplishment a magnificent rainbow

appears reflecting the most beautiful colors imaginable. These colors are also there for you as they offer powerful healing so you maintain peace of mind, harmony and balance within your life. Select now the colors that you personally need for reinforcing the desired positives you have brought into your life and for releasing any future Negative Energy that is other than supportive of your well-being. The name or names of the colors instantly are within your knowing. This is part of your intuitive knowing. Summon them now from the sun. Immediately you may perceive your entire body is blanketed with comforting, soothing, gentle lights. You feel them on the surface of your body with their healing, gentle, warm glow. Next, they enter your body through your feet and travel up to the top of your head continuously cleansing and healing, cleansing and healing from the darkness that you have already expelled. Feel those lights as they lovingly supply your body with healing energy for every atom within every cell.

Imagine the beautiful color or colors. Notice how bright or soft they are, how clear or how muted. Imagine them quietly flowing throughout your organs like miniature, soft waves that wash over your cells, your thoughts, your dreams. Fortunately you have the power to request reinforcements of these colors at any time. Request more and they return and replenish, cleanse and make whole all areas within your complete body that are in need of their magnificent energies.

Remember answers may be found within you. You are self-empowered. So you are positive as you approach each day with courage and confidence. What a wonderful journey this has been! In essence you have transformed yourself and you continue processing the desired changes over the rest of this day and evening in a very comfortable, non-invasive, easy and time efficient way. Whatever positive changes you have programmed, they are part of you now and feel just as comfortable as if they have been part of you always. Yet you are aware of your hypnosis tool and its power to make these comfortable changes. Your subconscious computer has been cleansed and updated. You are truly renewed!

And now if it is your appropriately selected time to sleep, begin sleeping … NOW. If you already have begun sleeping, and it is your appropriate time to sleep, continue sleeping. Sleep peacefully, deeply and uninterrupted while of course you are always able to awaken instantly if there were an emergency. Sleep wonderfully all the selected hours until it is your appropriate time to awaken. Process gently, comfortably, compassionately and time efficiently all that these words have done to serve you. If anything were to attempt to interfere with your sleep, simply put it in a big soup pot and put the lid on it. Put it on the back burner until your normal waking hours when you have appropriate time to process it. When you arise from your sleep, you are totally refreshed and feel like your batteries have been recharged. You feel absolutely great! Continue sleeping now and if it is your appropriate time to sleep, disregard the end of this recording that would bring you to your conscious state. For these instructions then only help you to sleep more deeply and peacefully in the most relaxed sleep. Enjoy your nourishing, peaceful, relaxing sleep …

However, if it is your time to return to your conscious state, continue following the instructions as you listen to my voice and I do bring you back to your conscious state as I count from one to five. Remember that when you return to your normal State of Consciousness, you are completely alert, able to think clearly, focus and concentrate extremely well. You are able to drive safely and easily. Remember though, tonight or whenever it is your time for sleep, as soon as your head touches the pillow and your eyes close for sleep, you enjoy a deep, peaceful, relaxed, and wonderful sleep. During your sleep time, you process easily anything resulting from this recording. You continue sleeping uninterrupted just as I described previously until it is your selected time to awaken.

Only if now is your time to return to your conscious state, do you follow my instructions to bring you out of deep relaxation by counting from one to five, the same way you bring yourself out of self-hypnosis … However, if it is your appropriate time to sleep, the following instructions and suggestions only help you to sleep more deeply, more relaxed and more peacefully … Now if it is truly your appropriate time to come back to your natural, normal State of Consciousness, then begin with: *One*, it is time now to come back to your normal Beta Consciousness State, coming out of deep, deep relaxation … *Two*, your entire body feels great. It has been cleansed and healed, revitalized and re-energized

... *Three*, your mind feels great! It has been cleansed and healed, revitalized and re-energized. It has gently, easily, comfortably, compassionately and time efficiently processed everything ... *Four*, your eyelashes are starting to gently flutter open as you are returning to your totally aware, alert, conscious state feeling so refreshed, able to drive easily and safely ... *Five, Six, Seven, Eight, Nine* and *Ten* your eyes are now open wide, comfortably focusing. Your eyes are now wide open. You are back to your completely normal conscious state, alert, clear headed, able to focus and concentrate better than before, remembering everything from this recording and feeling absolutely great!! Totally ALERT, AWAKE NOW!

APPENDIX THREE

YOUR BONUS FREE AUDIO DOWNLOAD

It is highly recommended that at your earliest convenience you listen to Relax, Release and Dream On: hypnotic guided imagery for relaxing mind and body, releasing negative emotions and sleeping peacefully.

This audio serves to take away doubts and concerns about going into hypnosis. Since 2002, this audio has assisted people to experience hypnosis. Of course, you can learn self-hypnosis and Reprogramming Self-hypnosis without this audio. Yet, you will find listening to Relax, Release and Dream On takes away uncertainty about the hypnosis process while it relaxes you with enjoyable guided imagery. It also will be a source of other long-term benefits for you.

HOW TO OBTAIN YOUR FREE BONUS AUDIO DOWNLOAD, *RELAX, RELEASE AND DREAM ON*:

1. Using the Internet, type the following address into your browser: http://www.GaleGlassnerTwersky.com/book-bonus-audio

2. Then follow the directions when you land on the next page. Fill in the requested information so we may send you a link to your email address for this audio.

3. Make sure you have confirmed the destination where your audio will be downloaded.

4. If you need any assistance, please use our Contact page

on galeglassner.com to message us and we will get back to you.

- PLEASE REMEMBER THE CAUTION: For your safety, avoid listening to this hypnosis audio or any hypnosis audio while you are a driver of a car or operating any machinery. Also avoid listening as a passenger in a car when the driver also may hear the audio. The audio will relax you into hypnosis and you will be focused only on the audio.

GLOSSARY

Abreaction: The release of emotional tension achieved through recalling a repressed traumatic experience.

Achilles Heel: portion, spot, area, or something of the sort that is an especially or solely vulnerable point; the tendon joining the calf muscles to the heel bone.

Acupressure: A type of massage therapy using finger pressure on specific bodily sites; as in Acupuncture. It is most often correlated with the Meridians in the body. Acupressure is also used to test the body's flow of energy and interruptions of energy flow; its finger pressure techniques help return the body's energy system back into balance, promote healing, and alleviate fatigue.

Adjunct Therapy: Additional therapy used together with main therapy or treatment, purposeful to assist primary treatment.

Alopecia Areata: Loss of hair in circumscribed patches, baldness.

American Board of Hypnotherapy (ABH): A leading organization of over 4,000 hypnosis professionals and hypnosis advocates, promoting use of hypnosis for well-being, founded by Dr. A.M. Krasner in 1982.

American Board of Neuro-Linguistic Programming (ABNLP): A sister professional organization of the ABH, for Neuro-linguistic Programming practitioners, promoting use of NLP for well-being.

Amygdala (also referred to as amygdale): An anatomic structure of the limbic system adjoining the temporal lobe of the brain; involved in emotions of fear and aggression, also associated with the sense of smell.

Applied Kinesiology: (see Muscle Testing, Acupressure) A form of chiropractic care involving the manipulation of muscles in order to achieve alignment for the body and well-being; also used by other wellness practitioners for testing and correcting alignment of body's electrical energy system.

Atrial Fibrillation: Medical care applied to revive someone who is having a heart attack and/or difficulty of breathing.

Auditory Learner: Someone who learns most efficiently through hearing spoken instructions or information.

Autonomic Bodily Functions: The autonomic nervous system (ANA) monitors your basic functions for life including those that are involuntary or have the ability to be carried out while you are not conscious; the visceral organs, blood pressure, cardiac output, blood glucose levels and body temperature.

Auto-suggestion: The subconscious adoption of an idea that one has originated within oneself through visual or verbal messages or statements that result in changing behavior.

Belay: To be made secure.

Belief System: One's way in which he/she accepts statements or existence as true or false with a firm opinion or conviction; faith based on a series of beliefs but not formalized into a religion; also a fixed organized set of beliefs common in a community or society.

Bi-polar disorder: A diagnosis of a mental illness characterized by fluctuating moods; containing alternating periods of elation (mania) and depression.

Buddhism: A religious and spiritual practice originating in India by Buddha and later spreading to China, Burma, Japan, Tibet and parts of Southeast Asia. The Buddhist philosophy is that life is full of suffering caused by desire and that the end to this suffering is through enlightenment.

Catharsis: The process of releasing emotions and providing relief of strong or repressed emotional tensions.

Cellular memory: Memories and experiences stored in our body cells relating to something very meaningful especially meaningful as a result of an impact or trauma.

Chi or Qi: A life force of energy, often referred to in martial arts, Chinese medicine and Acupuncture.

Cleared Vessel: A term as used in Judeo-Christian beliefs, applies to the concept of clearing oneself (the vessel symbol) of anything that is other than of God so as to allow God, using one's free will, to enter and to completely guide one's life in accordance with God's will and purpose.

Colitis: A condition often associated with stress; an irritable colon marked by diarrhea and stomach spasms caused by inflammation of the lining of the colon.

Collective Unconscious: A famous term that psychologist, Carl Jung, used in order to explain symbolism, dreams and images of the other than conscious mind; refers to a body of all knowledge that is accessed through the unconscious and functions to assist people in their waking lives.

Convincers: Techniques or ways as used in hypnosis to demonstrate and thereby convince someone to firmly believe that they are in hypnosis.

Dementia: A chronic, persistent disorder of the mental processes that causes severely impaired memory and reasoning ability, along with disturbed behavior.

Detoxifying: A cleansing period, most often a process of eliminating toxins out of your body through the aid of herbs, lymphatic massage and eating pure organic foods, also may refer to cleansing anything negative from your Mind/Body/Spirit.

Eastern Medicine: Eastern medicine encompasses a wide variety of practices that perceive the whole person including their Mind/Body/Spirit as important in treating the person, Eastern Medicine includes homeopathy, herbs, Acupuncture and other alternative avenues that are considered for well-being.

Ego, Super Ego: Freudian terms used to distinguish urge and drive within individuals. The super ego is a heightened consciousness and overly responsible. In order to function, the ego is often split between that and the Id (see Glossary definition), an aggressive, untamed part of oneself.

Emotional Payoff: A spontaneous association of pleasurable satisfaction one receives whenever thinking, feeling or behaving in a particular way(s).

Endorphins: Any of a group of peptide hormones that bind to opiate receptors and are found mainly in the brain.

Energy Balancing: See Acupressure.

Energy Vampire: A person who drains another person of his feelings of personal energy.

Entertainment Hypnosis: Hypnosis performed in front of audiences for entertainment purposes only. Those who volunteer do so to have fun and be part of the experience. The people chosen for this experience are typically very suggestible subjects.

Epiphany: An appearance or experience of manifestation; a sudden intuitive perception of or insight into reality, or the essential meaning of something.

Eye Fixation: As used in hypnosis, a technique of staring at an object until one goes into an Altered State of Consciousness such as Alpha consciousness.

Fable: A story told that often instills faith and inspiration; a story that may have a moral lesson that it is intentionally communicating.

Facilitator: Person responsible for leading or coordinating a technique or doing the work of a group in order to make an action or process possible or easier.

Family-ism: A belief system or mindset that members of the same family have been raised to believe as true even though the beliefs/mindsets may or may not be true. Family members will think and behave based on the accepted Family-ism without conscious knowledge or control of it.

Faulty Subconscious Program: A Reprogramming Hypnosis term that refers to a person's subconsciously accepted, held and defended mindset, mental/emotional association and/or belief system that adversely affects the person's thoughts, feelings, attitudes and/or behaviors; the person is most likely unaware of the existence and resulting influence of the Faulty Subconscious Program.

Fibromyalgia: A chronic disorder characterized by severe, widespread pain in the muscles and soft tissues surrounding joints, causes fatigue, and tenderness at various specific sites in the body. Also referred to as: fibromyalgia syndrome, fibromyositis, fibrositis.

Frequencies-electrical: A measurement of energy related to the electrical magnetic field.

Gigabytes: In computer science, a unit of measurement approximately equal to 1 billion bytes. A gigabyte is used to quantify memory or disk capacity. One gigabyte equals 1,000MB (actually 1,024 megabytes). One thousand megabytes or one billion bytes.

Grounded: A gestalt term used to refer to someone who is well anchored in their body or stable in their life with the issues that they are dealing with.

Guided Imagery: A therapeutic relaxing technique that involves closing one's eyes (sometimes guided by music) and creates an imagined picture of a pleasant scene(s) in order to help a person feel safe, secure, happy and restful; also used in hypnosis to present Indirect Suggestions to the person's subconscious mind.

Hepatology: The science that treats the liver; a treatise on the liver.

Hertz Frequencies: The number of repetitions per unit time of a complete waveform, as of an electric current; the SI (International System of Units) unit of frequency, equal to one cycle per second.

Higher Power (also called: Superior Power, Divine Intelligence, Greater Power, or Divine Source): The source that is responsible for one's life; one's Creator; the Source that provides meaning and purpose to one's life; the All Mighty, All Knowing Force in one's life such as God, Jesus or Allah.

Highest Good: Related to God or the Creator of the Universe, a sense of transcendence and trust from this source, what is in one's best interests in the long run of one's life from God's vantage point.

Hinduism: The common religion of India, based upon the religion of the original Aryan settlers as expounded and evolved in the Vedas, the Upanishads; the Bhagavad-Gita is used frequently as a guide and source for spiritual living; includes large pantheon symbolizing many attributes of a single god.

HypnoCounselor: A professional counselor who practices hypnosis; one who is certified to facilitate hypnosis to assist in relieving the stress of personal issues through hypnotic suggestions.

Hypnotherapist: One who professionally (either through certification or licensure) practices hypnosis to support the client's well-being.

Hypnotic Suggestibility: The ability for someone to be hypnotized; an indicator of how easily someone can transition from Beta consciousness to the Alpha or Theta consciousness, the hypnotized state of being subconsciously suggestible.

Hypnotic Trance: An induced State of Consciousness similar to deep relaxation yet more focused; the trance transitions the subconscious mind into its suggestible state.

Hypnotist: A person who uses hypnosis for entertainment or self-improvement issues; person who may or may not be certified to use hypnosis as a self-healing venue for others.

Hypnotizability: (See Hypnotic Suggestibility) the degree of ease in which one obtains the altered state of hypnosis.

Id: In psychological terms, commonly known to be an aggressive, untamed part of someone.

Ideomotor Cue: A physical act chosen to induce an intentionally associated emotional and/or physical response.

Ideomotor Response: Of or pertaining to involuntary motor activity caused by responding to an idea or statement; in hypnosis terms, a technique of responding to hypnotic questions/suggestions.

"In the Flow" or "In the Zone": Referring to when a person

is actualizing their life purpose and are not fighting anyone or anything; rather they are in a state of harmony, balance and cooperation with higher universal principles.

Indigo Children: Children who are believed to represent a higher state of human evolution; the term references the belief that these children have indigo-colored auras; these children are said to have paranormal abilities such as the ability to read minds or simply have increased empathy and creativity; children wise way beyond their years.

Induction: The act of inducing, bringing about, or causing the hypnotic state; one of a variety of methods used to facilitate a person entering into a trance state.

Inner Peace, Harmony and Balance: States of being in which one feels tranquil and calm; reflecting emotional health, feeling strong, centered and in a good place emotionally.

Intuition, Intuitive Knowing: The quality or ability of having direct perception or keen insight that comes from a Sixth Sense, outside of your five senses.

Irritable Bowel Syndrome: Also known as IBS; a condition of stomach disturbance: flatulence, diarrhea and discomfort frequently related to stress.

Jung, Carl, Jungian psychology: Originally a student of Freud, Jung placed emphasis on dreams, symbols and their meanings related to understanding emotions; founder of Analytical Psychology.

Kinesthetic learner: One who learns more easily using the physical movement of the body following natural patterns, e.g. learning typing by the physical practice of fingers moving on the keyboard as opposed to reading a book about it (visual learner) or listening to the teacher explain it (auditory learner).

Left brain (dominant): Describes a person who operates most efficiently from the left hemisphere of his/her brain — usually people who are more mathematical oriented, appreciate logic, order and calculations in a linear mode.

Meditation: The state of being present within oneself; often involves concentration on one's breath to quiet the mind and relax; some use a mantra for focus to help them reach meditative state; heighten states of relaxation that can bring enlightenment through an Altered State of Consciousness.

Meridian: Often classified within Acupuncture; any of the pathways in the body along which vital energy flows.

Mindset: Established set of attitudes held by someone, consciously and/or subconsciously.

Mind/Body/Spirit: A description of the physical, mental, emotional and spiritual makeup of the total person; parts of ourselves that cooperate together for transformation and wellness as one strives to be whole and well.

Negative Cleansing: A hypnosis technique of releasing Negative Energy that has been interfering with a person's harmony, balance and well-being.

Negative Energy: Vibrations of energy that are negatively charged similar to how electrical energy can have a negative charge; implies negative emotional energy.

Negativity: The quality or state of being negative, often marked by denial, opposition, gloomy outlook, opposite to something regarded as positive; may have bad effects.

Neo-cortex Brain: Top layer of the cerebral hemispheres made of six layers, involved in functions such as sensory perception, generation of motor commands, spatial reasoning, conscious thought and language.

Neuropsychoimmunology: (scientific term created by Candace Pert, PhD and her partner Michael Ruff, PhD): The study of how the connected Mind/Body/Spirit influences health and can affect healing; a holistic approach to understanding the brain, emotions and the body's immune system.

Neuroscientist, Biophysics: The field of study encompassing the various scientific disciplines dealing with the structure, development, function, chemistry, pharmacology, and pathology of the nervous system.

Opiate Receptors of the brain: Discovered and named by Candace Pert, PhD and Michael Ruff, PhD neuroscientists and research professors; a type of protein found in the brain, spinal cord and gastrointestinal tract that are activated once opiates reach the brain and they produce effects that correlate with the area of the brain involved; stimulation of opiate receptors by opiates results in feelings of reward and activates pleasure circuits that causes a rush by releasing a large amount of dopamine and this release of dopamine can lead to addiction.

Parable: A short allegorical story designed to illustrate or teach some truth, religious principle or moral lesson.

Patch: A medical treatment for nicotine dependency of cigarette smokers; often a bandage type application of a chemical to reduce nicotine craving; assists people for smoking cessation.

Positive Thinking: Consciously and/or subconsciously thinking optimistically; having good, healthy thoughts that can bring happiness and peace of mind.

Post Traumatic Stress: Reactions to stresses that a person experiences that result from and remain after a trauma of any kind; may be diagnosed as PTSD (Post Traumatic Stress Disorder) if it continues to cause problems that interfere in a person's life such as panic attacks, anxiety and fear related to the Traumatic event(s).

Post-hypnotic Suggestion: A suggestion given to a person while in hypnosis and intended to be direct the person's thoughts, beliefs, feelings, and or actions at a later time after coming out of hypnosis.

Power Source: see Higher Power.

Psychosis: A mental disorder characterized by symptoms such as delusions or hallucinations that indicate impaired contact with reality such as in paranoia or Schizophrenia.

RAM: In computer science, a main memory device in which information can be accessed in any order.

Right Brain Dominant Person: Someone who naturally excels

in right brain functions responsible for creative, intuitive and artistic ways of operating and seeing the world.

Reality: The state of being real, seeing things as they are factual and logical in this world.

Rectal Mucosal: The mucus-secreting membrane lining of the rectum.

Reincarnation: The belief that a person's soul has experienced one or more lives previously and that the soul returns again within another person on earth to learn spiritual lessons and/or correct a karmic imbalance.

Relaxation Response: A result of the mind and body letting go of tension and distracting thoughts and entering an altered state; used in hypnosis and meditation; offers many positive feel-good results for relaxing the body as well as the mind.

Reprogramming Hypnosis: A specialty hypnosis system with specific protocols and unique vocabulary that was created by hypnotherapist, Gale Glassner Twersky, A.C.H. The theory supporting Reprogramming Hypnosis was first published in 2005 in a 9-CD Series: Reprogram Your Subconscious: how to use hypnosis to get what you really want. The Reprogramming Hypnosis System compares the way computers operate to many aspects of how the subconscious mind operates.

Reprogramming Self-hypnosis: Same definition as for Reprogramming Hypnosis, except that the hypnosis protocol is led by the person himself/herself instead of being led by a facilitator.

Safe Place: Image of a haven or scene that you create in your mind that encourages you to feel safe while you receive rejuvenation and comfort during hypnosis.

Schizophrenia: (also referred to as dementia praecox) A severe mental disorder characterized by some, but not necessarily all, of the following features: emotional blunting, intellectual deterioration, social isolation, disorganized speech and behavior, delusions, and hallucinations.

Secondary Gain: A type of reward, satisfaction or goal that people achieve that is created from the existence of an issue that only appears to be their main issue or problem. It is an underlying reason that motivates them to display certain thoughts, beliefs and behaviors that are not the primary issue.

Self-empowerment: When a person feels in control, confident, high self esteem and in charge of decision-making processes that gives feelings that the person is in charge of himself/herself.

Self-esteem: HA belief or opinion of how someone views and feels about himself/herself in regard to self-worth and self-image; High Self-esteem builds self-confidence while Low Self-esteem lowers self-confidence.

Self-fulfilling Prophesy: The act of saying and believing in particular ideas, concepts or things that may occur and then later observing that they come true.

Self-healing: The knowledge and art of being in tune with oneself to correct areas within oneself that are unbalanced, undernourished or depleted; healing can take the form of body work, emotional/therapy work and/or spiritual work — which is the most effective and core of healing.

Shaman, (adj. Shamanic): A person acting as a medium between the visible and spirit worlds; one who practices healing or divination, a spiritual medicine person.

Soul Sisters: Women who have a close spiritual relationship to each other, being of like minds; or having had a supportive relationship in a Past Life; they often believe and feel that their connection is spiritual and/or predestined; the name used by a group of women who meet monthly to discuss personal and spiritual growth.

Spiritual, Spirituality: The quality or fact of being spiritual, attuned to a Divine Source or Higher Power such as God, Jesus, Buddha or Nature; involving a state of transforming problems and events into a higher purpose; a sense of faith, trust, hope and peace associated with a Higher Power beyond human abilities.

Subconscious Conference: A hypnosis technique used for receiving information from different parts of the subconscious for a person's benefit and understanding.

Subconscious Mind: The part of the brain that controls the autonomic bodily functions and the totality of mental and emotional processes of which the individual is not aware.

Subconscious Reprogramming: Method of changing the information that is stored in a person's subconscious (or unconscious mind); may be used with the goal of specific, positive attitudinal, emotional and behavioral modifications.

Subconscious Resistance: A hypnosis term that describes the blocking of your conscious desires by a part of your mind that is operating outside of your conscious awareness, your subconscious mind; implies that your subconscious mind is defending a subconsciously held belief, mindset and/or association and thus refuses to accept something that conflicts with any of those beliefs, mindsets and/or associations.

Subliminal: Existing or operating below the threshold of consciousness; being or employing stimuli insufficiently intense to produce a discrete sensation but often being or designed to be intense enough to influence the mental processes or the behavior of the individual.

Suggestible Subconscious: The State of Consciousness and hertz frequency when a person is in an Altered State of Consciousness that allows for his subconscious to become open to receiving, accepting and integrating the person's suggestions.

Synchronicity: The recognition from occurrence of events that everything in life is in harmony with your needs; describes events that are related more randomly rather than causally; yet they have a special significance or meaning that gives one a sense that there is righteousness and order from a Higher Power.

Tactile: The sensory act of touching or the sensation of being in tune with touch.

Ten Hertz Frequency: The electromagnetic frequency in which it is estimated the earth is vibrating.

Tinnitus: A prolonged condition of uncontrollable ringing or background noises or other similar sensations of sound in the ears.

Trauma: Something that has occurred to one or more people

that involves involuntary participation, threat, neglect, abuse or damage either spiritually, emotionally, physically or mentally.

Tribal Mentality: a belief that an entire community holds as true, such as we are only good if we sacrifice for others, and if we show concern for ourselves then we are considered conceited and selfish.

Trichotillomania: A stress-related condition that manifests in the behavior of uncontrollable hair pulling from any part of the body as in head, eyebrows, arms.

Unconscious Mind: Not conscious; where exists an awareness outside the boundaries of the Beta Consciousness State.

Western Medicine: A system in which licensed medical doctors and other health care professionals (such as nurses, pharmacists), treat symptoms and diseases using drugs, radiation, or surgery; may also be referred to as: allopathic medicine, bio-medicine, conventional medicine, mainstream medicine, and orthodox medicine.

BIBLIOGRAPHY

Albom, Mitch. *Tuesdays with Morrie: An Old Man, a Young Man*, and Life's Greatest Lesson. New York: Broadway, 2002.

Alvarez-Nemegyei, J., A. Negreros-Castillo, B. L. Nuno-Gutierres, J. Alvares-Berunza, and L. M. Alcocer-Martinez. "Ericksonian Hypnosis in Women with Fibromyalgia Syndrome." *PubMed*. July & Aug. 2007 <http://www.pubmed.gov>.

"Brain Scans Of The Future—Psychologists Use MRI To Understand Ties Between Memo- ries And The Imagination." *Science Daily: News & Articles in Science, Health, Environment & Technology*. 28 Mar. 2009 <http://www.sciencedaily.com/videos/2007/0710-brain_scans_ of_the_future.htm>.

Carlson, L. E., and BD Bultz. "Mind-Body Interventions in Oncology." *PubMed*. 13 Aug. 2008. <http://www.pubmed.gov>.

Carmody, T. P., C. Duncan, J. A. Solkowitz, J. Huggins, S. Lee, and K. Delucchi. "Hypno- sis for Smoking Cessation: A Randomized Trial." *PubMed*. 10 May 2008. <http://www. pubmed.gov>.

Davis, Judith. *Emotional Comfort: The Gift of Your Inner Guide*. New York: Wilder P, Inc., 2005.

Durlacher, James V. *Freedom From Fear Forever: The Acu-POWER Way To Overcoming Your Fears, Phobias, and Inner Problems*. Tempe, Ariz: Van Ness Pub. Co., 1995.

Elkins, G., J. Marcus, V. Stearns, and M. Hasan Rajab. "Pilot evaluation of hypnosis for the treatment of …[*Psychooncology*. 2007] – *PubMed* Result." NCBI HomePage. 28 Mar. 2009 <http://www.ncbi.nlm.nih.gov/pubmed/17048223>.

"Emotional Memories Function In Self-Reinforcing Loop." *Science Daily: News & Articles in Science, Health, Environment & Technology*. 28 Mar. 2009 <http://www.sciencedaily. com/releases/2005/03/ 050323130625.htm>.

"Frequency." *Merriam-Webster Online Dictionary*. 2009. Merriam-Webster Online. 21 May 2009 <http://www.merriam-webster.com/ dictionary/frequency>

Goleman, Daniel. *Emotional Intelligence: Why It Can Matter More Than IQ*. Los Angeles: Audio Renaissance, 2001.

Goodman, A. "Hypnosis, Hypnotizability and Treatment." *PubMed*. Oct. 2008. <http:// www.pubmed.gov>.

Gottlieb, David and Tatz, Akiva. *Letters to a Buddhist Jew*. Southfield, MI: Targum P, 2005.

Hammond, D. C. "Review of the Efficacy of Clinical Hypnosis with Headaches and Mi- graines." *PubMed*. Apr. 2007. <http://www.pubmed.gov>.

"Happiness Is 'Infectious' In Network Of Friends: Collective—Not Just Individual—Phe- nomenon." *Science Daily: News & Articles in Science, Health, Environment & Technology*. 28 Mar. 2009 <http://www.sciencedaily.com/releases/2008/12/ 081205094506.htm>.

"Happiness Lengthens Life." *Science Daily: News & Articles in Science, Health, En- vironment & Technology*. 28 Mar. 2009 <http://www.sciencedaily.com/releas- es/2008/08/ 080805075614.htm>.

Hay, Louise L. *You Can Heal Your Life*. Santa Monica, CA: Hay House, 1987.

"Hypnosis As An Alternative To Drug-Induced Sedation." *Science Daily: News & Articles in Science, Health, Environment & Technology*. 28 Mar. 2009 <http://www.sciencedaily.com/ releases/2003/02/ 030207072158.htm>.

"Hypnosis Shown to Reduce Symptoms of Dementia." *Science Daily: News & Articles in Science, Health, Environment & Technology*. Ed. Dan Hogan. 29 July 2008. <http://www. sciencedaily.com>.

"Hypnotherapy An Effective Treatment for Treatment for Irritable Bowel Syndrome." *Sci- ence Daily: News & Articles in Science, Health, Environment & Technology*. Ed. Dan Hogan. 28 Sept. 2005. <http://www.sciencedaily.com>.

Iglesias, A. "Hypnosis as a Vehicle for Choice and Self-Agency in the Treatment of Children with Trichotillomania." *PubMed*. Oct. 2003. <http://www.pubmed.gov>.

Jung, C. G. "THE CONCEPT OF THE COLLECTIVE UNCONSCIOUS." *Collective Unconscious*. 21 May 2009 <http://www.timestar.org>.

Maudouax, A., S. Bonnet, F. Lhonneux-Ledoux, and P. Lefebvre. "Ericksonian Hypnosis in Tinnitus Therapy." *PubMed. 2007.* <http://www.pubmed.gov>.

Mawdsley, J. E., D. G. Jenkins, M. G. Macey, and L. Langmead. "The Effect of Hypnosis on Systemic and Rectal Mucosal Measures of Inflammation in Ulcerative Colitis." *PubMed*. June 2008. <http://www.pubmed.gov>.

"Media Violence Cited As 'Critical Risk Factor' For Aggression." *Science Daily: News & Ar- ticles in Science, Health, Environment & Technology*.

28 Mar. 2009 <http://www.science- daily.com/releases/2008/11/
081119122632.htm>.

"Memorizing In Your Sleep." *Science Daily: News & Articles in Science,
Health, Environment & Technology.* 28 Mar. 2009
<http://www.sciencedaily.com/releases/1999/10/991026074517.
htm>.

"Methods of reducing discomfort during colonoscopy. [*Dig Dis Sci.*
2008] – *PubMed* Result. "NCBI HomePage. 28 Mar. 2009
<http://www.ncbi.nlm.nih.gov/pubmed/17999189>.

Morton, P. A. "The Hypnotic Belay in Alpine Mountaneering: The Use
of Self-Hypnosis for the Resolution of Sports Injuries and for
Performance Enhancement." *PubMed.* July 2003.
<http://www.pubmed.gov>.

Novoa, R., and T. Hammonds. "Clinical Hypnosis for Reduction of Atrial
Fibrillation After Coronary Artery Bypass Graft Surgery." *PubMed.*
Mar. 2008. <http://www.pubmed.gov>.

Pekala, R. J., R. Maurer, V. K. Kumar, N. C. Elliott, E. Masten, E. Moon,
and M. Salinger. "Self-Hypnosis Relapse Prevention Training with
Chronic Drug/Alcohol Users: Effects on Self-Esteem, Affect, and
Relapse." *PubMed.* Apr. 2004. <http://www.pubmed.gov>.

Pert, Candace. *Your Body Is Your Subconscious Mind.* Riverside: Sounds
True, 2004.

"Positive Thinking May Protect Against Breast Cancer." *Science Daily:
News & Articles in Science, Health, Environment & Technology.* 28 Mar.
2009   <http://www.sciencedaily.com/   releases/2008/08/
080821194717.htm>.

"Put On A Happy Face: It Helps You See The Big Picture." *Science Daily:
News & Articles in Science, Health, Environment & Technology.* 28 Mar.

2009   <http://www.sciencedaily.   com/releases/2008/11/
081117121229.htm>.

Rinpoche, Sogyal. *The Tibetan Book of Living and Dying*. New York,
NY:HarperSanFrancisco division of HarperCollins, 1993.

Ruiz, Don Miguel. *The Four Agreements: A Practical Guide to Personal
Freedom, A Toltec Wisdom Book*. Grand Rapids: Amber-Allen, 2001.

Saxe, John G. "The Blind Men and the Elephant." 28 Mar. 2009
<http://www.noogenesis.   com/pineapple/
blind_men_elephant.html>."

Science Of Stress—Dermatologists Detail The Scary Signs Of Stress
Revealed By Skin." *Science Daily: News & Articles in Science, Health,
Environment   &   Technology.   28   Mar.   2009
<http://www.sciencedaily.com/videos/2008/
0411-science_of_stress.htm>.

"Spirituality, Religious Practice May Slow Progression Of Alzheimer's
Disease." *Science Daily: News & Articles in Science, Health, Environment
& Technology*. 28 Mar. 2009 <http:// www.sciencedaily.com/
releases/2005/04/050430222301.htm>.

"Stanford Study Shows Hypnosis Helps Kids Undergoing Difficult
Procedure." *Science Daily: News & Articles in Science, Health,
Environment & Technology*. Ed. Dan Hogan. Jan. 2005.
<http://www.sciencedaily.com>.

Sunnen, Gerard V. "Spiritual Epiphanies During Hypnosis." *The Great
Plains: Turning off the taps*. 28 Mar. 2009 <http://www.triroc.com/
sunnen/topics/spiritualepiphanies.htm>.

Walsh, B. J. "Hypnotic Alteration of Body Image in the Eating
Disordered." *PubMed*. July 2008. <http://www.pubmed.gov>.

Warren, Rick. The *Purpose-Driven Life: What on Earth Am I Here For?* Grand Rapids: Zondervan, 2002.

Willemsen, R., and J. Vanderlinden. "Hypnotic Approaches for Alopecia Areata." *PubMed.* July 2008. <http://www.pubmed.gov>.

Winfrey, Oprah. "Love: It's All In Your Head." *O Magazine* Apr. 2004.

Xu, Y., and E. Cardena. "Hypnosis as an Adjunct Therapy in the Management of Diabetes."
PubMed. Jan. 2008. <http://www.pubmed.gov>.

INDEX

ABOUT THE AUTHOR

Gale Glassner Twersky, A.C.H., is a HypnoCounselor/ hypnotherapist, Motivational Speaker and President of Glassner Associates Hypnosis for Personal Growth and Wellness since 1999. Gale conducted her HypnoCounseling practice in Montclair, NJ, from 1999 to 2009. In 2009, she relocated Glassner Associates Hypnosis to the Los Angeles, CA, area. Besides being an experienced certified teacher of English and Oral Communications, Gale is certified in Advanced Clinical Hypnotherapy and has several specialty certifications including Past Life Hypnosis, Hypno-anesthesia and Spiritual Counseling. Additionally, Gale is a certified Instructor of Hypnosis and leads the Glassner Associates Hypnosis Certification Program. In 2010, Gale was honored as the recipient of the International Hypnosis Federation Award of Excellence in Communication. In 2013, Gale initiated and now leads the Reprogramming Hypnosis Specialist Certification through International Hypnosis Federation.

In 1993, Gale founded Soul Sisters, a personal growth and spiritual development group, still active in Randolph, NJ. For seven years Gale wrote a column featuring hypnosis for the Montclair Life and Leisure newspaper in NJ. In 2005, she authored and recorded in partnership with the highly respected Nightingale-Conant Corp. her nine-CD series, *Reprogram Your Subconscious: How to Use Hypnosis to Get What You Really Want* that quickly became and remained a Top Seller. In 2006, Gale published the CD, *Relax, Release and Dream On* that has been Number One Spoken Word MP3 Download on *Amazon.com*. In 2010, Gale completed the updated and expanded book edition of *Reprogram Your Subconscious: How to Use Hypnosis to Get What You Really Want* that is a culmination of over thirty years of her dedicated life's work in the personal growth, wellness and spiritual development fields. In 2016, the well-respected Gildan Media partnered with Gale to publish their Reprogram Your Subconscious Audiobook (revised 2016 edition) plus eight additional single audios that founded their Hypnotic Guided Imagery series. Being a professional and a pioneer in how to Reprogram Your Subconscious, Gale's passion is to empower and enrich people's lives. She seeks to accomplish this by sharing her subconscious mind theories and applications using the system of Reprogramming Hypnosis because they have been so effective for so many.

JOURNAL WITH AFFIRMATIONS

Each day I have a fresh start because I have forgiven everyone
including myself.

Forgiveness benefits the giver as much as or more than the receiver. I practice forgiveness daily.

When I live my life according to my heart, I live in serenity, living my truth.

No one is better than I am. I am no better than anyone else. We are all of the same energy, from the same Source.

I am deeply grateful for all I have.

I avoid judging other people. They are just being themselves at
their present soul development level.

I love and accept myself unconditionally.
Therefore, I love and accept others unconditionally as well.

I enjoy consistent peace. All is going well.

It is safe to love and to be loved. I carry love with me in
every cell of my body. I am loved.

My acts of kindness bring eternal joy to my Spirit.

I listen best when I listen with both my head and my heart.

I pay attention to what needs to be accomplished while
I am here on earth.
I contribute my part to the best of my abilities.

A thought is just a thought that I can keep or delete. I remember
to replace any deleted thought with an exceptionally positive
thought that supports my internal peace.

I surround myself with truly positive people who support me with
their words and with their kindness.
I do the same for them.

I am worthy and deserve to have all that I need. There is enough for everyone.

Whenever I perceive stress whether consciously or unconsciously,
I instantly relax myself.

I value as important every person who crosses my path, as well as those who travel along my path beside me.

Just giving someone a smile can be a gift of recognition and acceptance.

I have much that I can give to others.

I avoid making assumptions. I have learned to simply ask for the facts or wait for them to be clear.

Competition may be good in sports and in business, but I keep it out of my personal relationships.

My past is one of my greatest teachers. It teaches me how to
avoid repeating my mistakes.
It teaches me how to improve my results.

I am my own best friend; I treat myself respectfully as such.

I am intelligent. I am wise. I am loved. I am good

I have chosen to live in freedom from fear. I live in freedom within
my Mind/Body/Spirit.

One of the most important characteristics I possess is my
willingness to seek and allow change for my self-improvement.

Truth is often difficult to discern; yet, time will confirm it.

I release all negative emotions that are other than for my
Highest Good.

Today is the most important day of my life. Today is all I have and I
live it with that in mind.

There is something positive and good in everyone.

I have a positive, optimistic attitude about everything in my life.

I act as though in all things I am expressing my Spirit, because I am.

Children are blessings. Children remind me to appreciate the
simple and ordinary things in life.

I always have all that I need. With extreme gratitude I accept my positive abundance in all aspects of my life.

I have retrieved all subconscious parts of me. I am whole and complete. My self-healing is complete.

I believe in the positive gifts and positive opportunities in each moment of my life.

I am improving and getting better each and every day and in each and every way.

I am a work in progress.

I practice compassion for others, recognizing that each person is precious and everyone has challenges.

I am aware of my intuitive Inner Knowing. I allow it to guide me in positive ways for my Highest Good.

Not everyone would make the choices I would make. That is okay.
We all have our own path.

I am unique. Yet, everyone is unique. Not everyone thinks
the way I do.

Whatever I look for within my day, I find it. I look for the beauty
and the good.

I respect and appreciate all living things. Everyone and everything has a purpose.

Happiness is a state of mind that I have an option of choosing each day. Today I choose to be happy and tomorrow it is the same.

I always have faith that I can cope with whatever comes my way and I am fine. I trust and believe in myself.

Everything that is happening is significant and meaningful even
though its meaning may be unclear for now.

My responsibility to myself is to live my life in harmony with my ethics, morals and spiritual beliefs.

My High Self-esteem is intrinsic and invincible. Nothing that I or anyone else can think, say or do, can affect my High Self-esteem in any other way other than in a positive or neutral way.

One of the most important characteristics I possess is my willingness to seek and allow change for my self-improvement.

Truth is often difficult to discern; yet, time will confirm it.

I release all negative emotions that are other than for my
Highest Good.

Today is the most important day of my life. Today is all I have and I live it with that in mind.

There is something positive and good in everyone.

I have a positive, optimistic attitude about everything in my life.

I act as though in all things I am expressing my Spirit, because I am.

Children are blessings. Children remind me to appreciate the
simple and ordinary things in life.

I always have all that I need. With extreme gratitude I accept my
positive abundance in all aspects of my life.

I am also Spirit; I am always in good company and never alone.

CPSIA information can be obtained
at www.ICGtesting.com
Printed in the USA
JSHW021503170420
5131JS00007B/76

9 781722 500306